POEMS

For Every Day
of the Year

POEMS

For Every Day of the Year

366 Beautiful Poems of
Love, Inspiration and
Encouragement

EDITED BY

KAREN McCOSKER & NICHOLAS ALBERY

gb GALAHAD BOOKS

First Galahad Books edition published in 2003

Galahad Books
A division of BBS Publishing Corporation
450 Raritan Center Parkway
Edison, New Jersey 08837

Galahad Books is a registered trademark of BBS Publishing Corporation.

Published by arrangement with Steerforth Press

The Steerforth Press edition published under the title: *Poem a Day*

ISBN: 1-57866-127-7

Printed in the United Sates of America.

Foreword

In the early 1970s I was living in Athens. After a year, I was hoping that my father would find the courage to make the trip to see me. But despite the fact that he hated flying, loathed being away from his small, self-owned business and hometown where he knew everyone and everyone recognized him, my father did accompany my mother on this visit. While making the arduous ascent towards the Acropolis, I sensed a trepidation in his steps. He had a bad heart; it was suffocatingly hot and windless; the landscape was utterly foreign to him. He had become something he had rarely been: a stranger. I feared he might lose the psychological surefootedness that being on his own terrain gave him, want to turn back, go home. Pausing, he began to recite a poem, one by Edna St. Vincent Millay:

> . . . Euclid alone
> Has looked on Beauty bare. Fortunate they
> Who, though once only and then but far away,
> Have heard her massive sandal set on stone.

Recalling what he knew oriented my father. The poem gave him breathing space in the crowd, and time to recover from the anxiety of feeling off balance. Hearing the words he had memorized helped him make his way because they suggested an association between the strange place and the familiar poem, gathering up the distance between Athens and his upstate New York home.

Though my father often recited (no Thanksgiving or Christmas went unmarked by verse), I hadn't realized until that morning in Athens how a single poem, even a few lines, learned by heart can transform the person who needs to hear those words at a particular time; how they can make what otherwise might have been abandoned possible.

When trying to piece together our pasts, memory can be notoriously selective, choosing, even creating, one detail at the expense of another, transposing incidents, disregarding time; yet I can recall, again with certainty, when I experienced the effect a recitation of memorized poems can have on an audience. I was one person in a formidable auditorium of people come to hear Andrei Voznesensky. The poet did not read his work; he declaimed it in Russian from the stage and I, an undergraduate and fledgling writer of poetry, listened in awe. Such was the force of this reciting that at the pauses between stanzas, the silence in the room was so charged that it rang in my ears. It was as if we had become a single entity whose collective wind had just been knocked out of our chest.

I have since heard moving readings where poets have the page at hand; yet there is always the sense that the page is only for reference, and that the poem is an intimate and urgent offering, brought from a place inside, not external to, the poet.

To memorize a poem is much more than a mental exercise. Indeed, it is the only way to truly know a poem, but to "know" in the case of poetry requires a kind of emotional cognition. If we are drawn to a poem enough to reread it, for whatever reason, it is a candidate for memorization. During the process of continually repeating words, phrases, lines, and stanzas, we must make decisions about when to use emphasis, how long to pause, what shading of voice will best convey meaning. In order to justify our grasp of the poem, we inhabit it and, not unusually, glimpse the mind of the poet in the act of creating, so intently are we assuming its structure and words. In a sense, we put on the poem like a garment, and view the world in poetic guise. The poem then becomes ours during the interpretation of it since that is when we claim it, fully, with our critical and emotional insight, independent of the text.

Drama instructors who teach Shakespeare have told me that their students do not question the meaning of what they are reading until a passage is to be memorized. Only when committing the text to memory do they begin to see themselves in relationship to the text. It is not until then that they engage themselves, personally and fundamentally, with the words.

No matter if we are speaking from a stage to an audience, from the front porch to the wind, or from a Barcalounger to our cat, this reciprocity between poem and person underlies the way we come to make a poem ours.

Lately, at three a.m., my insomnia in overdrive and a long road ahead, I call on poetry for the most dire yet common of reasons: to convince me I am not alone, that there have been other victims of such extended, after hours introspection, that somewhere someone is also trying to make sense of a life. It is their words I borrow, always grateful and astonished at having them, to wrap about me in the night.

Recently, at a gathering of teachers, I asked a woman who had memorized much poetry what use there was in doing so. "It gives me the opportunity to comfort someone," she responded without pausing to consider the question, since she had done so many years and many poems before. Indeed, the poems we memorize are gifts to ourselves, but they are consolations, revelations and joys to others as well, and they must be accessible, ready to the tongue, for if we have to dig in our luggage for the dog-eared book or run home to our desk, we have lost the moment.

On the plane home, I was seated next to a graduate in Russian studies whom I had met two nights before when we exchanged poems: my Akhmatova in English, his in the original. Beginning our descent, the plane dropped precipitously through the clouds, then pitched from side to side. Strangers instinctively seized the forearms of their neighbors. "This is it," I thought, reading the same fearfully alert expression on the faces of those near me. "Look, Paul," I said, gripping his wrist while attempting to convey in an unconcerned tone what I hoped was not my last request, "if we go down, just say the poem again." We laughed, but I meant it.

As I drive the thirteen miles to work, five days a week, aware that statistics for mishaps on the highway are far higher than for those in the air, I practice the poems I've chosen to learn. They are my antidote for the blatant cry of pop culture, the encroachment of technospeak, the demoralizing debates over downsizing and megamergers. With the constant repetition of these poems, I begin to feel like one of the characters at the end of Ray Bradbury's *Fahrenheit 451*, a novel in which a society's leaders enforce the idea that it is every citizen's duty to burn books. It is the Book People, wandering in the woods, who eradicate their identities in order to take on those of the works they are committing to memory in an act of political defiance necessary to preserve a culture. One of them says, "It doesn't matter what you do . . . so long as you change something from the way it was before you touched it into something that's like you after you take your hands away."

It is true that when you commit a poem to memory, it undergoes a personal interpretation; yet, ultimately, it is you who are changed into something other than you were before the poet touched you with the hands of the heart.

Karen McCosker
Westfield, Maine

NEW EVERY MORNING

Every day is a fresh beginning,
Listen my soul to the glad refrain.
  And, spite of old sorrows
    And older sinning,
    Troubles forecasted
    And possible pain,
Take heart with the day and begin again.

Susan Coolidge
(29 January 1835 - 9 April 1905)

This poem has been used in a UK hospice to bring comfort to patients. Susan Coolidge (the pseudonym of Sarah Chauncey Woolsey) was born in Cleveland, Ohio, in January 1835. She composed three volumes of verse, wrote the *Katy* books and other unsentimental stories in a natural style for girls, and edited the letters of Jane Austen and Fanny Burney.

BLOODY MEN

Bloody men are like bloody buses –
You wait for about a year
And as soon as one approaches your stop
Two or three others appear.

You look at them flashing their indicators,
Offering you a ride.
You're trying to read the destinations,
You haven't much time to decide.

If you make a mistake, there is no turning back.
Jump off, and you'll stand there and gaze
While the cars and the taxis and lorries go by
And the minutes, the hours, the days.

Wendy Cope
(21 July 1945 -)

Wendy Cope notes: "When I wrote this, in 1987, I must already have been a bit short-sighted. Nowadays, if I'm wearing glasses, I have no difficulty in reading the destination on buses."

Infant joy

'I have no name:
'I am but two days old.'
What shall I call thee?
'I happy am,
'Joy is my name.'
Sweet joy befall thee!

Pretty joy!
Sweet joy but two days old,
Sweet joy I call thee:
Thou dost smile,
I sing the while,
Sweet joy befall thee!

William Blake

(28 November 1757 - 12 August 1827)

There are children in Shakespeare and there were nursery rhymers aplenty, but Blake was the first poet to speak to and for small children in their own right, in their condition of innocence.

SYMPATHY

I know what the caged bird feels, alas!
  When the sun is bright on the upland slopes;
When the wind stirs soft through the springing grass,
And the river flows like a stream of glass;
  When the first bird sings and the first bud opes,
And the faint perfume from its chalice steals –
I know what the caged bird feels!

I know why the caged bird beats his wing
  Till its blood is red on the cruel bars;
For he must fly back to his perch and cling
When he fain would be on the bough a-swing;
  And a pain still throbs in the old, old scars
And they pulse again with a keener sting –
I know why he beats his wing!

I know why the caged bird sings, ah me,
  When his wing is bruised and his bosom sore, –
When he beats his bars and he would be free;
It is not a carol of joy or glee,
  But a prayer that he sends from his heart's deep core,
But a plea, that upward to Heaven he flings –
I know why the caged bird sings!

Paul Laurence Dunbar
(27 June 1872 – 9 February 1906)

The importance of Dunbar's success to the black writers who would follow him was so significant that one wrote, "A Negro poet had not won recognition in the United States in the century and a quarter since the family of John Wheatly of Boston emancipated their slave girl, Phillis, in recognition of her *Poems* . . . (1773)."

POET-TREE

i fear that i shall never make
a poem slippier than a snake
or oozing with as fine a juice
as runs in girls or even spruce
no i wont make not now nor later
pnomes as luverlee as pertaters
trees is made by fauns or satyrs
but only taters make pertaters
& trees is grown by sun from sod
& so are the sods who need a god
but poettrees lack any clue
they just need me   & maybe you

Earle Birney
(13 May 1904 –)

This poem is a parody of the six-stanza poem 'Trees' by Joyce Kilmer, published in 1914, which starts "I think that I shall never see / A poem lovely as a tree" and which ends "Poems are made by fools like me, / But only God can make a tree."

Earle Birney grew up in Calgary and on a farm in British Columbia. In the 1930s he had to leave the States because of his involvement in Trotskyist causes. He served in the Canadian Army from 1942 to 1945, and was an active writer until a severe heart attack in 1980. His poetry collections include *Pnomes*, and *Jukollages and Other Stanzas*, his memoirs are entitled *Child Addict in Alberta*, and he edited *Twentieth Century Canadian Poetry*.

from TWELFTH NIGHT
SWEET-AND-TWENTY

O mistress mine, where are you roaming?
  O, stay and hear! your true love's coming,
    That can sing both high and low:
Trip no further, pretty sweeting;
Journeys end in lovers meeting,
    Every wise man's son doth know.
    What is love? 'tis not hereafter;
Present mirth hath present laughter;
    What's to come is still unsure:
In delay there lies no plenty;
Then come kiss me, sweet-and-twenty!
    Youth's a stuff will not endure.

William Shakespeare
(23 April 1564 – 23 April 1616)

On this day in 1601 *Twelfth Night* was entered on the Stationers Register.

This song is sung by the clown Feste in *Twelfth Night*, to two of the comic characters, Andrew Aguecheek and Sir Toby Belch. Feste offers a love song, or a song of good life. Sir Toby replies, "A love song, a love song," and Andrew agrees, saying, "Ay, ay. I care not for good life."

Also on 6 January in 1586, John Shakespeare, William's father, was deprived of his alderman's gown, as a consequence of his long absence from Stratford-on-Avon council meetings.

SONNET 115

All we were going strong last night this time,
the *mots* were flying & the frozen daiquiris
were downing, supine on the floor lay Lise
listening to Schubert grievous & sublime,
my head was frantic with a following rime:
it was a good evening, an evening to please,
I kissed her in the kitchen – ecstasies –
among so much good we tamped down the crime.

The weather's changing. This morning was cold,
as I made for the grove, without expectation,
some hundred Sonnets in my pocket, old,
to read her if she came. Presently the sun
yellowed the pines & my lady came not
in blue jeans & a sweater. I sat down & wrote.

John Berryman
(25 October 1914 - 7 January 1972)

When Berryman was still a child, his father died of gunshot wounds, probably by suicide. Berryman won a scholarship to Cambridge University. At Princeton University, where he was a Creative Writing Fellow from 1943 to 1944, he completed many of the poems later published as *Berryman's Sonnets*. In *Dream Songs* (1969) he wrote: "I'm cross with God who has wrecked this generation . . . he gorged on Sylvia Plath. That was a first rate haul. He left alive fools I could number with a kitchen knife." His novel *Recovery* admitted his struggle with alcoholism. He married three times.

MOONLIGHT

It will not hurt me when I am old,
  A running tide where moonlight burned
  Will not sting me like silver snakes;
The years will make me sad and cold,
  It is the happy heart that breaks.

The heart asks more than life can give,
  When that is learned, then all is learned;
  The waves break fold on jewelled fold,
But beauty itself is fugitive,
  It will not hurt me when I am old.

Sara Teasdale
(8 August 1884 – 29 January 1933)

Strange Victory, Teasdale's final volume of poetry, containing just twenty-two short poems, is arguably her best. In retrospect, the title seems not without its irony since this literary achievement could not sustain the poet as her health declined and she faced the fear of spending her last days as an invalid dependent on others. Teasdale died from taking an overdose of barbiturates.

ACCIDENTS OF BIRTH

Je vois les effroyables espaces de l'Univers qui m'enferment, et je me trouve attaché à un coin de cette vaste étendue, sans savoir pourquoi je suis plutôt en ce lieu qu'en un autre, ni pourquoi ce peu de temps qui m'est donné à vivre m'est assigné à ce point plutôt qu'à un autre de toute l'éternité qui m'a précédé, et de toute qui me suive.

(*Pensées sur la Religion*, Pascal)[1]

The approach of a man's life out of the past is history, and the approach of time out of the future is mystery. Their meeting is the present, and it is consciousness, the only time life is alive. The endless wonder of this meeting is what causes the mind, in its inward liberty of a frozen morning, to turn back and question and remember. The world is full of places. Why is it that I am here?

(*The Long-Legged House*, Wendell Berry)

Spared by a car- or airplane-crash or
cured of malignancy, people look
around with new eyes at a newly
praiseworthy world, blinking eyes like these.

For I've been brought back again from the
fine silt, the mud where our atoms lie
down for long naps. And I've also been
pardoned miraculously for years
by the lava of chance which runs down
the world's gullies, silting us back.
Here I am, brought back, set up, not yet
happened away.
                        But it's not this random
life only, throwing its sensual
astonishments upside down on
the bloody membranes behind my eyeballs,
not just me being here again, old
needer, looking for someone to need,
but you, up from the clay yourself,

Accidents of Birth

as luck would have it, and inching
over the same little segment of earth-
ball, in the same little eon, to
meet in a room, alive in our skins,
and the whole galaxy gaping there
and the centuries whining like gnats –
you, to teach me to see it, to see
it with you, and to offer somebody
uncomprehending, impudent thanks.

William Meredith
(9 January 1919 -)

William Meredith was born in New York City. He served as a naval aviator in World War II. His first poetry collection, *Love Letter from an Impossible Land*, was published in 1944. He has served as a chancellor of the Academy of American Poets as well as the Consultant in Poetry to the Library of Congress.

1. I see the terrifying spaces of the universe that enclose me, and I find myself attached to a corner of this vast expanse, without knowing why I am more in this place than in another, nor why this little time that is given me to live is assigned me at this point more than another out of all the eternity that has preceded me and out of all that will follow me (*Thoughts on Religion*, Pascal).

MEETING AT NIGHT

The grey sea and the long black land;
And the yellow half-moon large and low;
And the startled little waves that leap
In fiery ringlets from their sleep,
As I gain the cove with pushing prow,
And quench its speed i' the slushy sand.

Then a mile of warm sea-scented beach;
Three fields to cross till a farm appears;
A tap at the pane, the quick sharp scratch
And blue spurt of a lighted match,
And a voice less loud, thro' its joys and fears,
Than the two hearts beating each to each!

Robert Browning
(7 May 1812 - 12 December 1889)

Elizabeth Barrett was a 39-year-old invalid confined by illness and a possessive father to the family house in Wimpole Street when Robert Browning first contacted her. Browning had read her poem "Lady Geraldine's Courtship" containing a brief tribute to the humanity of his poetry and was moved to respond.

His letter begins "I love your verses with all my heart, dear Miss Barrett, – and this is no off-hand complimentary letter that I shall write." For a page or so the critical compliments continue until, quite suddenly, he insists, "I do, as I say, love these books with all my heart – and I love you too."

On 20 May 1845 she agreed to allow him to visit her in her room, and on 12 September 1846 they were married secretly at St. Marylebone Church, leaving almost immediately for the milder climate and cheaper living in Italy. Hearing news of the marriage, Wordsworth is reported to have commented, "Well, I hope they understand one another – nobody else would."

On 27 October 1845, Elizabeth Barrett saw "Meeting at Night" in printer's proof and wrote to Robert Browning: "You throw largesses out on all sides without counting the cost: how beautiful."

THE VOICE

Woman much missed, how you call to me, call to me,
Saying that now you are not as you were
When you had changed from the one who was all to me,
But as at first, when our day was fair.

Can it be you that I hear? Let me view you, then,
Standing as when I drew near to the town
Where you would wait for me: yes, as I knew you then,
Even to the original air-blue gown!

Or is it only the breeze, in its listlessness
Travelling across the wet mead to me here,
You being ever dissolved to wan wistlessness,
Heard no more again far or near?

Thus I; faltering forward,
Leaves around me falling,
Wind oozing thin through the thorn from norward,
And the woman calling.

Thomas Hardy
(2 June 1840 – 11 January 1928)

Hardy's strained marriage to his first wife Emma Gifford nevertheless resulted in moving love poetry after her death in 1912. At his own death in 1928, his heart was buried with Emma in Dorset and his ashes were placed in Westminster Abbey next to those of Charles Dickens.

DON'T BE LITERARY, DARLING

Don't be literary, darling, don't be literary
If you're James in the morning you're Hemingway in bed
Don't talk of yourself in the style of your own obituary –
For who cares what they say of you after you're dead.

Don't be always a thought ahead and a move behind
Like a general reconnoitring dangerous ground,
This is a game it's much better to enter blind
And the one who wins is the one who is caught and bound.

If you can't be straight then just say nothing instead.
I'll know what you mean much better than if it was said.

Sasha Moorsom
(25 January 1931 – 22 June 1993)

Sasha Moorsom was one of the BBC's first female producers. Encouraged by Dylan Thomas, she brought the poems of Ted Hughes, Philip Larkin, and her friend Thom Gunn to a radio audience while they were still relatively unknown. The author of two novels, she also edited the education magazine *Where?* and had a regular column in *The Listener*. Married to Michael Young (see his poem "The Metronomic Moon" in this present volume), she became involved with many of his projects, including the Open College of the Arts and the Consumer's Association. As well as being a poet, she was a painter, photographer, sculptor, and talented organizer. Her poems were published for the first time, jointly with Michael Young's, by Carcanet, in November 1994, in a book entitled *Your Head in Mine*.

13   J A N U A R Y

My life closed twice before its close

My life closed twice before its close –
It yet remains to see
If Immortality unveil
A third event to me

So huge, so hopeless to conceive
As these that twice befell.
Parting is all we know of heaven,
And all we need of hell.

Emily Dickinson
(10 December 1830 – 15 May 1886)

On this day in 1854, Emily Dickinson wrote from Amherst to the Revd. Edward Everett Hale: "You were the Pastor of B. F. Newton, . . . and I have often hoped to know if his last hours were cheerful, and if he was willing to die . . . Mr. Newton was with my Father two years . . . [He] became to me a gentle, yet grave Preceptor, teaching me what to read, what authors to admire, what was most great or beautiful in nature, and that sublime lesson, a faith in things unseen, and in a life again. . . . [He] was an elder brother, loved indeed very much, and mourned and remembered."

Benjamin Newton had been a law student with her father, and she had been 18 when he left. He married and died not long after, in 1853. This has been conjectured to be the first "parting" to which Emily refers in this poem. The second could be the loss of her much loved spiritual adviser, Revd. Charles Wadsworth, who left New York for California in 1862. As she put it in a letter to Thomas Wentworth Higginson, written when she was 32:

"When a little girl, I had a friend who taught me Immortality; but venturing too near, himself, he never returned. Soon after my tutor died, and for several years, my lexicon was my only companion. Then I found one more, but he was not contented I be his scholar, so he left the land."

First they came for the jews

First they came for the Jews
and I did not speak out –
because I was not a Jew.
Then they came for the communists
and I did not speak out –
because I was not a communist.
Then they came for the trade unionists
and I did not speak out –
because I was not a trade unionist.
Then they came for me –
and there was no one left
to speak out for me.

Pastor Niemöller
(14 January 1892 – 6 March 1984)

German Lutheran pastor Martin Niemöller was an ace submarine commander in World War I and offered to serve in the German navy in World War II, despite his outspoken opposition to Hitler. In retaliation for his preaching against the Führer, his house was ransacked by the Gestapo and he was imprisoned for seven years in Sachsenhausen and Dachau concentration camps. His memoirs were entitled *Vom U-Boot zur Kanzel* (*From U-Boat to the Pulpit*).

PROPHECY

I shall lie hidden in a hut
   In the middle of an alder wood,
With the back door blind and bolted shut,
   And the front door locked for good.

I shall lie folded like a saint,
   Lapped in a scented linen sheet,
On a bedstead striped with bright-blue paint,
   Narrow and cold and neat.

The midnight will be glassy black
   Behind the panes, with wind about
To set his mouth against a crack
   And blow the candle out.

Elinor Wylie
(7 September 1885 – 16 December 1928)

In a poetic gender reversal, Percy Bysshe Shelley often served as a muse to Elinor Wylie; she referred to him as "that archangel." In what seems an example of bold promotion, some of Wylie's family went so far as to propose Elinor as the twentieth-century female Shelley. Wylie, herself, in her novel *The Orphan Angel*, imagines that Shelley escapes drowning when he's rescued by a Yankee ship, which brings him to frontier America, a rather unaccommodating landscape for the English Romantic poet.

MY LOVE IS LIKE TO ICE

My love is like to ice, and I to fire:
How comes it then that this her cold so great
Is not dissolved through my so hot desire,
But harder grows the more I her entreat?
Or how comes it that my exceeding heat
Is not allayed by her heart-frozen cold,
But that I burn much more in boiling sweat,
And feel my flames augmented manifold?
What more miraculous thing may be told,
That fire, which all things melts, should harden ice,
And ice, which is congealed with senseless cold,
Should kindle fire by wonderful device?
Such is the power of love in gentle mind,
That it can alter all the course of kind.

Edmund Spenser
(c. 1552 - 16 January 1599)

Spenser was the son of a clothmaker in East Smithfield, and became a "sizar" or poor scholar at Pembroke Hall, Cambridge. He entered the household of the Earl of Leicester in 1579 and got to know Sir Philip Sidney. In return for crushing rebellion and settling Munster, he acquired Kilcolman Castle in County Cork. Sir Walter Raleigh visited him there and persuaded him to take the first three books of his epic poem *Faerie Queene* to Court. Spenser's previous published attack on Queen Elizabeth's match with the Duc d'Alençon helped prevent preferment, however (although he secured a royal pension), and he returned to his Irish "exile." A rebellion destroyed his home and he fled with his second wife and his children to London, where he died in poverty the following year and was buried in Westminster Abbey.

I AM NOT I

I am not I.
       I am this one
Walking beside me whom I do not see,
Whom at times I manage to visit,
And at other times I forget.
The one who remains silent when I talk,
The one who forgives, sweet, when I hate,
The one who takes a walk when I am indoors,
The one who will remain standing when I die.

Juan Ramón Jiménez
(24 December 1881 – 29 May 1958)
translated by Robert Bly
(23 December 1926 –)

Jiménez was born in Moguer, Huelva, the setting for his story of the young poet and his donkey, *Platero y Yo* (1914). Giving up the law, he moved to Madrid. When the Civil War started he remained in the capital for a time, caring for the wounded and collecting children from the ruined streets. He moved to Havana and then to Florida, losing many of his manuscripts in the process. Influenced by Verlaine in his youth, he in turn influenced Lorca and other Spanish poets. He was awarded the Nobel prize for literature in 1957, the year before his death.

GERTRUDE'S PRAYER

That which is marred at birth Time shall not mend,
    Nor water out of bitter well make clean;
All evil thing returneth at the end,
    Or elseway walketh in our blood unseen.
Whereby the more is sorrow in certaine –
Dayspring mishandled cometh not againe.

To-bruizèd be that slender, sterting spray
    Out of the oake's rind that should betide
A branch of girt and goodliness, straightway
    Her spring is turnèd on herself, and wried
And knotted like some gall or veiney wen. –
Dayspring mishandled cometh not agen.

Noontide repayeth never morning-bliss –
    Sith noon to morn is incomparable;
And, so it be our dawning goth amiss,
    None other after-hour serveth well.
Ah! Jesu-Moder, pitie my oe paine –
Dayspring mishandled[1] cometh not againe!

Rudyard Kipling
(30 December 1865 - 18 January 1936)

G. M. Young wrote: "Kipling, though short, was lithe and slim, with beautifully balanced movements. His most arresting feature was his heavy eyebrows, which shot up and down with his talk: under them twinkled bright blue eyes."

1. *Dayspring Mishandled* is the title of a late short story by Kipling in which one theme is a character's mishandling of the dawning of inspiration within him.

19 JANUARY

from THE TRIUMPH OF CHARIS

Have you seen but a bright lily grow,
  Before rude hands have touched it?
Ha' you marked but the fall o' the snow
  Before the soil hath smutched it?
Ha' you felt the wool o' the beaver?
    Or swan's down ever?
Or have smelt o' the bud o' the brier?
    Or the nard[1] in the fire?
Or have tasted the bag o' the bee?
O so white, O so soft, O so sweet is she!

Ben Jonson
(probably 11 June 1572 - 6 August 1637)

On this day in 1619 Ben Jonson left the home of William Drummond of Hawthornden after some weeks with him, towards the end of his Scottish tour, which began in June 1618. Drummond's notes of their talks are a main source of biographical information on Jonson.

Also on this day, in 1623, Ben Jonson's piece *Time Vindicated to Himself and to His Honors* was performed.

Ben Jonson was born in Westminster and brought up by his stepfather, a bricklayer, as his own father, who had been a minister, died a month before the birth. Having fought for the Dutch against the Spanish, killing an enemy champion in single combat, Jonson became an actor, then a playwright, and was an admiring friend of Shakespeare's ("Sweet swan of Avon . . . The applause, delight, the wonder of our stage.").

Jonson killed an actor in a duel in 1598, escaping the gallows by pleading benefit of clergy. In 1605 he was imprisoned and in danger of having his nose and ears split for his share in a comedy that was derogatory to the Scots. In 1616 James I appointed him as in effect the first Poet Laureate, with the grant of a royal pension. Jonson became London's "literary dictator," with younger writers in his "tribe" calling themselves the "sons of Ben."

1. spikenard: an aromatic plant.

from LOVE'S LABOUR'S LOST
ACT V SCENE II

When icicles hang by the wall,
　And Dick the shepherd blows his nail,[1]
And Tom bears logs into the hall,
　And milk comes frozen home in pail,
When blood is nipped and ways be foul,
Then nightly sings the staring owl,
　　　Tu-whit,
Tu-who! a merry note,
While greasy Joan doth keel the pot.

When all aloud the wind doth blow,
　And coughing drowns the parson's saw,
And bird sits brooding in the snow,
　And Marian's nose looks red and raw,
When roasted crabs hiss in the bowl,
Then nightly sings the staring owl,
　　　Tu-whit,
Tu-who! a merry note,
While greasy Joan doth keel the pot.

William Shakespeare
(23 April 1564 ‒ 23 April 1616)

Coming as it does at the very end of the play, this simple rustic song contrasts sharply with the cleverness and pedantry that permeate *Love's Labour's Lost*. Granville-Barker remarked: "The play finishes, as a play of merry-making should, with everyone ranged for our last look at them."

1. blowing on his nails to warm his hands, a phrase asssociated with enforced idleness during cold spells.

GIVING UP SMOKING

There's not a Shakespeare sonnet
Or a Beethoven quartet
That's easier to like than you
Or harder to forget.

You think that sounds extravagant?
I haven't finished yet –
I like you more than I would like
To have a cigarette.

Wendy Cope
(21 July 1945 –)

"I gave up smoking on 21st January 1985 and wrote this a couple of weeks later," Wendy Cope comments, adding: "People who have never been addicted to nicotine don't understand what an intense love poem it is."

THE DIVINE IMAGE

To Mercy, Pity, Peace, and Love
All pray in their distress;
And to these virtues of delight
Return their thankfulness.

For Mercy, Pity, Peace, and Love
Is God, our father dear,
And Mercy, Pity, Peace, and Love
Is Man, his child and care.

For Mercy has a human heart,
Pity a human face,
And Love, the human form divine,
And Peace, the human dress.

Then every man, of every clime,
That prays in his distress,
Prays to the human form divine,
Love, Mercy, Pity, Peace.

And all must love the human form,
In heathen, Turk, or Jew;
Where Mercy, Love, & Pity dwell
There God is dwelling too.

William Blake
(28 November 1757 - 12 August 1827)

As a young man Blake was greatly influenced by the work of Emmanuel Swedenborg –
though disillusionment crept in later on in life. A central tenet of Swedenborg's teaching
argued that, created in God's image, humans are in their true nature divine.

AN IRISH AIRMAN FORSEES HIS DEATH

I know that I shall meet my fate
Somewhere among the clouds above;
Those that I fight I do not hate,
Those that I guard I do not love;
My country is Kiltartan Cross,
My countrymen Kiltartan's poor,
No likely end could bring them loss
Or leave them happier than before.
Nor law, nor duty bade me fight,
Nor public men, nor cheering crowds,
A lonely impulse of delight
Drove to this tumult in the clouds;
I balanced all, brought all to mind,
The years to come seemed waste of breath,
A waste of breath the years behind
In balance with this life, this death.

William Butler Yeats
(13 June 1865 - 28 January 1939)

The Irish airman in this poem was Robert Gregory, who was killed in action in Italy on 23 January 1918 and buried in the Pavoda main cemetery. He was the son of Sir William and Lady Gregory, and had designed the sets of early Abbey Theatre productions. Yeats thought of him as a Renaissance man: "painter, classical scholar, scholar in painting and in modern literature, boxer, horseman, airman;" and after Gregory's death he commented: "Major Gregory [said] ... that the months since he joined the Army had been the happiest of his life. I think this brought him peace of mind ... from his constant struggle to resist those other gifts that brought him ease and friendship. Leading his squadron in France or in Italy, mind and hand were at one, will and desire." Yeats wrote this poem in 1918.

STORY OF A HOTEL ROOM

Thinking we were safe – insanity!
We went in to make love. All the same
Idiots to trust the little hotel bedroom.
Then in the gloom . . .
. . . And who does not know that pair of shutters
With the awkward hook on them
All screeching whispers? Very well then, in the gloom
We set about acquiring one another
Urgently! But on a temporary basis
Only as guests – just guests of one another's senses.

But idiots to feel so safe you hold back nothing
Because the bed of cold, electric linen
Happens to be illicit. . . .
To make love as well as that is ruinous.
Londoner, Parisian, someone should have warned us
That without permanent intentions
You have absolutely no protection
 – If the act is clean, authentic, sumptuous,
The concurring deep love of the heart
Follows the naked work, profoundly moved by it.

Rosemary Tonks
(1932 -)

Rosemary Tonks has apparently ceased to publish since converting to Christianity in the 1970s. Her published work includes poetry volumes such as *Notes on Cafés and Bedrooms* (1963), novels such as *Businessmen as Lovers*, and writings for children such as *On Wooden Wings*. She was expelled from Wentworth School at 16 and married at 19.

MY LOVE IS LIKE A RED RED ROSE

My love is like a red red rose
  That's newly sprung in June:
My love is like the melody
  That's sweetly play'd in tune.

As fair art thou, my bonnie lass,
  So deep in love am I:
And I will love thee still, my dear,
  Till a' the seas gang dry.

Till a' the seas gang dry, my dear,
  And the rocks melt wi' the sun:
And I will love thee still, my dear,
  While the sands o' life shall run.

And fare thee weel, my only love,
  And fare thee weel a while!
And I will come again, my love,
  Tho' it were ten thousand mile.

Robert Burns
(25 January 1759 – 21 July 1796)

Maurice Lindsey commented: "And did ever lover, vowing human constancy in terms of eternity, swear more movingly than Burns, who apparently knew so little of the meaning of constancy where women's love was concerned." This song and "Auld Lang Syne" are among the two hundred that Burns wrote or collected for The Scots Musical Museum. Burns is Scotland's national poet with Burns Night on 25 January celebrated by his fellow-countrymen around the world. In 1859, at a dinner to mark the centenary of Burns' birth, Ralph Waldo Emerson declared that "The Confession of Augsburg, The Declaration of Independence, the French Rights of Man, and the 'Marseillaise' are not more weighty documents in the history of freedom than the songs of Burns."

AUSTRALIA

Last sea-thing dredged by sailor Time from Space,
Are you a drift Sargasso, where the West
In halcyon calm rebuilds her fatal nest?
Or Delos of a coming Sun-God's race?
Are you for Light, and trimmed, with oil in place,
Or but a Will o' Wisp on marshy quest?
A new demesne for Mammon to infest?
Or lurks millennial Eden 'neath your face?

The cenotaphs of species dead elsewhere
That in your limits leap and swim and fly,
Or trail uncanny harp-strings from your trees,
Mix omens with the auguries that dare
To plant the Cross upon your forehead sky,
A virgin helpmate Ocean at your knees.

Bernard O'Dowd
(11 April 1866 – 1 September 1953)

January 26th is Australia's National Day. On this day in 1788 Captain Arthur Phillip landed at Sydney Cove with a fleet of convict ships: "We . . . had the satisfaction of finding the finest harbour in the world in which a thousand sail of the line may ride with the most perfect security."

The poet Bernard O'Dowd was born in Beaufort, Australia, the son of Ulster immigrants, and he grew up in Ballarat, Victoria. He gained both arts and law degrees and ended up as a chief parliamentary legal draftsman. He married Eva Fryer in 1889 but left her for the socialist poet Marie E. J. Pitt. In his 1909 address *Poetry Militant*, he declared that the poet has a socialist obligation to further humanity's best interests.

This sonnet "Australia" is from his first collection published in 1903, entitled *Dawnward?*, with the question mark perhaps indicating his doubts as to Australia's direction. In his poem "The Bush," however, he envisages for Australia a future as glorious as that of ancient Greece and Rome. A later volume of poetry, *The Silent World* (1909), speculates about a mystic world beyond the physical world; and his *Alma Venus* (1921) is a poetic exploration of the mysteries of sex. He wrote almost no poetry after 1921.

JABBERWOCKY
(from *Through the Looking-Glass*)

'Twas brillig, and the slithy toves
  Did gyre and gimble in the wabe:
All mimsy were the borogoves,
  And the mome raths outgrabe.

'Beware the Jabberwock, my son!
  The jaws that bite, the claws that catch!
Beware the Jubjub bird, and shun
  The frumious Bandersnatch!'

He took his vorpal sword in hand:
  Long time the manxome foe he sought –
So rested he by the Tumtum tree,
  And stood awhile in thought.

And, as in uffish thought he stood,
  The Jabberwock, with eyes of flame,
Came whiffling through the tulgey wood,
  And burbled as it came!

One, two! One, two! And through and through
  The vorpal blade went snicker-snack!
He left it dead, and with its head
  He went galumphing back.

'And hast thou slain the Jabberwock?
  Come to my arms, my beamish boy!
O frabjous day! Callooh! Callay!'
  He chortled in his joy.

'Twas brillig, and the slithy toves
  Did gyre and gimble in the wabe:
All mimsy were the borogoves,
  And the mome raths outgrabe.

Lewis Carroll
(27 January 1832 - 14 January 1898)

Some critics consider "Jabberwocky," with its portmanteau words, to be a burlesque of Edmund Spenser's word-coinages. "Take care of the sounds," Carroll advised "and the sense will take care of itself." Some of the nonsense words in it, such as "chortle" and "burble," have since entered normal usage. The poem appeared in *Through the Looking-Glass,* published in 1871, a sequel to Carroll's *Alice's Adventures in Wonderland* of 1865.

SAILING TO BYZANTIUM

That is no country for old men. The young
In one another's arms, birds in the trees
– Those dying generations – at their song,
The salmon-falls, the mackerel-crowded seas,
Fish, flesh, or fowl, commend all summer long
Whatever is begotten, born, and dies.
Caught in that sensual music all neglect
Monuments of unageing intellect.

An aged man is but a paltry thing,
A tattered coat upon a stick, unless
Soul clap its hands and sing, and louder sing
For every tatter in its mortal dress,
Nor is there singing school but studying
Monuments of its own magnificence;
And therefore I have sailed the seas and come
To the holy city of Byzantium.

O sages standing in God's holy fire
As in the gold mosaic of a wall,
Come from the holy fire, perne in a gyre,°   *reel in spiral revolutions*
And be the singing-masters of my soul.
Consume my heart away; sick with desire
And fastened to a dying animal
It knows not what it is; and gather me
Into the artifice of eternity.

Once out of nature I shall never take
My bodily form from any natural thing,
But such a form as Grecian goldsmiths make

SAILING TO BYZANTIUM

Of hammered gold and gold enamelling
To keep a drowsy Emperor awake;
Or set upon a golden bough to sing
To lords and ladies of Byzantium
Of what is past, or passing, or to come.

William Butler Yeats
(13 June 1865 - 28 January 1939)

The typescript of this poem is dated 26 September 1926. For a BBC Belfast broadcast of his poems in 1931, Yeats wrote: "Now I am trying to write about the state of my soul, for it is right for an old man to make his soul, and some of my thoughts on that subject I have put into a poem called "Sailing to Byzantium." When Irishmen were illuminating the *Book of Kells* [8th/9th century] and making the jewelled croziers in the National Museum, Byzantium was the centre of European civilization and the source of its spiritual philosophy, so I symbolize the search for the spiritual life by a journey to that city."

SISTRUM

Triune, shaping, restless power,
Life-flow from life's natal hour,
No music chords are in thy sound;
By some thou'rt but a rattle found;
Yet, without thy ceaseless motion,
To ice would turn their dead devotion.
Life-flow of my natal hour,
I will not weary of thy power,
Till in the changes of thy sound
A chord's three parts distinct are found.
I will faithful move with thee,
God-ordered, self-fed energy,
Nature in eternity.

Margaret Fuller
(23 May 1810 – 19 July 1850)

As foreign correspondent for the *New York Tribune*, Fuller departed for Europe in 1846. In Italy, she was introduced to the Marchese Angelo Ossoli, a Roman nobleman with scant funds, and bore him a son in 1848. Two years later she sailed with Ossoli and their son for America, but was shipwrecked and drowned with her family off Fire Island. At Emerson's urging, Thoreau went to the site of the disaster hoping to salvage Fuller's belongings and manuscripts, but all was lost.

RICHARD CORY

Whenever Richard Cory went down town,
  We people on the pavement looked at him:
He was a gentleman from sole to crown,
  Clean favored, and imperially slim.

And he was always quietly arrayed,
  And he was always human when he talked;
But still he fluttered pulses when he said,
  "Good morning," and he glittered when he walked.

And he was rich – yes, richer than a king –
  And admirably schooled in every grace:
In fine, we thought that he was everything
  To make us wish that we were in his place.

So on we worked, and waited for the light,
  And went without the meat, and cursed the bread;
And Richard Cory, one calm summer night,
  Went home and put a bullet through his head.

Edwin Arlington Robinson
(22 December 1869 – 6 April 1935)

Robinson's parents so wanted a girl that the poet went without a name for six months after his birth until people outside the family had the idea to put male names on pieces of paper and draw them from a hat. The man who wrote "Edwin" happened to live in Arlington, Massachusetts.

THE SONG OF WANDERING AENGUS

I went out to the hazel wood,
Because a fire was in my head,
And cut and peeled a hazel wand,
And hooked a berry to a thread;
And when white moths were on the wing,
And moth-like stars were flickering out,
I dropped the berry in a stream
And caught a little silver trout.

When I had laid it on the floor
I went to blow the fire aflame,
But something rustled on the floor,
And some one called me by my name:
It had become a glimmering girl
With apple blossom in her hair
Who called me by my name and ran
And faded through the brightening air.

Though I am old with wandering
Through hollow lands and hilly lands,
I will find out where she has gone,
And kiss her lips and take her hands;
And walk among long dappled grass,

THE SONG OF WANDERING AENGUS

And pluck till time and times are done
The silver apples of the moon,
The golden apples of the sun.

William Butler Yeats
(13 June 1865 – 28 January 1939)

This poem was written on 31 January (1893?). Yeats' note reads, in part: "An old man who was cutting a quickset hedge near Gort, in Galway, said, only the other day, 'One time I was cutting timber over in Inchy, and about eight o'clock one morning, when I got there, I saw a girl picking nuts, with her hair hanging down over her shoulders; brown hair; and she had a good clean face, and she was tall, and nothing on her head, and her dress no way gaudy, but simple. And when she felt me coming up, she gathered herself up, and was gone, as if the earth had swallowed her up. And I followed her, and looked for her, but I never could see her again from that day to this, never again.'"

WHY SO PALE AND WAN?

Why so pale and wan, fond lover?
    Prithee, why so pale?
Will, when looking well can't move her,
    Looking ill prevail?
    Prithee, why so pale?

Why so dull and mute, young sinner?
    Prithee, why so mute?
Will, when speaking well can't win her,
    Saying nothing do 't?
    Prithee, why so mute?

Quit, quit for shame! This will not move;
    This cannot take her.
If of herself she will not love,
    Nothing can make her:
    The devil take her!

Sir John Suckling
(1 February 1609 – c. 1642)

The poet was said by Aubrey to have invented the game of cribbage. He led the life of a rich man's son, at the age of 17 inheriting an enormous fortune from his father. Suckling immediately left Trinity College, Cambridge, and traveled on the Continent. At the age of 28, he insisted on lavish staging for his play *Aglaura* (from which the above is a song) – the actors had to wear real lace and embroideries of "pure gold and silver." In 1639 he raised a troop of one hundred mounted men for Charles I's Scottish expedition, clothing them in luxurious scarlet coats. In 1641, he failed in his conspiracy to rescue the Earl of Strafford from the Tower of London and fled to France. Some accounts say he committed suicide; others, that he was stabbed to death by a servant. He was 33.

SONG

O blush not so! O blush not so!
  Or I shall think you knowing;
And if you smile the blushing while,
  Then maidenheads are going.

There's a blush for won't, and a blush for shan't,
  And a blush for having done it:
There's a blush for thought, and a blush for naught,
  And a blush for just begun it.

O sigh not so! O sigh not so!
  For it sounds of Eve's sweet pippin;
By those loosened lips you have tasted the pips
  And fought in an amorous nipping.

Will you play once more at nice-cut-core,
  For it only will last our youth out?
And we have the prime of the kissing time,
  We have not one sweet tooth out.

There's a sigh for yes, and a sigh for no,
  And a sigh for I can't bear it !
O what can be done, shall we stay or run?
  O, cut the sweet apple and share it!

John Keats
(31 October 1795 – 23 February 1821)

Keats began an effervescent letter to John Hamilton Reynolds and made up a song of five stanzas (above), and then stopped, saying: "I proposed to write you a serious political letter." But he soon had had enough of being serious: "I cannot write in prose. It is a sun-shiny day," and proceeded to add further impromptu poetry to his letter.

THE SCHOLARS

Bald heads forgetful of their sins,
Old, learned, respectable bald heads
Edit and annotate the lines
That young men, tossing on their beds,
Rhymed out in love's despair
To flatter beauty's ignorant ear.

All shuffle there; all cough in ink;
All wear the carpet with their shoes;
All think what other people think;
All know the man their neighbour knows.
Lord, what would they say
Did their Catullus walk that way?

William Butler Yeats
(13 June 1865 – 28 January 1939)

The manuscript of this poem is dated April 1915.

TO MARGO

In life's rough-and-tumble
you're the crumble on my apple crumble
and the fairy on my Christmas tree!
In life's death-and-duty
you've the beauty of the Beast's own Beauty –
I feel humble as a bumble-bee!

In life's darkening duel
I'm the lighter, you're the lighter fuel –
and the tide that sways my inland sea!
In life's meet-and-muster
you've the lustre of a diamond cluster –
a blockbuster – just a duster, me!

Gavin Ewart
(4 February 1916 – 23 October 1995)

Gavin Ewart commented: "This is a birthday poem for my wife (29th December)."

THE WAKING

I wake to sleep, and take my waking slow.
I feel my fate in what I cannot fear.
I learn by going where I have to go.

We think by feeling. What is there to know?
I hear my being dance from ear to ear.
I wake to sleep, and take my waking slow.

Of those so close beside me, which are you?
God bless the Ground! I shall walk softly there,
And learn by going where I have to go.

Light takes the Tree; but who can tell us how?
The lowly worm climbs up a winding stair;
I wake to sleep, and take my waking slow.

Great Nature has another thing to do
To you and me; so take the lively air,
And, lovely, learn by going where to go.

The Waking

This shaking keeps me steady. I should know.
What falls away is always. And is near.
I wake to sleep, and take my waking slow.
I learn by going where I have to go.

Theodore Roethke
(25 May 1908 – 1 August 1963)

Roethke was born in Saginaw, Michigan. His father was of Prussian extraction and owned a large greenhouse. Roethke wrote about his youth among the greenhouse flowers in his collection *The Lost Son* (1948). He taught creative writing at Lafayette College and elsewhere, before becoming poet-in-residence at the University of Washington in Seattle. In 1953, he married Beatrice Heath O'Connell, a student at Bennington College from the time he taught there. In that year too, several of Roethke's more autobiographical poems appeared in his collection *The Waking*.

Jay Parini describes Roethke as "a latter-day Transcendentalist, finding spiritual correspondences in physical things."

Roethke was institutionalized on several occasions for brief periods, and liked "to identify himself with 'mad' poets of the past such as William Blake and Christopher Smart." When Roethke writes (last verse above) "This shaking keeps me steady," the words are in keeping with his view of his breakdowns as in essence spiritual crises.

There is an echo of this poem "The Waking" in his poem "Words for the Wind" where he writes "What falls away will fall; / All things bring me love."

THE PASSIONATE SHEPHERD TO HIS LOVE

Come live with me, and be my love,
And we will all the pleasures prove,
That valleys, groves, hills, and fields,
Woods, or steepy mountain yields.

And we will sit upon the rocks,
Seeing the shepherds feed their flocks,
By shallow rivers to whose falls
Melodious birds sing madrigals.

And I will make thee beds of roses,
And a thousand fragrant posies,
A cap of flowers, and a kirtle,°   *gown or skirt*
Embroidered all with leaves of myrtle;

A gown made of the finest wool,
Which from our pretty lambs we pull;
Fair linèd slippers for the cold,
With buckles of the purest gold;

A belt of straw and ivy buds,
With coral clasps and amber studs:
And if these pleasures may thee move,
Come live with me, and be my love.

The shepherds' swains shall dance and sing
For thy delight each May morning.
If these delights thy mind may move,
Then live with me, and be my love.

Christopher Marlowe
(6 February 1564 – 30 May 1593)

Marlowe was born in Canterbury, the son of a shoemaker. He graduated from Corpus Christi College, Cambridge, and wrote his four best-known plays – *Tamburlaine, Dr. Faustus, The Jew of Malta,* and *Edward II* – within a six-year period. He was involved in a street fight where a man was killed, was deported from the Netherlands for trying to forge gold coins, and was on the point of being arrested for spreading atheistic opinions when he too was killed in a brawl. It was a tavern argument with one Ingram Frizer about paying the bill; Marlowe attacked him and was himself then stabbed, dying instantly. His contemporary writers paid tribute to his work – he was Shakespeare's "dead shepherd" in *As You Like It.*

The above poem was published in *The Passionate Pilgrim* in 1599 and a year later again, this time with a poem in response by Sir Walter Raleigh, beginning:

If all the world and love were young,
And truth in every shepherd's tongue,
These pretty pleasures might me move,
To live with thee and be thy love.

from KING RICHARD II
ACT II SCENE I

Gaunt. This royal throne of kings, this sceptered isle,
This earth of majesty, this seat of Mars,
This other Eden, demi-Paradise;
This fortress built by Nature for herself
Against infection and the hand of war;
This happy breed of men, this little world;
This precious stone set in the silver sea,
Which serves it in the office of a wall,
Or as a moat defensive to a house,
Against the envy of less happier lands;
This blessed plot, this earth, this realm, this England,
This nurse, this teeming womb of royal kings,
Feared by their breed, and famous by their birth,
Renowned for their deeds as far from home,
For Christian service and true chivalry,
As is the sepulchre, in stubborn Jewry,
Of the world's ransom, blessed Mary's Son;
This land of such dear souls, this dear dear land,
Dear for her reputation through the world,
Is now leased out – I die pronouncing it –
Like to a tenement or pelting farm:
England, bound in with the triumphant sea,
Whose rocky shore beats back the envious siege
Of watery Neptune, is now bound in with shame,

from KING RICHARD II

With inky blots, and rotten parchment bonds:
That England, that was wont to conquer others,
Hath made a shameful conquest of itself.

William Shakespeare
(23 April 1564 - 23 April 1616)

On this day in 1601, the day before the Earl of Essex's planned rebellion against Elizabeth I, Essex's agents bribed the Chamberlain's Men to put on a performance of *Richard II*, believing that the play's deposition scene (Act IV, Scene i, in which the unpopular monarch willingly abdicates his reign) would steel the rebels in their purpose. Essex was executed on 25 February 1603.

ONE ART

The art of losing isn't hard to master;
so many things seem filled with the intent
to be lost that their loss is no disaster.

Lose something every day. Accept the fluster
of lost door keys, the hour badly spent.
The art of losing isn't hard to master.

Then practice losing farther, losing faster:
places, and names, and where it was you meant
to travel. None of these will bring disaster.

I lost my mother's watch. And look! my last, or
next-to-last, of three loved houses went.
The art of losing isn't hard to master.

I lost two cities, lovely ones. And, vaster,
some realms I owned, two rivers, a continent.
I miss them, but it wasn't a disaster.

One art

– Even losing you (the joking voice, a gesture
I love) I shan't have lied. It's evident
the art of losing's not too hard to master
though it may look like (*Write* it!) like disaster.

Elizabeth Bishop
(*8 February 1911 – 6 October 1979*)

Elizabeth Bishop's father died when she was 8 months old and she never saw her mother again once the latter was confined to a mental hospital. Her biographer Brett Miller attributes this poem to 1975, an alcoholic time in Elizabeth's life when she was barely functioning or even writing letters. The draft of this villanelle started out with the title "How to Lose Things," and referred to her companion Alice Methfesell "an average-sized not exceptionally / beautiful or dazzlingly intelligent person" (who in fact later returned to her, and was invaluable as her secretary, chauffeur, traveling companion, and nurse). Miller identifies the lost houses as in Key West, Petrópolis, and Ouro Pêtro, one of the cities as Rio de Janeiro, and the continent as South America (lost to her since her friend Lota Soares' suicide). In addition to alcoholism, Elizabeth Bishop suffered from depression and physical ailments. She died of cerebral aneurysm. "Awful but cheerful" were the words she had wanted Alice to put on her tombstone.

from THE JUNGLE BOOKS
QUIQUERN (CHAPTER HEADING)

The People of the Eastern Ice, they are melting like the snow –
They beg for coffee and sugar; they go where the white men go.
The People of the Western Ice, they learn to steal and fight;
They sell their furs to the trading-post; they sell their souls to the white.
The People of the Southern Ice, they trade with the whaler's crew;
Their women have many ribbons, but their tents are torn and few.
But the People of the Elder Ice, beyond the white man's ken –
Their spears are made of the narwhal-horn, and they are the last of the Men!

Rudyard Kipling
(30 December 1865 – 18 January 1936)

Rudyard Kipling was born in Bombay. He was separated from his parents at the age of six by being sent for five years to boarding schools in England, and it was perhaps the cruelties he experienced there that made him sensitive later in life to the sufferings of victimized natives and Tommies. His tales for children, the two *Jungle Books*, were published in 1894-5. He won the Nobel prize for literature in 1907.

SONNET 116

Let me not to the marriage of true minds
Admit impediments. Love is not love
Which alters when it alteration finds,
Or bends with the remover to remove:
Oh no, it is an ever fixèd mark
That looks on tempests and is never shaken;
It is the star to every wandering bark,
Whose worth's[1] unknown, although his height[2] be taken.
Love's not Time's fool, though rosy lips and cheeks
Within his bending sickle's compass come;
Love alters not with his brief hours and weeks,
But bears it out even to the edge of doom.
   If this be error and upon me proved,
   I never writ, nor no man ever loved.

William Shakespeare
(23 April 1564 - 23 April 1616)

On this day in 1616, Shakespeare's younger daughter Judith married his old friend Thomas Quiney, four years her junior, at the Stratford-on-Avon parish church.

Shakespeare's wording in this sonnet of course echoes that of the marriage service ("If any of you know cause, or just impediment, why these two persons should not be joined together in holy Matrimony, ye are to declare it.").

1. Astral influence.
2. A height taken so as to calculate longitude.

WORDS

Axes
After whose stroke the wood rings,
And the echoes!
Echoes traveling
Off from the center like horses.

The sap
Wells like tears, like the
Water striving
To re-establish its mirror
Over the rock

That drops and turns,
A white skull,
Eaten by weedy greens.
Years later I
Encounter them on the road –

Words dry and riderless,
The indefatigable hoof-taps.
While
From the bottom of the pool, fixed stars
Govern a life.

Sylvia Plath
(27 October 1932 – 11 February 1963)

On this day in 1960, exactly three years before taking her own life, Sylvia Plath had written to her mother and brother with news of her first book of poems, *The Colossus*, being accepted by Heinemann. "Amaze of amaze," she wrote.

The sound of the sea

The sea awoke at midnight from its sleep,
And round the pebbly beaches far and wide
I heard the first wave of the rising tide
Rush onward with uninterrupted sweep;
A voice out of the silence of the deep,
A sound mysteriously multiplied
As of a cataract from the mountain's side,
Or roar of winds upon a wooded steep.
So comes to us at times, from the unknown
And inaccessible solitudes of being,
The rushing of the sea-tides of the soul;
And inspirations, that we deem our own,
Are some divine foreshadowing and foreseeing
Of things beyond our reason or control.

Henry Wadsworth Longfellow
(27 February 1807 - 24 March 1882)

Grief in his personal life often undercut Longfellow's literary and academic success. Eight years after losing his first wife, Longfellow married Fanny Appleton. They had six children, one of whom died in 1848. In addition, Longfellow had endured partial loss of vision since 1843. In 1861, while together in their Cambridge home, Craigie House, Fanny died as a result of her dress catching fire from burning sealing wax. In 1884, Longfellow became the first American poet to have a commemorative bust placed in Westminster Abbey.

Rain – Birdoswald

I stand under a leafless tree
more still, in this mouse-pattering
thrum of rain,
than cattle shifting in the field.
It is more dark than light.
A Chinese painter's brush of deepening grey
moves in a subtle tide.

The beasts are darker islands now.
Wet-stained and silvered by the rain
they suffer night,
marooned as still as stone or tree.
We sense each other's quiet.

Almost, death could come
inevitable, unstrange
as is this dusk and rain,
and I should be no more
myself, than raindrops
glimmering in last light
on black ash buds

or night beasts in a winter field.

Frances Horovitz
(13 February 1938 – 2 October 1983)

Frances Horovitz began to write poetry after her marriage to the performance poet Michael Horovitz. In 1980, inspired by a commission on the theme of Hadrian's Wall, she lived in a farmhouse at Kiln Hill, near the Roman fort of Birdoswald in Cumbria. Many of her poems at that time took their inspiration from the Irthing Valley below Birdoswald. She died at the age of 45 after a long struggle with cancer.

VALENTINE

Not a red rose or a satin heart.

I give you an onion.
It is a moon wrapped in brown paper.
It promises light
like the careful undressing of love.

Here.
It will blind you with tears
like a lover.
It will make your reflection
a wobbling photo of grief.

I am trying to be truthful.

Not a cute card or a kissogram.

I give you an onion.
Its fierce kiss will stay on your lips,
possessive and faithful
as we are,
for as long as we are.

Take it.
Its platinum loops shrink to a wedding-ring,
if you like.

Valentine

Lethal.
Its scent will cling to your fingers,
cling to your knife.

Carol Ann Duffy
(23 December 1955 -)

Carol Ann Duffy writes: "This was written for radio one February. There was a basket of onions on the kitchen table, where I was sitting with my notebook. A couple of years later, a reader sent me a lovely watercolor based on the poem. More recently, a proof copy from a publisher misprinted 'onion' throughout as 'opinion.' An improvement, perhaps."

Harp song of the dane women

What is a woman that you forsake her,
And the hearth-fire and the home-acre,
To go with the old grey Widow-maker?

She has no house to lay a guest in –
But one chill bed for all to rest in,
That the pale suns and the stray bergs nest in.

She has no strong white arms to fold you,
But the ten-times-fingering weed to hold you –
Out on the rocks where the tide has rolled you.

Yet, when the signs of summer thicken,
And the ice breaks, and the birch-buds quicken,
Yearly you turn from our side, and sicken –

Sicken again for the shouts and the slaughters.
You steal away to the lapping waters,
And look at your ship in her winter-quarters.

You forget our mirth, and talk at the tables,
The kine in the shed and the horse in the stables –
To pitch her sides and go over her cables.

Then you drive out where the storm-clouds swallow,
And the sound of your oar-blades, falling hollow,
Is all we have left through the months to follow.

Harp song of the Dane women

Ah, what is Woman that you forsake her,
And the hearth-fire and the home-acre,
To go with the old grey Widow-maker?

Rudyard Kipling
(30 December 1865 – 18 January 1936)

Embittered by a quarrel with his brother-in-law in America, and by the death of his daughter and the loss of his son in the Great War, Kipling lived in relative seclusion in Burwash, Sussex, but continued to venture forth on travels to South Africa and elsewhere.

LOVE'S PHILOSOPHY

The fountains mingle with the river
  And the rivers with the Ocean,
The winds of Heaven mix for ever
  With a sweet emotion;
Nothing in the world is single;
  All things by a law divine
In one spirit meet and mingle.
  Why not I with thine ? –

See the mountains kiss high Heaven
  And the waves clasp one another;
No sister-flower would be forgiven
  If it disdained its brother;
And the sunlight clasps the earth
  And the moonbeams kiss the sea:
What is all this sweet work worth
  If thou kiss not me ?

Percy Bysshe Shelley
(4 August 1792 – 8 July 1822)

Shelley flirted with the young and attractive Sophia Stacey, a ward of one of his uncles, who came with her chaperone to visit Mary Shelley and him in Florence in December 1819. Mary commented that "the younger one was *entousiasmée* to see him – the elder said he was a very shocking man." While Mary stayed at home looking after their child, Shelley would take Sophia and her chaperone out to galleries. Sophia, Mary admitted, "sings well for an English dilettante" and Shelley wrote her several love lyrics, including this one.

UP-HILL

Does the road wind up-hill all the way?
  Yes, to the very end.
Will the day's journey take the whole long day?
  From morn to night, my friend.

But is there for the night a resting-place?
  A roof for when the slow dark hours begin.
May not the darkness hide it from my face?
  You cannot miss that inn.

Shall I meet other wayfarers at night?
  Those who have gone before.
Then must I knock, or call when just in sight?
  They will not keep you standing at that door.

Shall I find comfort, travel-sore and weak?
  Of labour you shall find the sum.
Will there be beds for me and all who seek?
  Yea, beds for all who come.

Christina Rossetti
(5 December 1830 – 29 December 1894)

Christina Rossetti was born in London, her father Italian and her mother half-Italian. The house was a magnet for literary refugees and she was educated at home, and lived there all her life, retiring from work as a governess as a result of ill health. "Differing from her Bohemian brother, Dante Gabriel, and more like her older sister, she found the world evil. She repudiated pleasure: 'I cannot possibly use the word "happy" without meaning something beyond this present life.'" (Louis Untermeyer).

LONG-LEGGED FLY

That civilisation may not sink,
Its great battle lost,
Quiet the dog, tether the pony
To a distant post;
Our master Caesar is in the tent
Where the maps are spread,
His eyes fixed upon nothing,
A hand under his head.
Like a long-legged fly upon the stream
His mind moves upon silence.

That the topless towers be burnt
And men recall that face,
Move most gently if move you must
In this lonely place.
She thinks, part woman, three parts a child,
That nobody looks; her feet
Practise a tinker shuffle
Picked up on a street.
Like a long-legged fly upon the stream
Her mind moves upon silence.

That girls at puberty may find
The first Adam in their thought,
Shut the door of the Pope's chapel,
Keep those children out.
There on that scaffolding reclines
Michael Angelo.
With no more sound than the mice make

Long-legged Fly

His hand moves to and fro.
Like a long-legged fly upon the stream
His mind moves upon silence.

William Butler Yeats
(13 June 1865 – 28 January 1939)

Michelangelo does not recline on the scaffolding in his own poem "On the Painting of the Sistine Chapel" : "I've grown a goitre by dwelling in this den / . . . crosswise I strain me like a Syrian bow: / . . . foul I fare and painting is my shame" (see John Addington Symonds's version in 99 *Poems in Translation*, edited by Pinter and others).

It was Helen's beauty that led to the burning of Troy's "topless towers" (in the second stanza).

from CYMBELINE
ACT IV SCENE II

Gui   Fear no more the heat o' the sun,
        Nor the furious winter's rages,
        Thou thy worldly task hast done,
        Home art gone, and ta'en thy wages.
        Golden lads, and girls all must,
        As chimney-sweepers come to dust.

Arv   Fear no more the frown o' th' great,
        Thou art past the tyrant's stroke,
        Care no more to clothe and eat,
        To thee the reed is as the oak;
        The sceptre, learning, physic must
        All follow this, and come to dust.

Gui   Fear no more the lightning flash,
Arv   Nor th' all-dreaded thunderstone.
Gui   Fear not slander, censure rash.
Arv   Thou hast finish'd joy and moan.
Both   All lovers young, all lovers must,
        Consign to thee and come to dust.

Gui   No exorciser harm thee,
Arv   Nor no witch-craft charm thee.
Gui   Ghost unlaid forbear thee.

from CYMBELINE

Arv   Nothing ill come near thee.
Both   Quiet consummation have,
        And renowned be thy grave.

William Shakespeare
(23 April 1564 - 23 April 1616)

This dirge is spoken in turns by Guiderius and Arviragus, the two lost sons of
Cymbeline, King of Britain, who live as the children of Bellarius in a cave in Wales. They
have found Fidele, their page (actually their sister Imogen in disguise), apparently dead.
She revives quickly enough once they leave her alone.
    Dr. Johnson found the play ridiculous: "To remark the folly of the fiction, the absurdity
of the conduct, the confusion of the names and manners of different times, and the im-
possibility of the events in any system of life, were to waste criticism upon unresisting
imbecility, upon faults too evident for detection, and too gross for aggravation."
Tennyson, who was rather fonder of the play, died with a copy of it lying next to him on
his bed.

THE STARLIGHT NIGHT

Look at the stars! look, look up at the skies!
　O look at all the fire-folk sitting in the air!
　The bright boroughs, the circle-citadels there!
Down in dim woods the diamond delves! the elves'-eyes!
The grey lawns cold where gold, where quickgold lies!
　Wind-beat whitebeam! airy abeles¹ set on a flare!
　Flake-doves sent floating forth at a farmyard scare! –
Ah well! it is all a purchase, all is a prize.

Buy then! bid then! – What? – Prayer, patience, alms, vows.
Look, look: a May-mess, like on orchard boughs!
　Look! March-bloom, like on mealed-with-yellow sallows!²
These are indeed the barn; withindoors house
The shocks.³ This piece-bright paling⁴ shuts the spouse
　Christ home, Christ and his mother and all his hallows.

Gerard Manley Hopkins
(28 July 1844 – 8 June 1889)

Hopkins described this poem and "God's Grandeur" to his mother (1 March 1877) as "two sonnets I wrote in a freak the other day ... They are not so queer, but have a few metrical effects, mostly after Milton." And to Robert Bridges he added the note "to be read, both of them, slowly, strongly marking the rhythms and fetching out the syllables."

1. White poplars with waving (flaring) leaves.
2. Goat willows with yellow catkins.
3. Piles of sheaves.
4. Perhaps paling-boards of the barn with "pieces" of light shining through the gaps.

from TO HIS COY MISTRESS

Had we but world enough, and time,
This coyness, Lady, were no crime.
We would sit down, and think which way
To walk, and pass our long love's day.
Thou by the Indian Ganges' side
Shouldst rubies find: I by the tide
Of Humber would complain. I would
Love you ten years before the Flood:
And you should, if you please, refuse
Till the conversion of the Jews.
My vegetable love should grow
Vaster than empires, and more slow.
An hundred years should go to praise
Thine eyes, and on thy forehead gaze.
Two hundred to adore each breast:
But thirty thousand to the rest.
An age at least to every part,
And the last age should show your heart.
For, Lady, you deserve this state;
Nor would I love at lower rate.
  But at my back I always hear
Time's wingèd chariot hurrying near:
And yonder all before us lie
Deserts of vast eternity.
Thy beauty shall no more be found;
Nor, in thy marble vault, shall sound
My echoing song: then worms shall try
That long preserved virginity:

from TO HIS COY MISTRESS

And your quaint honour turn to dust;
And into ashes all my lust.
The grave's a fine and private place,
But none I think do there embrace.
   Now therefore, while the youthful hue
Sits on thy skin like morning dew,
And while thy willing soul transpires
At every pore with instant fires,
Now let us sport us while we may;
And now, like amorous birds of prey,
Rather at once our time devour,
Than languish in his slow-chapt power.
Let us roll all our strength, and all
Our sweetness, up into one ball:
And tear our pleasures with rough strife,
Through the iron gates of life.
Thus, though we cannot make our sun
Stand still, yet we will make him run.

Andrew Marvell
(31 March 1621 - 16 or 18 August 1678)

Andrew Marvell was born in Yorkshire in 1621. His mother died when he was 16; his father drowned three years later. Marvell traveled through Europe between 1643 and 1647 to avoid the Civil War – "The Cause was too good to have been fought for," he said.
   In the realm of love, "To His Coy Mistress" remains to this day one of the most effective poetic weapons in the seducer's arsenal.

FIRST FIG

My candle burns at both ends;
  It will not last the night;
But ah, my foes, and oh, my friends
  It gives a lovely light!

Edna St. Vincent Millay
(22 February 1892 – 19 October 1950)

Concerning the rewards and pitfalls of her profession, Edna St. Vincent Millay once re-marked : "A person who publishes a book wilfully appears before the populace with his pants down . . . If it is a good book nothing can hurt him. If it is a bad book, nothing can help him."

from[1] ADONAIS[2]

AN ELEGY ON THE DEATH OF JOHN KEATS,
AUTHOR OF ENDYMION, HYPERION, &C.

He is made one with Nature: there is heard
His voice in all her music, from the moan
Of thunder, to the song of night's sweet bird;
He is a presence to be felt and known
In darkness and in light, from herb and stone,
Spreading itself where'er that Power may move
Which has withdrawn his being to its own;
Which wields the world with never-wearied love,
Sustains it from beneath, and kindles it above.

He is a portion of the loveliness
Which once he made more lovely: he doth bear
His part, while the one Spirit's plastic stress[3]
Sweeps through the dull dense world, compelling there,
All new successions to the forms they wear;
Torturing th' unwilling dross that checks its flight
To its own likeness, as each mass may bear;
And bursting in its beauty and its might
From trees and beasts and men into the Heaven's light.

The splendours of the firmament of time
May be eclipsed, but are extinguished not;
Like stars to their appointed height they climb,
And death is a low mist which cannot blot
The brightness it may veil. When lofty thought
Lifts a young heart above its mortal lair,

from ADONAIS

And love and life contend in it, for what
Shall be its earthly doom, the dead live there
And move like winds of light on dark and stormy air.

Percy Bysshe Shelley
(4 August 1792 - 8 July 1822)

"Adonais" was completed on 16 June 1821. Shelley wrote to John Gisborne: "It is a highly wrought piece of art, perhaps better in point of composition than anything I have written." In his preface, Shelley gives his highly partial version of Keats's death: "The savage criticism of his "Endymion," which appeared in the *Quarterly Review*, produced the most violent effect on his susceptible mind; the agitation thus originated ended in the rupture of a blood vessel in the lungs; a rapid consumption ensued, and the succeeding acknowledgments from more candid critics, of the true greatness of his powers, were ineffectual to heal the wound thus wantonly inflicted."

1. Stanzas 42-44.
2. The name derives from Adonis, the young hunter and god of beauty and fertility in Greek legend who was loved by Aphrodite and killed by a boar.
3. "Plastic stress" means roughly "shaping force."

SPLEEN

I was not sorrowful, I could not weep,
And all my memories were put to sleep.

I watched the river grow more white and strange,
All day till evening I watched it change.

All day till evening I watched the rain
Beat wearily upon the window pane.

I was not sorrowful, but only tired
Of everything that ever I desired.

Her lips, her eyes, all day became to me
The shadow of a shadow utterly.

All day mine hunger for her heart became
Oblivion, until the evening came,

And left me sorrowful, inclined to weep,
With all my memories that could not sleep.

Ernest Dowson
(2 August 1867 - 23 February 1900)

Born into an eminent family at Belmont Hill in Kent, Dowson left Queen's College, Oxford, without finishing his studies, and became part of Wilde's and Beardsley's set in London. He inherited a dry dock from his father, but, having become a heavy drinker, he lived there in squalor, later moving to France and converting to Roman Catholicism. He died at the age of 32.

THOSE WINTER SUNDAYS

Sundays too my father got up early
and put his clothes on in the blueblack cold,
then with cracked hands that ached
from labor in the weekday weather made
banked fires blaze. No one ever thanked him.

I'd wake and hear the cold splintering, breaking.
When the rooms were warm, he'd call,
and slowly I would rise and dress,
fearing the chronic angers of that house,

Speaking indifferently to him,
who had driven out the cold
and polished my good shoes as well.
What did I know, what did I know
of love's austere and lonely offices?

Robert Hayden
(4 August 1913 – 25 February 1980)

Robert Hayden was born in Detroit and educated at Wayne State University. His poetry
books included *Heart-Shape in the Dust* (1940) and *Words in the Mourning Time* (1970). He
was the editor of *Kaleidoscope – Poems by American Negro Poets* (1967). In this book, he
warned against the black writer being consigned to "a kind of literary ghetto" where he
would be "not considered as a writer but a species of race-relations man."

What the bullet sang

O joy of creation
        To be!
O rapture to fly
        And be free!
Be the battle lost or won,
  Though its smoke shall hide the sun,
I shall find my love – The one
        Born for me!

I shall know him where he stands,
        All alone,
With the power in his hands
        Not o'erthrown;
I shall know him by his face,
  By his god-like front and grace;
I shall hold him for a space,
        All my own!

It is he – O my love!
        So bold!
It is I – All thy love
        Foretold!
It is I. O love what bliss!

WHAT THE BULLET SANG

Dost thou answer to my kiss?
Oh! sweetheart, what is this!
      Lieth there so cold!

Bret Harte
(25 August 1836 – 5 May 1902)

Francis Brett Harte was his own source of financial support from the age of fifteen, having left school in New York City two years earlier. After his mother remarried, he followed her to California, where his articles and poems were published in local newspapers. His short stories soon attracted a national audience. Eventually, he lived solely in London, supporting himself completely by his pen after having lost his appointment to the U. S. consulate in Glasgow. Mark Twain, with whom Harte collaborated on the poorly received drama *Ah Sin*, said of him "He trimmed and trained and schooled me patiently ... changed me from an awkward utterer of coarse grotesqueness...."

The lesson

'Your father's gone,' my bald headmaster said.
His shiny dome and brown tobacco jar
Splintered at once in tears. It wasn't grief.
I cried for knowledge which was bitterer
Than any grief. For there and then I knew
That grief has uses – that a father dead
Could bind the bully's fist a week or two;
And then I cried for shame, then for relief.

I was a month past ten when I learnt this:
I still remember how the noise was stilled
In school-assembly when my grief came in.
Some goldfish in a bowl quietly sculled
Around their shining prison on its shelf.
They were indifferent. All the other eyes
Were turned towards me. Somewhere in myself
Pride, like a goldfish, flashed a sudden fin.

Edward Lucie-Smith
(27 February 1933 -)

Edward Lucie-Smith comments: "This is set in Jamaica, where I was brought up, during World War II. I was at a boys' prep school, where I was badly bullied. My father worked for the old colonial government, and died rather rapidly of lung cancer in 1943. I never saw him during his illness, and was in fact only rather remotely aware that something was wrong. In any case I had been largely brought up by servants before being sent to boarding school: I wasn't close to my parents and today have very few memories of my father as a result. The poem is essentially about the difference between what one is supposed to feel and what one actually does feel, when faced with some sort of 'shaping' event. I think I wrote the poem itself sometime in the 1950s, and it reflects my then interest in strict verse forms."

THE SOLDIER

If I should die, think only this of me:
  That there's some corner of a foreign field
That is for ever England. There shall be
  In that rich earth a richer dust concealed;
A dust whom England bore, shaped, made aware,
  Gave, once, her flowers to love, her ways to roam,
A body of England's, breathing English air,
  Washed by the rivers, blessed by suns of home.

And think, this heart, all evil shed away,
  A pulse in the eternal mind, no less
    Gives somewhere back the thoughts by England given;
Her sights and sounds; dreams happy as her day;
  And laughter, learnt of friends; and gentleness,
    In hearts at peace, under an English heaven.

Rupert Brooke
(3 August 1887 – 23 April 1915)

On 28 February 1915, Brooke's naval ship sailed for the Dardanelles. On the way there, and weakened by sunstroke, he died of blood-poisoning at the Greek island of Skyros. Winston Churchill telegrammed that he should be buried there, and added: "We shall not see his like again." The grave is in an olive grove in the far south of Skyros, a Greek heaven with air and sun and sights and sounds to rival any English delights, although somewhat encroached on of late by Greek naval emplacements.

Rupert Brooke in his brief life showed enormous energy and enthusiasm. Before the war, he had written to a friend: "I want to walk a thousand miles, and write one thousand plays, and drink one thousand pots of beer, and kiss one thousand girls." Walter de la Mare remarked that "he flung himself into the world, as a wasp into a cake shop, Hotspur into the fighting."

TIME IS . . .

I fear time's tumbril hurrying us
    – bare wee foetuses
hardly rubbed with God's pleasure –
    to the place of execution.
"Stay!" My beloved, Giacometti above,
    Renoir below,
spirit shining, horse to horse,
    leaps in the way.
An angel rapes a neuron in her brain:
"Celebrate! Our rescue remedy is
    the timeless now –
    her handmaids
commitment, compassion and conspiracy,
the breathing together of love.
    Life *is* delightful
from womb bliss to birth bliss,
from home bliss to death bliss
    and beyond
our lives ripple through eternity.
    Enjoy!"

Alan Beam
(29 February 1948 –)

Alan Beam comments: "I was here imagining my wife sharing with me a sudden illumination as to how a belief in the timelessness of the present might offer some reassurance about life's fleetingness as we entered middle age."

Alan Beam was born on this day in St. Albans in 1948 and is primarily a nonfiction writer and editor.

FOR K. R. ON HER SIXTIETH BIRTHDAY

Blow out the candles of your cake.
They will not leave you in the dark,
Who round with grace this dusky arc
Of the grand tour which souls must take.

You who have sounded William Blake,
And the still pool, to Plato's mark,
Blow out the candles of your cake.
They will not leave you in the dark.

Yet, for your friends' benighted sake,
Detain your upward-flying spark;
Get us that wish, though like the lark
You whet your wings till dawn shall break:
Blow out the candles of your cake.

Richard Wilbur
(1 March 1921 –)

Richard Wilbur writes: "This poem, which fell into the form of a rondel, was written for Kathleen Raine, a scholar of Blake and of the Neo-Platonists, one of whose poems is entitled 'The Still Pool.' I used the word 'mark' in the nautical sense, as a measure of the depth of water."

from THE SHIP OF DEATH

5

Build then the ship of death, for you must take
the longest journey, to oblivion.

And die the death, the long and painful death
that lies between the old self and the new.

Already our bodies are fallen, bruised, badly bruised,
already our souls are oozing through the exit
of the cruel bruise.

Already the dark endless ocean of the end
is washing in through the breeches of our wounds,
already the flood is upon us.

O build your ship of death, your little ark
and furnish it with food, with little cakes, and wine
for the dark flight down oblivion.

D. H. Lawrence
(11 September 1885 – 2 March 1930)

Lawrence worked on this poem as he lay dying of tuberculosis in the South of France. In *Etruscan Places* he had described the tomb of an Etruscan prince: "The sacred treasures of the dead, the little bronze ship of death that should bear him over to the other world, the vases of jewels for his arraying, the vases of small dishes, the little bronze statuettes and tools, the armour."

"Do I fear the invisible dark hand of death," Lawrence had once asked, "plucking me into the darkenss, gathering me blossom by blossom from the stem of life into the unknown of my afterwards? I fear it only in reverence and with strange satisfaction."

LOVE

Love bade me welcome; yet my soul drew back,
  Guilty of dust and sin.
But quick-eyed Love, observing me grow slack
  From my first entrance in,
Drew nearer to me, sweetly questioning
  If I lack'd anything.

'A guest,' I answer'd, 'worthy to be here':
  Love said, 'You shall be he.'
'I, the unkind, ungrateful? Ah, my dear,
  I cannot look on Thee.'
Love took my hand and smiling did reply,
  'Who made the eyes but I?'

'Truth, Lord: but I have marr'd them: let my shame
  Go where it doth deserve.'
'And know you not,' says Love, 'Who bore the blame?'
  'My dear, then I will serve.'
'You must sit down,' says Love, 'and taste my meat.'
  So I did sit and eat.

George Herbert
(3 April 1593 – 3 March 1633)

George Herbert, brother of Lord Herbert of Cherbury, was born in Montgomery. He was elected a fellow at Trinity College, Cambridge, in 1614, at the age of 22; he became an MP for Montgomery in 1624; and was ordained a priest in 1630.

Of the role of the country parson, Herbert wrote, "Love is his business and aime"; he himself was revered by his contemporaries as "holy George Herbert," a kindly, saintly man with a love of music. His first biographer Izaak Walton recounts how he died of consumption in his 39th year, on his deathbed composing "such hymns and anthems as the angels and he now sing in heaven."

NO, I'M NOT AFRAID

No, I'm not afraid: after a year
Of breathing these prison nights
I will survive into the sadness
To name which is escape.

The cockerel will weep freedom for me
And here – knee-deep in mire –
My gardens shed their water
And the northern air blows in draughts.

And how am I to carry to an alien planet
What are almost tears, as though towards home . . .
It isn't true, I *am* afraid, my darling!
But make it look as though you haven't noticed.

Irina Ratushinskaya
(4 March 1954 -)
translated by David McDuff

On 4 March 1983, her 29th birthday, Irina Ratushinskaya was sentenced to seven years in the Soviet "strict regime" labor camp at Barashevo where she was beaten frequently, starved, frozen, force-fed, and kept in solitary confinement. Her crime was the "manufacture and dissemination" of her poetry, coupled with "anti-Soviet agitation and propaganda." After worldwide campaigns on her behalf, Ratushinskaya was released from prison on 9 October 1986, and on 18 December 1986 she was allowed to leave the Soviet Union for Britain, accompanied by her husband, the human rights activist Igor Gerashchenko.

As kingfishers catch fire

As kingfishers catch fire, dragonflies dráw fláme;
  As tumbled over rim in roundy wells
  Stones ring; like each tucked[1] string tells, each hung bell's
Bow[2] swung finds tongue to fling out broad its name;
Each mortal thing does one thing and the same:
  Deals out that being indoors each one dwells;
  Selves[3] – goes itself; *myself* it speáks and spells;
Crying *Whát I dó is me: for that I came.*

I say móre: the just man justices;
  Kéeps gráce: thát keeps all his goings graces;
Acts in God's eye what in God's eye he is –
  Christ – for Christ plays in ten thousand places,
Lovely in limbs, and lovely in eyes not his
  To the Father through the features of men's faces.

Gerard Manley Hopkins
(28 July 1844 – 8 June 1889)

This poem was probably composed in March or April of 1877. Hopkins wrote elsewhere that "every workman has a use for every object he makes. Much more has God . . . The thunder speaks of his terror, the lion is like his strength, . . . the honey like his sweetness, . . . they tell of him, they give him glory." His justification as a Jesuit for loving the material world so intensely he derived from a medieval Franciscan theologian, Duns Scotus, who argued that the material world was necessary to make God available to the human senses. The discovery of Duns Scotus's work left Hopkins "flush with a new stroke of enthusiasm."

1. plucked, touched.
2. "sound-bow," the part of the bell struck by the hammer.
3. realizes its individuality.

HOW DO I LOVE THEE?
LET ME COUNT THE WAYS

How do I love thee? Let me count the ways.
I love thee to the depth and breadth and height
My soul can reach, when feeling out of sight
For the ends of being and ideal grace.
I love thee to the level of every day's
Most quiet need, by sun and candlelight.
I love thee freely, as men strive for right;
I love thee purely, as they turn from praise.
I love thee with the passion put to use
In my old griefs, and with my childhood's faith.
I love thee with a love I seemed to lose
With my lost saints – I love thee with the breath,
Smiles, tears, of all my life! – and, if God choose,
I shall but love thee better after death.

Elizabeth Barrett Browning
(6 March 1806 - 29 June 1861)

An invalid living in Wimpole Street under the possessive eye of her father, who refused to allow any of his children to marry, Elizabeth Barrett Browning was approaching her forties and seemed destined to the life of a recluse. On 20 May 1845, after a long exchange of letters, she allowed Robert Browning, who was six years her junior, to visit her. In his first letter he had written: "I love your verses with all my heart, dear Miss Barrett . . . And I love you too." On 12 September 1846, she secretly married him, eventually settling in Florence, giving birth to a son in her 45th year.

This sonnet was the penultimate poem from the 43 "Sonnets from the Portuguese," written during the Brownings' courtship (Robert Browning called her "little Portuguese" because of her olive skin). The sonnets mark her passage from hesitation, through doubt and disbelief, to joy at their mutual love.

She kept the sonnets secret from Robert for the first three years of marriage. She chose to reveal them when the death of his mother precipitated a crisis of faith in him. It seems that her intention was to demonstrate the fluid, shape-changing, but eternal nature of love – love defying death.

NOT WAVING BUT DROWNING

Nobody heard him, the dead man,
But still he lay moaning:
I was much further out than you thought
And not waving but drowning.

Poor chap, he always loved larking
And now he's dead
It must have been too cold for him his heart gave way,
They said.

Oh, no no no, it was too cold always
(Still the dead one lay moaning)
I was much too far out all my life
And not waving but drowning.

Stevie Smith
(20 September 1902 – 7 March 1971)

On this day in 1971, Stevie Smith died of a brain tumor at Ashburton College Hospital in Devon. She was born in Hull, but lived most of her life with her aunt in Palmers Green, London. She is known for her witty, acerbic poetry, adorned with her drawings and doodling, that often have loneliness and death as their themes. In conversation with her friend, the novelist Kay Dick, Stevie Smith said: "I'm terribly pro old age really, because it's so relaxed, you know, oh so marvellous. You just go around and do exactly what you like, and somehow it's so delightful.

"I love death, I think it's the most exciting thing. As one gets older one gets into this – well it's like a race, before you get to the waterfall, when you feel the water slowly getting quicker and quicker, and you can't get out, and all you want to do is get to the waterfall and over the edge. How exciting it is! Why do people grumble about old age so much?"

Stevie Smith's collection *Not Waving But Drowning* was published in 1957.

LITTLE ELEGY
FOR A CHILD WHO SKIPPED ROPE

Here lies resting, out of breath,
Out of turns, Elizabeth
Whose quicksilver toes not quite
Cleared the whirring edge of night.

Earth whose circles round us skim
Till they catch the lightest limb,
Shelter now Elizabeth
And for her sake trip up death.

X. J. Kennedy
(21 August 1929 -)

X. J. Kennedy remarks, "This very early poem – it dates from about 1958 – owes whatever merit it may have to those brief elegies for children written by Herrick ('Here she lies, a pretty bud'), Ben Jonson (elegy for his son), and Wordsworth ('A Slumber Did My Spirit Seal'). Young poets learn by imitation."

X. J. Kennedy (the pseudonym for Joseph Charles Kennedy) was born in Dover, New Jersey, educated at Columbia University and the Sorbonne and served in the United States Navy for four years till 1955. In 1977 he gave up a tenured professorship to concentrate on writing and editing, and has edited the best-selling *An Introduction to Poetry*. His verse for children includes *Brats* (1986) and *Ghastlies, Goops, and Pincushions* (1989).

X. J. Kennedy once referred to himself as "one of an endangered species: people who still write in meter and rime." He published with his wife Dorothy the magazine *Counter/Measures*, in defense of traditional poetry.

THE GREATER CATS

The greater cats with golden eyes
Stare out between the bars.
Deserts are there, and different skies,
And night with different stars.
They prowl the aromatic hill,
And mate as fiercely as they kill,
And hold the freedom of their will
To roam, to live, to drink their fill;
But this beyond their wit know I:
Man loves a little, and for long shall die.

Their kind across the desert range
Where tulips spring from stones,
Not knowing they will suffer change
Or vultures pick their bones.
Their strength's eternal in their sight,
They rule the terror of the night,
They overtake the deer in flight,
And in their arrogance they smite;
But I am sage, if they are strong:
Man's love is transient as his death is long.

Yet oh what powers to deceive!
My wit is turned to faith,
And at this moment I believe
In love, and scout at death.
I came from nowhere, and shall be
Strong, steadfast, swift, eternally:
I am a lion, a stone, a tree,
And as the Polar star in me

THE GREATER CATS

Is fixed my constant heart on thee.
Ah, may I stay forever blind
With lions, tigers, leopards, and their kind.

Vita Sackville-West
(9 March 1892 - 2 June 1962)

Victoria Mary Sackville-West, the author of some 50 books, was born at Knole House in Kent, the palatial home of the Sackvilles since the 16th century.

In her diary, Virginia Woolf writes: "One of these days, I shall sketch here, like a grand historical picture, the outlines of all my friends . . . . It might be a way of writing the memoirs of one's own times during people's lifetimes. It might be a most amusing book. The question is how to do it. Vita should be Orlando, a young nobleman."

from THE PRINCESS

Ask me no more: the moon may draw the sea;
  The cloud may stoop from heaven and take the shape
  With fold to fold, of mountain or of cape;
But O too fond, when have I answer'd thee?
        Ask me no more.

Ask me no more: what answer should I give?
  I love not hollow cheek or faded eye:
  Yet, O my friend, I will not have thee die!
Ask me no more, lest I should bid thee live;
        Ask me no more.

Ask me no more: thy fate and mine are seal'd:
  I strove against the stream and all in vain:
  Let the great river take me to the main:
No more, dear love, for at a touch I yield;
        Ask me no more.

Alfred, Lord Tennyson
(6 August 1809 - 6 October 1892)

On this day in 1843, Charles Dickens sent copies of his work to Tennyson in homage to the "Truth and Beauty" of his works.

  "Ask me no more" was one of the songs that Tennyson added as an afterthought to the third edition of *The Princess* in 1850, the year in which he was appointed Poet Laureate in succession to Wordsworth.

SAY NOT THE STRUGGLE NOUGHT AVAILETH

Say not the struggle nought availeth,
  The labour and the wounds are vain,
The enemy faints not, nor faileth,
  And as things have been, things remain.

If hopes were dupes, fears may be liars;
  It may be, in yon smoke concealed,
Your comrades chase e'en now the fliers,
  And, but for you, possess the field.

For while the tired waves, vainly breaking,
  Seem here no painful inch to gain,
Far back through creeks and inlets making
  Comes, silent, flooding in, the main,

And not by eastern windows only,
  When daylight comes, comes in the light,
In front the sun climbs slow, how slowly,
  But westward, look, the land is bright.

Arthur Hugh Clough
(1 January 1819 - 13 November 1861)

Churchill quoted from this poem on several occasions in 1941 – the last line helped him to emphasize Britain's expectations of her ally in the West. On this day in 1941, the American Lend-Lease Act was passed, which allowed President Roosevelt to provide equipment to Britain, whose reserves were almost totally exhausted.

In a speech broadcast from Chequers in the spring of 1941, Churchill spoke of how the United States were "very closely bound up with us now" and he recited from Clough's poem, remarking how its sentiments were "apt and appropriate to our fortunes tonight" and would be so judged "wherever the English language is spoken or the flag of freedom flies."

To daffodils

Fair daffodils, we weep to see
  You haste away so soon:
As yet the early-rising sun
  Has not attained his noon
    Stay, stay,
  Until the hasting day
    Has run
  But to the evensong;
And, having prayed together, we
  Will go with you along.

We have short time to stay as you;
  We have as short a spring;
As quick a growth to meet decay,
  As you or anything.
    We die,
  As your hours do, and dry
    Away
  Like to the summer's rain;
Or as the pearls of morning's dew,
  Ne'er to be found again.

Robert Herrick
(24 August 1591 – 15 October 1674)

Herrick took up his position as vicar of Dean Prior with some reluctance, expecting to find himself surrounded by dull and uncultured country people. One Sunday he is supposed to have thrown his sermon at an inattentive congregation, cursing them from the pulpit in his frustration. Gradually, though, he came to develop a feeling for the Devonshire rural life, becoming fascinated by folk-custom and festivals, and learning to appreciate the land.

BINSEY POPLARS

FELLED 1879

My aspens dear, whose airy cages quelled,
  Quelled or quenched in leaves the leaping sun,
All felled, felled, are all felled;
    Of a fresh and following folded rank
        Not spared, not one
        That dandled a sandalled
    Shadow that swam or sank
On meadow and river and wind-wandering
    weed-winding bank.

  O if we but knew what we do
      When we delve or hew –
    Hack and rack the growing green!
        Since country is so tender
    To touch, her being só slender,
    That, like this sleek and seeing ball
    But a prick will make no eye at all,
    Where we, even where we mean
        To mend her we end her,
      When we hew or delve:
After-comers cannot guess the beauty been.
  Ten or twelve, only ten or twelve
    Strokes of havoc únselve

Binsey poplars

The sweet especial scene,
Rural scene, a rural scene,
Sweet especial rural scene.

Gerard Manley Hopkins
(28 July 1844 – 8 June 1889)

One of Hopkins's favorite walks took him from Oxford across Port Meadow and toward Binsey, passing a double row of aspens that hung over the towpath. Writing to his friend R. W. Dixon on this day in 1879, he added a postscript to the letter: "I have been up to Godstow this afternoon. I am sorry to say that the aspens that lined the river are everywhere felled." Irony piled on insult for Hopkins once he learned that the trees had been felled to make brake shoes for locomotives of the Great Western Railway, a company whose noisy, land-devouring works he considered responsible for the destruction of beautiful landscapes right across the region.

ODE (WE ARE THE MUSIC MAKERS)

We are the music-makers,
And we are the dreamers of dreams,
Wandering by lone sea-breakers,
And sitting by desolate streams;
World-losers and world forsakers,
On whom the pale moon gleams:
Yet we are the movers and shakers
Of the world for ever, it seems.

With wonderful deathless ditties
We build up the world's great cities.
And out of a fabulous story
We fashion an empire's glory:
One man with a dream, at pleasure,
Shall go forth and conquer a crown;
And three with a new song's measure
Can trample an empire down.

We, in the ages lying
In the buried past of the earth,
Built Nineveh with our sighing,
And Babel itself with our mirth;
And o'erthrew them with prophesying

ODE (WE ARE THE MUSIC MAKERS)

To the old of the new world's worth;
For each age is a dream that is dying,
Or one that is coming to birth.

Arthur William Edgar O'Shaughnessy
(14 March 1844 - 30 January 1881)

The anthologist Palgrave improved this poem by cutting it down from nine stanzas to three, and it is for this shortened poem alone that O'Shaughnessy is nowadays remembered. He was born in London, and at the age of 19 started work in the British Museum, ending up in the zoological department, specializing in icthyology. This ode and some of his other "Victorian escapist verse" appeared in his book *Music and Moonlight* published in 1874. He died of influenza in his 39th year.

SONNET 30

When to the sessions of sweet silent thought
I summon up remembrance of things past,
I sigh the lack of many a thing I sought,
And with old woes new wail my dear times' waste:
Then can I drown an eye, unus'd to flow,
For precious friends hid in death's dateless night,
And weep afresh love's long since cancell'd woe,
And moan the expense of many a vanish'd sight:
Then can I grieve at grievances foregone,
And heavily from woe to woe tell o'er
The sad account of fore-bemoaned moan,
Which I new pay as if not paid before.
　But if the while I think on thee, dear friend,
　All losses are restor'd and sorrows end.

William Shakespeare
(23 April 1564 - 23 April 1616)

On this day in 1604, Shakespeare's company walked in the procession from Tower Bridge to Westminster that accompanied the new king, James I, on his formal entry into London. Ben Jonson and Thomas Dekker were among those who had penned a series of speeches for the day's entertainment.

from HAMLET
ACT III SCENE I

Hamlet. To be, or not to be: that is the question:
Whether 'tis nobler in the mind to suffer
The slings and arrows of outrageous fortune,
Or to take arms against a sea of troubles,
And by opposing end them? To die: to sleep;
No more; and, by a sleep to say we end
The heart-ache and the thousand natural shocks
That flesh is heir to, 'tis a consummation
Devoutly to be wish'd. To die, to sleep;
To sleep: perchance to dream: ay, there's the rub;
For in that sleep of death what dreams may come
When we have shuffled off this mortal coil,
Must give us pause. There's the respect
That makes calamity of so long life;
For who would bear the whips and scorns of time,
The oppressor's wrong, the proud man's contumely,
The pangs of dispriz'd love, the law's delay,
The insolence of office, and the spurns
That patient merit of the unworthy takes,
When he himself might his quietus° make   *exit*
With a bare bodkin?° Who would fardels° bear,   *small dagger / burdens*
To grunt and sweat under a weary life,
But that the dread of something after death,
The undiscover'd country from whose bourn
No traveller returns, puzzles the will,
And makes us rather bear those ills we have
Than fly to others that we know not of?

from HAMLET

Thus conscience does make cowards of us all;
And thus the native hue of resolution
Is sicklied o'er with the pale cast of thought,
And enterprises of great pitch and moment
With this regard their currents turn awry,
And lose the name of action.

William Shakespeare
(23 April 1564 – 23 April 1616)

On this day in 1976 a performance of *Hamlet* with Albert Finney in the lead role opened
the National Theatre in London, some 25 years after work on the building first started.
Charles Lamb wrote in his essay *On the Tragedies of Shakespeare*: "I confess myself utterly
unable to appreciate that celebrated soliloquy . . . 'To be or not to be,' or to tell whether it
be good, bad or indifferent, it has been so handled and pawed about by declamatory boys
and men."

17 MARCH

COME TO THE EDGE

Come to the edge.
We might fall.
Come to the edge.
It's too high!
COME TO THE EDGE!
And they came,
And he pushed,
And they flew.

Christopher Logue
(23 November 1926 -)

On this day in 1918, the French poet Guillaume Apollinaire was wounded in the head by a shell splinter (subsequently dying in the influenza epidemic on 9 November 1918).

Editorial apology: In previous printings of *A Poem A Day*, this poem was attributed to 'Anonymous' and there were textual differences. The poem in fact appears in Christopher Logue's *Selected Poems* published by Faber and Faber Ltd. in 1988. I am grateful to both Christopher Logue and Faber and Faber Ltd. for their forbearance and for their permission to continue using this poem.

Christopher Logue writes: "The poem was written in — I think — 1968. Michael Kustow curated an exhibition of Apollinaire's work at the ICA and asked me for a poem to go on a poster to advertise the show.

"I cannot say that the poem was the result of my reading Apollinaire, more by the idea of the man, his life, as much as his poetry. A daring figure."

Christopher Logue was born in Portsmouth, where he went to the grammar school. His years in the British Army (1944-48) included two years in army prison. He translated and adapted the poetry of Pablo Neruda in *Red Bird Dancing on Ivory* and *The Man Who Told His Love*. His Brechtian musical, *The Lily White Boys*, was put on by the English Stage Company in 1960. His very free adaptations of Homer's *Iliad* started appearing in the early sixties. A pioneer of jazz poetry and a political poet, he has produced a series of poster poems, including "I Shall Vote Labour" (1966). His collection *True Stories* from *Private Eye* was published in 1973.

FUTILITY

Move him into the sun –
Gently its touch awoke him once,
At home, whispering of fields unsown.
Always it woke him, even in France,
Until this morning and this snow.
If anything might rouse him now
The kind old sun will know.

Think how it wakes the seeds –
Woke, once, the clays of a cold star.
Are limbs, so dear-achieved, are sides,
Full-nerved – still warm – too hard to stir?
Was it for this the clay grew tall?
– O what made fatuous sunbeams toil
To break earth's sleep at all?

Wilfred Owen
(18 March 1893 – 4 November 1918)

In his preface to the collection of his poems that included "Futility," Wilfred Owen wrote:

This book is not about heroes. English Poetry is not yet fit to speak of them.
Nor is it about deeds, or lands, nor anything about glory, honor, might, majesty,
dominion, or power, except War.
Above all I am not concerned with Poetry.
My subject is War, and the pity of War.
The poetry is in the pity.
Yet these elegies are to this generation in no sense consolatory. They may be to the
next. All a poet can do today is warn. That is why the true Poets must be truthful.
If I thought the letter of this book would last, I might have used proper names;
but if the spirit of it survives – survives Prussia – my ambition and those names
will have achieved themselves fresher fields than Flanders . . .

from LESSONS OF THE WAR
TO ALAN MITCHELL
Viri duellis nupet idoneus
Et militavi non sine gloria[1]

NAMING OF PARTS

Today we have naming of parts. Yesterday,
We had daily cleaning. And tomorrow morning,
We shall have what to do after firing. But today,
Today we have naming of parts. Japonica
Glistens like coral in all of the neighbouring gardens,
          And today we have naming of parts.

This is the lower sling swivel. And this
Is the upper sling swivel, whose use you will see,
When you are given your slings. And this is the piling swivel,
Which in your case you have not got. The branches
Hold in the gardens their silent, eloquent gestures,
          Which in our case we have not got.

This is the safety-catch, which is always released
With an easy flick of the thumb. And please do not let me
See anyone using his finger. You can do it quite easy
If you have any strength in your thumb. The blossoms
Are fragile and motionless, never letting anyone see
          Any of them using their finger.

And this you can see is the bolt. The purpose of this
Is to open the breech, as you see. We can slide it
Rapidly backwards and forwards: we call this
Easing the spring. And rapidly backwards and forwards

Naming of Parts

The early bees are assaulting and fumbling the flowers:
        They call it easing the Spring.

They call it easing the Spring: it is perfectly easy
If you have any strength in your thumb: like the bolt,
And the breech, and the cocking-piece, and the point of balance,
Which in our case we have not got; and the almond-blossom
Silent in all of the gardens and the bees going backwards and forwards,
        For today we have naming of parts.

Henry Reed
(22 February 1914 -)

On this day in 1941 several hundred people were killed in air raids on Glasgow and Clydeside.

1. "Lately I have lived in the midst of battles, creditably enough, / And have soldiered, not without glory." Reed plays on the opening lines of a poem by Horace (III.26), substituting "duellis" (war/battles) for Horace's word "puellis" (girls).

SPRING

Nothing is so beautiful as spring –
  When weeds, in wheels, shoot long and lovely and lush;
  Thrush's eggs look little low heavens, and thrush
Through the echoing timber does so rinse and wring
The ear, it strikes like lightnings to hear him sing;
  The glassy peartree leaves and blooms, they brush
  The descending blue; that blue is all in a rush
With richness; the racing lambs too have fair their fling.

What is all this juice and all this joy?
  A strain of the earth's sweet being in the beginning
In Eden garden. – Have, get, before it cloy,
  Before it cloud, Christ, lord, and sour with sinning,
Innocent mind and Mayday in girl and boy,
  Most, O maid's child, thy choice and worthy the winning.

Gerard Manley Hopkins
(28 July 1844 – 8 June 1889)

On this day in 1884, Coventry Patmore, a haughty Catholic poet to whom Hopkins had shown his poems, replied discouragingly: " ... to the already sufficiently arduous character of such poetry you seem to me to have added the difficulty of following several entirely novel and simultaneous experiments in versification and construction, together with an altogether unprecedented system of alliteration and compound words; – any one of which novelties would be startling and productive of distraction from the poetic matter ... "

Hopkins wrote this sonnet in the spring of 1877 while studying as a Jesuit at St. Beauno's in the valley of the Clwyd in Wales.

THE OLD MAN'S COMFORTS
AND HOW HE GAINED THEM

You are old, Father William, the young man cried,
   The few locks which are left you are grey;
You are hale, Father William, a hearty old man,
   Now tell me the reason, I pray.

In the days of my youth, Father William replied,
   I remember'd that youth would fly fast,
And abused not my health and my vigour at first,
   That I never might need them at last.

You are old, Father William, the young man cried,
   And pleasures with youth pass away;
And yet you lament not the days that are gone,
   Now tell me the reason, I pray.

In the days of my youth, Father William replied,
   I remember'd that youth could not last;
I thought of the future, whatever I did,
   That I never might grieve for the past.

You are old, Father William, the young man cried,
   And life must be hastening away;
You are cheerful, and love to converse upon death,
   Now tell me the reason, I pray.

THE OLD MAN'S COMFORTS

I am cheerful, young man, Father William replied,
    Let the cause thy attention engage;
In the days of my youth I remember'd my God!
    And He hath not forgotten my age.

Robert Southey
(12 August 1774 - 21 March 1843)

Southey was born in Bristol and from the age of two to six he was handed by his draper father and mother to his mother's half-sister to bring up. As an adult he would "kiss and weep on his mother" in his dreams. He was thrown out of Westminster School for starting *The Flagellant* magazine and at Oxford almost persuaded Coleridge to migrate to America to set up a Pantisocrat commune utopia. In June 1798, he set up home independently for the first time in a rented former ale-house at Westbury-on-Trym in Gloucestershire, with his wife and his now widowed mother. He wrote "Old Man's Comfort" at Westbury in the spring of 1799 at the age of 24, having undertaken to supply poems for the *Morning Post* at a guinea a week. "This was one of the happiest portions of my life," he wrote later. "I never before or since produced so much poetry in the same space of time."

He became very conservative in later life and was made Poet Laureate. At the age of 60 he wrote: "I have been parted from my wife by something worse than death. Forty years she has been the life of my life, and I have left her this day in a lunatic asylum." He remarried, but his own mind began to fail and he died at the age of 70.

NIGHT

The night has a thousand eyes,
    And the day but one;
Yet the light of the bright world dies
    With the dying sun.

The mind has a thousand eyes,
    And the heart but one;
Yet the light of a whole life dies,
    When love is done.

Francis William Bourdillon
(22 March 1852 – 30 January 1921)

Bourdillon was the son of a priest. He was educated at Worcester College, Oxford, became the resident tutor to the two sons of the Prince and Princess Christian at Cumberland Lodge, and later took private pupils for the University of Eastbourne. He produced a number of books and translations, including *Early Editions of the Roman de la Rose* and *Preludes and Romances*. He lived in Buddington near Midhurst in Sussex with his wife Agnes and they had two sons and a daughter.

IMAGINATION

There is a dish to hold the sea,
   A brazier to contain the sun,
A compass for the galaxy,
   A voice to wake the dead and done!

That minister of ministers,
   Imagination, gathers up
The undiscovered Universe,
   Like jewels in a jasper cup.

Its flame can mingle north and south;
   Its accent with the thunder strive;
The ruddy sentence of its mouth
   Can make the ancient dead alive.

The mart of power, the fount of will,
   The form and mold of every star,
The source and bound of good and ill,
   The key of all the things that are,

IMAGINATION

Imagination, new and strange
  In every age, can turn the year;
Can shift the poles and lightly change
  The mood of men, the world's career.

John Davidson
(11 April 1857 – 23 March 1909)

The Scottish playwright and poet John Davidson was born in Barrhead, Renfrewshire. His family background was somewhat unstable – he was the son of a minister from an extreme sect and had a brother who tried to kill his mother with a carving knife. At 13, he worked in a chemical works, and two years later became a pupil-teacher. Yeats described meeting him in the British Museum Reading Room in about 1894. "I am writing verse," Davidson told him. "I had been writing prose for a long time, and then one day I thought I might just as well write what I liked, as I must starve in any case. It was the luckiest thought I ever had, for my agent now gets me forty pounds for a ballad, and I made three hundred out of my last book of verse."

But a few months after this meeting, Yeats wrote, "Davidson had spent his inspiration. 'The fires are out', he said, 'and I must hammer the cold iron.' When I heard a few years ago that he had drowned himself [off Penzance], I knew that I had always expected some such end."

Nevertheless, Yeats spoke of his poetry as finding "new subject matter, new emotions"; and T. S. Eliot described Davidson's satiric Cockney monologue "Thirty Bob A Week" as a "great poem for ever."

DON'T LET THAT HORSE

Don't let that horse
            eat that violin

    cried Chagall's mother

                        But he
        kept right on
                    painting

And became famous

And kept on painting
                    The Horse With Violin In Mouth
And when he finally finished it
he jumped up upon the horse
                            and rode away
        waving the violin

And then with a low bow gave it
to the first naked nude he ran across

And there were no strings
                    attached

Lawrence Ferlinghetti
(24 March 1919 -)

Lawrence Ferlinghetti was born in Yonkers, New York, and educated at Columbia University and the Sorbonne. As the City Lights Books publisher of Allen Ginsberg's *Howl*, he is identified with the Beat movement.

THE DESTRUCTION OF SENNACHERIB

The Assyrian came down like a wolf on the fold,
And his cohorts were gleaming in purple and gold;
And the sheen of their spears was like stars on the sea,
When the blue wave rolls nightly on deep Galilee.

Like the leaves of the forest when Summer is green,
That host with their banners at sunset were seen;
Like the leaves of the forest when Autumn hath blown,
That host on the morrow lay withered and strown.

For the Angel of Death spread his wings on the blast,
And breathed in the face of the foe as he pass'd;
And the eyes of the sleepers wax'd deadly and chill,
And their hearts but once heaved, and for ever grew still!

And there lay the steed with his nostril all wide;
But through it there roll'd not the breath of his pride:
And the foam of his gasping lay white on the turf,
And cold as the spray of the rock-beating surf.

And there lay the rider, distorted and pale,
With the dew on his brow and the rust on his mail;
And the tents were all silent, the banners alone,
The lances uplifted, the trumpet unblown.

The destruction of Sennacherib

And the widows of Ashur are loud in their wail;
And the idols are broke in the temple of Baal;
And the might of the Gentile, unsmote by the sword,
Hath melted like snow in the glance of the Lord!

George Gordon, Lord Byron
(22 January 1788 – 19 April 1824)

On this day in 1812, Annabella Milbanke, a reserved and serious woman, saw Byron for the first time and recorded her impressions of this darling of fashionable society. "His mouth," she observed, "continually betrays the acrimony of his spirit." His pride and passion inflamed by her snubs, Byron launched a calculated courtship, posing as the hell-raising rake who longed to reform.

Once won round, Annabella quickly discovered that Byron's infatuation fell a long way short of love. Only hours after their wedding and still in the carriage that had brought them from the church, Byron taunted her: "Whatever induced you to marry me? What a dupe you have been to your imagination! How is it possible that a woman of your sense could form the wild hope of reforming me? It is enough for me that you are my wife for me to hate you! If you were the wife of any other man, I own you might have charm."

Exactly twelve months later she arranged a legal separation. Byron fought the action unsuccessfully, furious that she should have chosen to leave him.

"The Destruction of Sennacherib" was included in Byron's volume *Hebrew Melodies* published in 1815. The poem is based on the story of the siege of Jerusalem by the army of Sennacherib, King of Assyria, in 701 BC. Old Testament (2 Kings 19:35–36).

from A SHROPSHIRE LAD

XXXII

From far, from eve and morning
 And yon twelve-winded sky,
The stuff of life to knit me
 Blew hither: here am I.

Now – for a breath I tarry
 Nor yet disperse apart –
Take my hand quick and tell me,
 What have you in your heart.

Speak now, and I will answer;
 How shall I help you, say;
Ere to the wind's twelve quarters
 I take my endless way.

A. E. Housman
(26 March 1859 – 30 April 1936)

Housman formed a passionate friendship with Moses Jackson while at St. John's College, Oxford. Soon after Jackson's marriage and emigration to India, Housman began writing poetry, and he published *A Shropshire Lad* privately in 1896. Its poems became very popular during the First World War. Housman himself withdrew from the world to become the stiff, aloof, austere man who admitted: "The emotional part of my life was over when I was thirty-five years old."

from ODE: INTIMATIONS OF IMMORTALITY
from RECOLLECTIONS OF EARLY CHILDHOOD

There was a time when meadow, grove, and stream,
    The earth, and every common sight
        To me did seem
      Apparell'd in celestial light,
The glory and the freshness of a dream.
It is not now as it has been of yore; –
      Turn wheresoe'er I may,
        By night or day,
The things which I have seen I now can see no more!
      The rainbow comes and goes,
      And lovely is the rose;
      The moon doth with delight
Look round her when the heavens are bare;
      Waters on a starry night
      Are beautiful and fair;
    The sunshine is a glorious birth;
    But yet I know, where'er I go,
That there hath pass'd away a glory from the earth.

William Wordsworth
(7 April 1770 - 23 April 1850)

In her Grasmere Journal for 27 March 1802, Wordsworth's sister Dorothy wrote: "A divine morning. At breakfast Wm. wrote part of an ode [above]. Mr. Oliff sent the dung and Wm. went to work in the garden. We sat all day in the orchard."

My heart leaps up

My heart leaps up when I behold
    A rainbow in the sky:
So was it when my life began;
So is it now I am a man;
So be it when I shall grow old,
    Or let me die!
The Child is father of the Man;
And I could wish my days to be
Bound each to each by natural piety.

William Wordsworth
(7 April 1770 ‑ 23 April 1850)

This poem was written on 26 March 1802, as is noted by Wordsworth's sister Dorothy in her journal's account of the day: "A beautiful morning. William wrote to Annette, then worked on 'The Cuckoo.' I was ill and in bad spirits – After dinner I sat 2 hours in the or‑ chard. William and I walked together after tea, first to the top of White Moss, then to Mr. Oliff's. I left Wm. and while he was absent wrote out poems. I grew alarmed and went to seek him – I met him at Mr. Cliff's. He has been trying, without success, to alter a passage – in "Silver Hew" poem. He had written a conclusion just before he went out. While I was getting into bed, he wrote 'The Rainbow' [My heart leaps up]."

Their friend Coleridge considered this poem an expression of the truth that "men are ungrateful to others only when they have ceased to look back on their former selves with joy and tenderness. They exist in fragments."

Thou art indeed just, Lord

Justus quidem tu es, Domine, si disputem tecum: verumtamen justa loquar ad te:
Quare via impiorum prosperatur? &c.[1]

Thou art indeed just, Lord, if I contend
With thee; but, sir, so what I plead is just.
Why do sinners' ways prosper? and why must
Disappointment all I endeavour end?
 Wert thou my enemy, O thou my friend,
How wouldst thou worse, I wonder, than thou dost
Defeat, thwart me? Oh, the sots and thralls of lust
Do in spare hours more thrive than I that spend,
Sir, life upon thy cause. See, banks and brakes[2]
Now, leavèd how thick! lacèd they are again
With fretty chervil,[3] look, and fresh wind shakes
Them; birds build – but not I build; no, but strain,
Time's eunuch, and not breed one work that wakes.
Mine, O thou lord of life, send my roots rain.

Gerard Manley Hopkins
(28 July 1844 – 8 June 1889)

On this day in 1883, Hopkins wrote from Dublin to his old university friend Alexander Baillie: "It is a great help to have someone . . . that will answer my letters, and it supplies some sort of intellectual stimulus. I sadly need that and a general stimulus to being, so dull and yet harassed is my life."

Hopkins wrote this sonnet in the spring of 1889. Several months before he had felt a sense of despair while on a retreat at St. Stanislaus's College, Tullamore: "What is my wretched life? . . . All my undertakings miscarry: I am like a straining eunuch. . . ."

1. The Latin quotation comes from the Vulgate version of Chapter 12 of the Book of Jeremiah. The first three lines of the poem translate the Latin, while the "&c" suggests the relevance to the poem of the rest of the chapter.
2. Thickets.
3. Cow-parsley, an herb with leaves like lace or fretwork.

TO A FAT LADY SEEN FROM THE TRAIN

TRIOLET

O why do you walk through the fields in gloves,
　　Missing so much and so much?
O fat white woman whom nobody loves,
Why do you walk through the fields in gloves,
When the grass is soft as the breast of doves
　　And shivering-sweet to the touch?
O why do you walk through the fields in gloves,
　　Missing so much and so much?

Frances Cornford
(30 March 1886 – 19 August 1960)

Frances Cornford, the granddaughter of Charles Darwin, was born and lived in Cambridge. This is her best known poem. She married the philosopher Francis M. Cornford. Their son John, a Communist at the London School of Economics, was the first Englishman to enroll against Franco, and was killed in Spain in 1936.

G. K. Chesterton wrote a rejoinder to this poem, addressed to the "Fat-headed poet that nobody reads," which begins: "Why do you rush through the field in trains, / Guessing so much and so much."

DEATH, BE NOT PROUD

Death, be not proud, though some have called thee
Mighty and dreadful, for thou art not so:
For those whom thou think'st thou dost overthrow
Die not, poor Death; nor yet canst thou kill me.
From Rest and Sleep, which but thy pictures be,
Much pleasure, then from thee much more must flow;
And soonest our best men with thee do go –
Rest of their bones and souls' delivery.
Thou'rt slave to fate, chance, kings, and desperate men,
And dost with poison, war, and sickness dwell;
And poppy or charms can make us sleep as well
And better than thy stroke. Why swell'st thou then?
One short sleep past, we wake eternally,
And Death shall be no more: Death, thou shalt die.

John Donne
(c. June 1572 – 31 March 1631)

Donne wanted control of his own dying. He wrote a treatise entitled *Biathanatos* in defense of suicide in which he claimed that Jesus committed suicide. To a friend he wrote: "I would not that death should take me asleep. I would not have him merely seize me, and only declare me to be dead, but win me, and overcome me." He died dramatically, rising from his sickbed to preach a last sermon, getting dressed in his shroud to have his portrait painted, and then, according to Izaak Walton, "he was so happy to have nothing to do but to die . . . As . . . his last breath departed from him, he closed his own eyes, and then disposed his hands and body into such a posture, as required not the least alteration by those that came to shroud him."

A SONG OF A YOUNG LADY
TO HER ANCIENT LOVER

Ancient person, for whom I
All the flattering youth defy,
Long be it ere thou grow old,
Aching, shaking, crazy, cold;
  But still continue as thou art,
  Ancient person of my heart.

On thy withered lips and dry,
Which like barren furrows lie,
Brooding kisses I will pour
Shall thy youthful heat restore
(Such kind showers in autumn fall,
And a second spring recall);
  Nor from thee will ever part,
  Ancient person of my heart.

Thy nobler part, which but to name
In our sex would be counted shame,
By age's frozen grasp possessed,
From his ice shall be released,
And soothed by my reviving hand,
In former warmth and vigor stand.
All a lover's wish can reach

A SONG OF A YOUNG LADY
TO HER ANCIENT LOVER

For thy joy my love shall teach,
And for thy pleasure shall improve
All that art can add to love.
    Yet still I love thee without art,
    Ancient person of my heart.

John Wilmot, Earl of Rochester
(1 April 1647 - 26 July 1680)

John Wilmot was born in Ditchley in Oxfordshire, with a Royalist father and a mother with a Parliamentarian background, who was nevertheless in the 1650s forced into exile with her children. John became Earl of Rochester at the age of 12 and lived a recklessly brave and dissolute, bisexual existence at the court of Charles II. He married the rich heiress he had previously forcibly abducted (and been sent to the Tower for so doing). He died, either of kidney stones or syphilis, at the age of 32, having made his peace with both his wife and his maker. In Samuel Johnson's view, Rochester had "blazed out his youth and his health in lavish voluptuousness."

JOINING THE COLOURS
(WEST KENTS, DUBLIN, 1914)

There they go marching all in step so gay!
  Smooth-cheeked and golden, food for shells and guns.
Blithely they go as to a wedding day,
        The mothers' sons.

The drab street stares to see them row on row
  On the high tram-tops, singing like the lark.
Too careless-gay for courage, singing they go
        Into the dark.

With tin whistles, mouth-organs, any noise,
  They pipe the way to glory and the grave;
Foolish and young, the gay and golden boys
        Love cannot save.

High heart! High courage! The poor girls they kissed
  Run with them: they shall kiss no more, alas!
Out of the mist they stepped – into the mist
        Singing they pass.

Katharine Tynan
(23 January 1861 – 2 April 1931)

Katharine Tynan was born into a Catholic farming family in County Dublin. She became a friend of Yeats – indeed he wondered at one point whether he ought to propose to her – and played her part in the Celtic literary revival. Her two sons served in the First World War.

VIRTUE

Sweet day, so cool, so calm, so bright!
The bridal of the earth and sky –
The dew shall weep thy fall tonight;
    For thou must die.

Sweet rose, whose hue angry and brave
Bids the rash gazer wipe his eye,
Thy root is ever in its grave,
    And thou must die.

Sweet spring, full of sweet days and roses,
A box where sweets compacted lie,
My music shows ye have your closes,
    And all must die.

Only a sweet and virtuous soul,
Like season'd timber, never gives;
But though the whole world turn to coal,
    Then chiefly lives.

George Herbert
(3 April 1593 – 3 March 1633)

Herbert was born in Montgomery into a distinguished Anglo-Welsh family. His mother, Lady Magdalen, was Donne's patron, to whom Donne addressed his *Holy Sonnets*. Donne seems to have helped influence Herbert away from political and court life toward the church, which he entered shortly after marriage to Jane Danvers.

As a young man, Herbert was criticized for placing too much value on his noble ancestry, but as a priest he was noted for his humility and popularity, befriending all his parishioners and encouraging them to read.

STILL I RISE

You may write me down in history
With your bitter, twisted lies,
You may trod me in the very dirt
But still, like dust, I'll rise.

Does my sassiness upset you?
Why are you beset with gloom?
'Cause I walk like I've got oil wells
Pumping in my living room.

Just like moons and like suns,
With the certainty of tides,
Just like hopes springing high,
Still I'll rise.

Did you want to see me broken?
Bowed head and lowered eyes?
Shoulders falling down like teardrops,
Weakened by my soulful cries.

Does my haughtiness offend you?
Don't you take it awful hard
'Cause I laugh like I've got gold mines
Diggin' in my own back yard.

You may shoot me with your words,
You may cut me with your eyes,
You may kill me with your hatefulness,
But still, like air, I'll rise.

Still i rise

Does my sexiness upset you?
Does it come as a surprise
That I dance like I've got diamonds
At the meeting of my thighs?

Out of the huts of history's shame
I rise
Up from a past that's rooted in pain
I rise
I'm a black ocean, leaping and wide,
Welling and swelling I bear in the tide.

Leaving behind nights of terror and fear
I rise
Into a daybreak that's wondrously clear
I rise
Bringing the gifts that my ancestors gave,
I am the dream and the hope of the slave.
I rise
I rise
I rise.

Maya Angelou
(4 April 1928 -)

Maya Angelou has a volume of verse with the title *And Still I Rise*. Her spirit and joie de
vivre seem intact despite a difficult upbringing – her parents broke up, she was raped by
her mother's boyfriend, became mute for five years, and was for a time a prostitute. Her
passionate stories of life as a singer, performer, dancer, and Black activist unfold in her
autobiographies, starting with *I Know Why the Caged Bird Sings*. More recently she wrote
and recited a poem for Bill Clinton's inauguration as president.

LOVE AND SLEEP

Lying asleep between the strokes of night
　　I saw my love lean over my sad bed,
　　Pale as the duskiest lily's leaf or head,
Smooth-skinned and dark, with bare throat made to bite,
Too wan for blushing and too warm for white,
　　But perfect-coloured without white or red.
And her lips opened amorously, and said –
I wist not what, saving one word – Delight.

And all her face was honey to my mouth,
　　And all her body pasture to mine eyes;
　　　The long lithe arms and hotter hands than fire
The quivering flanks, hair smelling of the south,
　　The bright light feet, the splendid supple thighs
　　And glittering eyelids of my soul's desire.

Algernon Charles Swinburne
(5 April 1837 - 10 April 1909)

Swinburne was born in London, the son of Admiral Charles Swinburne and Lady Jane Ashburnham. Beating and bullying received at Eton left him with a masochistic preoccupation with flagellation. He failed to graduate from Balliol College, Oxford. This was the man who, according to Edgell Rickword, "shattered the virginal reticence of Victoria's serenest years. with a book of poems" – the uninhibited tone of Swinburne's *Poems and Ballads* of 1866 with their celebration of "the roses and raptures of vice" were a sensation at the time. But his constitution became too frail for his Bohemian lifestyle – Rossetti would have to pin Swinburne's address to his coat collar as the only way to ensure his safe return from drinking bouts. For the last forty years of his life he lodged with his friend Theodore Watts-Dunton at No. 2 The Pines, Putney. His friend weaned him from drink, but the exuberance and rebelliousness gradually faded from his writing.

6 APRIL

from THE GENERAL PROLOGUE
to THE CANTERBURY TALES

Whan that Aprill with his shoures soote°	*sweet*
The droghte of March hath perced to the roote,	
And bathed every veyne° in swich° licour°	*veins (i.e. in plants); such; liquid*
Of which vertu° engendred is the flour;	*potency*
When Zephirus° eek° with his sweete breeth	*the west wind; also*
Inspired° hath in every holt and heeth°	*Quickened; woodland and heathland*
The tendre croppes,° and the yonge sonne	*shoots*
Hath in the Ram° his halve cours yronne,	*Aries*
And smale foweles° maken melodye,	*birds*
That slepen al the nyght with open ye°	*eye*
(So priketh° hem° nature in hir corages°);	*incites; them; hearts*
Thanne longen folk to goon on pilgrames,	
And palmeres° for to seken straunge strondes,°	*professional pilgrims; shores*
To ferne halwes,° kowthe° in sondry londes;	*far-off shrines; known*
And specially from every shires ende	
Of Engelond to Caunterbury they wende,°	*go*
The hooly blisful° martir° for to seke,	*blessed; St. Thomas Beckett*
That hem hath holpen° whan that they were seeke°.	*helped; sick*

Geoffrey Chaucer
(ca. 1343 – 25 October 1400)

Many Latin and Italian works have introductory lines on spring. These Mediterranean models may account for March being described as a dry month. It has been suggested on very slender evidence that Chaucer himself went on a pilgrimage to Canterbury in April 1387 or 1388, perhaps because his wife Philippa was ill.

from ODE: INTIMATIONS OF IMMORTALITY
FROM RECOLLECTIONS OF EARLY CHILDHOOD

Our birth is but a sleep and a forgetting:
The Soul that rises with us, our life's Star,
> Hath had elsewhere its setting,
>> And cometh from afar:
>> Not in entire forgetfulness,
>> And not in utter nakedness,
But trailing clouds of glory do we come
>> From God, who is our home:
Heaven lies about us in our infancy!
Shades of the prison-house begin to close
>> Upon the growing Boy,
But He beholds the light, and whence it flows,
>> He sees it in his joy;
The Youth, who daily farther from the east
>> Must travel, still is Nature's Priest,
>> And by the vision splendid
>> Is on his way attended;
At length the Man perceives it die away,
And fade into the light of common day.

William Wordsworth
(7 April 1770 - 23 April 1850)

Wordsworth in his dictated memoirs says: "I was born at Cockermouth, in Cumberland, on 7 April 1770, the second son of John Wordsworth, attorney-at-law . . . The time of my infancy and early boyhood was passed partly at Cockermouth, and partly with my mother's parents at Penrith, where my mother, in the year 1778, died of a decline, brought on by a cold . . . My father never recovered his usual cheerfulness of mind after this loss, and died when I was in my fourteenth year, a schoolboy . . . [It was told me that I] was the only one of her five children about whose future . . . [my mother] was anxious . . . [that I would be] remarkable either for good or for evil. The cause of this was, that I was of a stiff, moody, and violent temper."

from THE JUNGLE BOOKS

MOWGLI'S BROTHERS (CHAPTER HEADING)

Now Chil the Kite brings home the night
That Mang the Bat sets free –
The herds are shut in byre and hut,
For loosed till dawn are we.
This is the hour of pride and power,
Talon and tush and claw.
Oh, hear the call! – Good hunting all
That keep the Jungle Law!

Rudyard Kipling

(30 December 1865 – 18 January 1936)

On this day in 1891, Kipling wrote to Hallam Tennyson in gratitude for his father's kind words about Kipling's work. If there is any good in it, "he knows more than I," and he added that Tennyson's commendation was worth more than a decoration in the field to him.

The Jungle Books appeared in 1894 and 1895. *Mowgli's Brothers* was inspired in part by a scene from H. Rider Haggard's *Nada the Lily*. The immutable Law of the Jungle to which Kipling refers above is partly defined in *The Jungle Books* as follows:

As the creeper that girdles the tree trunk, the Law runneth forward and back –
For the strength of the Pack is the Wolf, and the strength of the Wolf is the Pack.
The jackal may follow the tiger, but, Cub, when thy whiskers are grown,
Remember the wolf is a hunter – go forth and get food of thine own.
Keep peace with the Lords of the Jungle – the Tiger, the Panther, the Bear;
And trouble not Hathi the Silent, and mock not the Bear in his lair.
Now these are the Laws of the Jungle, and many and mighty are they;
But the head and the hoof of the Law and the haunch and the hump is –
Obey!

SHILOH

A REQUIEM (APRIL, 1862)

Skimming lightly, wheeling still,
　The swallows fly low
Over the field in clouded days,
　The forest-field of Shiloh –
Over the field where April rain
Solaced the parched ones stretched in pain
Through the pause of night
That followed the Sunday fight
　Around the church of Shiloh –
The church so lone, the log-built one,
That echoed to many a parting groan
　　　And natural prayer
　Of dying foemen mingled there –
Foemen at morn, but friends at eve –
　Fame or country least their care:
(What like a bullet can undeceive!)
　But now they lie low,
While over them the swallows skim,
　And all is hushed at Shiloh.

Herman Melville
(1 August 1819 – 28 September 1891)

Melville's first personal contact with the Civil War battlefield was in 1864 when he was at the front in Virginia. A collection of war poems was published in 1866. In that year, Melville took up his appointment as District Inspector of Customs in New York City, a post he held for 19 years. Years earlier, when he was 23, Melville ended his stint as a seaman for a whaling company by jumping ship in the Marquesas. His experience in the South Seas formed the basis for his widely read books *Typee* and *Omoo*. Approximately four years later, *Moby Dick* was tepidly received by the public.

from ENDYMION

BOOK I

A thing of beauty is a joy for ever:
Its loveliness increases, it will never
Pass into nothingness; but still will keep
A bower quiet for us, and a sleep
Full of sweet dreams, and health, and quiet breathing.
Therefore, on every morrow, are we wreathing
A flowery band to bind us to the earth,
Spite of despondence, of the inhuman dearth
Of noble natures, of the gloomy days,
Of all the unhealthy and o'er-darkened ways
Made of our searching; yes, in spite of all,
Some shape of beauty moves away the pall
From our dark spirits.

John Keats
(31 October 1795 - 23 February 1821)

John Keats dated his Preface to "Endymion" 10 April 1818. In it, he warned readers that they "must soon perceive great inexperience, immaturity, and every error denoting a feverish attempt, rather than a deed accomplished" in the poetry that followed. Reviewing the work for *Blackwood's Magazine*, John Gibson Lockhart, no lover of what he called "The Cockney School of Poetry," agreed and ventured the opinion that the poem was one of "calm, settled, imperturbable, drivelling idiocy."

from A SONG TO DAVID

Strong is the horse upon his speed;
Strong in pursuit the rapid glede,°   *bird of prey*
  Which makes at once his game:
Strong the tall ostrich on the ground;
Strong through the turbulent profound
  Shoots Xiphias to his aim.

Strong is the lion – like a coal
His eyeball, – like a bastion's mole
  His chest against the foes:
Strong the gier-eagle on his sail;
Strong against tide th' enormous whale
  Emerges as he goes.

But stronger still, in earth and air,
And in the sea, the man of prayer,
  And far beneath the tide:
And in the seat to faith assign'd,
Where ask is have, where seek is find,
  Where knock is open wide.

Christopher Smart
(11 April 1722 - 21 May 1771)

Christopher Smart was born in Shipbourne, near Tunbridge Wells. He was summed up by Odell Shepard as "a university wit and scholar, a translator of Horace and a Grub Street hack, a drunkard, a Bedlamite, and a radiantly happy Christian who died in a debtors' prison."

Denied the use of paper and pen in Bedlam, it is said that Smart scratched out "A Song to David" with a key on his room's wainscot. The poem was written in self-identification with David the psalmist and inspired poet-priest, "the great Author of the Book of Gratitude." His friend W. Mason, on reading "A Song to David," declared Smart "as mad as ever."

THE LOST

The fairest day that ever yet has shone,
Will be when thou the day within shalt see;
The fairest rose that ever yet has blown,
When thou the flower thou lookest on shalt be.
But thou art far away among Time's toys;
Thyself the day thou lookest for in them,
Thyself the flower that now thine eye enjoys,
But wilted now thou hang'st upon thy stem.
The bird thou hearest on the budding tree,
Thou hast made sing with thy forgotten voice;
But when it swells again to melody,
The song is thine in which thou wilt rejoice;
And thou new risen 'midst these wonders live,
That now to them dost all thy substance give.

Jones Very
(28 August 1813 - 8 May 1880)

Very's bizarre behavior after experiencing an episode of profound religious ecstasy was such that his colleagues at Harvard Divinity School asked that he leave his post as tutor in freshman Greek. Very spent one month in a private asylum. Eventually, his religious zeal diminished in intensity, though he continued to preach. One could assume that Thoreau, a student of Very's, received from his tutor not only a better understanding of Greek but an urgent sense of philosophical mysticism as well.

SUNLIGHT

from MOSSBAWN: TWO POEMS IN DEDICATION
for Marie Heaney

There was a sunlit absence.
The helmeted pump in the yard
heated its iron,
water honeyed

in the slung bucket
and the sun stood
like a griddle cooling
against the wall

of each long afternoon.
So, her hands scuffled
over the bakeboard,
the reddening stove

sent its plaque of heat
against her where she stood
in a floury apron
by the window.

Now she dusts the board
with a goose's wing,
now sits, broad-lapped,
with whitened nails

SUNLIGHT

and measling shins:
here is a space
again, the scone rising
to the tick of two clocks.

And here is love
like a tinsmith's scoop
sunk past its gleam
in the meal-bin.

Seamus Heaney
(13 April 1939 –)

Seamus Heaney was born in Mossbawn, County Derry, Northern Ireland, the eldest of 11 children, and the son of a Catholic farmer. He won a scholarship to St Columb's College, and in 1965 became a lecturer and married Marie Devlin. The next year saw the publication of his first book of poetry, *Death of a Naturalist*. Some of his recent poetry, *The Haw Lantern* (1987) and *Seeing Things* (1991), has been concerned with the death of his parents. *The Spirit Level* (1996) was Heaney's first book of poems after he was awarded the 1995 Nobel Prize for Literature.

O CAPTAIN! MY CAPTAIN!
from MEMORIES OF PRESIDENT LINCOLN
(in *Leaves of Grass*)

O Captain! my Captain! our fearful trip is done,
The ship has weathered every rack, the prize we sought is won,
The port is near, the bells I hear, the people all exulting,
While follow eyes the steady keel, the vessel grim and daring;
    But O heart! heart! heart!
     O the bleeding drops of red!
      Where on the deck my Captain lies,
       Fallen cold and dead

O Captain! my Captain! rise up and hear the bells;
Rise up–for you the flag is flung–for you the bugle trills,
For you bouquets and ribboned wreaths–for you the shores a-crowding,
For you they call, the swaying mass, their eager faces turning;
    Here, Captain! dear father!
     This arm beneath your head!
      It is some dream that on the deck
       You've fallen cold and dead.

My Captain does not answer, his lips are pale and still,
My father does not feel my arm, he has no pulse nor will;
The ship is anchored safe and sound, its voyage closed and done,
From fearful trip the victor ship comes in with object won;

O CAPTAIN! MY CAPTAIN!

Exult, O shores! and ring, O bells!
But I, with mournful tread,
Walk the deck my Captain lies,
Fallen cold and dead.

Walt Whitman
(31 May 1819 – 26 March 1892)

President Lincoln was shot on Good Friday, 14 April 1865, at Ford's Theatre in Washington by J. Wilkes Booth, an actor, and died the next morning. Walt Whitman was at home with his mother and family in Brooklyn at the time: "Mother prepared breakfast – and other meals afterwards as usual; but not a mouthful was eaten all day by any of us. We each drank half a cup of coffee: that was all. Little was said. We got every newspaper morning and evening, and the frequent extras of that period, and pass'd them silently to each other."

DOVER BEACH

The sea is calm tonight.
The tide is full, the moon lies fair
Upon the straits; on the French coast the light
Gleams and is gone; the cliffs of England stand,
Glimmering and vast, out in the tranquil bay.
Come to the window, sweet is the night-air!
Only, from the long line of spray
Where the sea meets the moon-blanched land,
Listen! you hear the grating roar
Of pebbles which the waves draw back, and fling,
At their return, up the high strand,
Begin, and cease, and then again begin
With tremulous cadence slow, and bring
The eternal note of sadness in.

Sophocles long ago
Heard it on the Aegean, and it brought
Into his mind the turbid ebb and flow
Of human misery; we
Find also in the sound a thought,
Hearing it by this distant northern sea.

The Sea of Faith
Was once, too, at the full, and round earth's shore
Lay like the folds of a bright girdle furled.
But now I only hear
Its melancholy, long, withdrawing roar,
Retreating, to the breath
Of the night-wind, down the vast edges drear
And naked shingles of the world.

DOVER BEACH

Ah, love, let us be true
To one another! for the world, which seems
To lie before us like a land of dreams,
So various, so beautiful, so new,
Hath really neither joy, nor love, nor light,
Nor certitude, nor peace, nor help for pain;
And we are here as on a darkling plain
Swept with confused alarms of struggle and flight,
Where ignorant armies clash by night.

Matthew Arnold
(24 December 1822 – 15 April 1888)

In 1851, Matthew Arnold married Fanny Lucy Wightman. "Dover Beach" dates from the beginning of their European honeymoon.

Most of Matthew Arnold's verse was written by the age of 45 and examined the theme of human alienation and disconnection from the changing world of the 19th century. Arnold continued to write as a literary critic until the end of his life, believing it was the best vehicle for social reform.

I WANDERED LONELY AS A CLOUD

I wandered lonely as a cloud
That floats on high o'er vales and hills,
When all at once I saw a crowd,
A host, of golden daffodils;
Beside the lake, beneath the trees,
Fluttering and dancing in the breeze.

Continuous as the stars that shine
And twinkle on the milky way,
They stretched in never-ending line
Along the margin of a bay:
Ten thousand saw I at a glance,
Tossing their heads in sprightly dance.

The waves beside them danced; but they
Out-did the sparkling waves in glee:
A poet could not but be gay,
In such a jocund company:
I gazed–and gazed–but little thought
What wealth the show to me had brought:

For oft, when on my couch I lie
In vacant or in pensive mood,
They flash upon that inward eye

I WANDERED LONELY AS A CLOUD

Which is the bliss of solitude;
And then my heart with pleasure fills
And dances with the daffodils.

William Wordsworth
(7 April 1770 – 23 April 1850)

William's sister Dorothy described these daffodils by Ullswater in her Grasmere Journal for 15 April 1802: "We set off after dinner from Eusemere . . . The wind was furious and we thought we must have returned . . . The wind seized our breath, the lake was rough . . . When we were in the woods beyond Gowbarrow park we saw a few daffodils close to the water side. We fancied that the lake had floated the seeds ashore and that the little colony had so sprung up. But as we went along there were more and yet more and at last under the boughs of the trees, we saw that there was a long belt of them along the shore, about the breadth of a country turnpike road. I never saw daffodils so beautiful they grew among the mossy stones about and about them, some rested their heads upon these stones as on a pillow for weariness and the rest tossed and reeled and danced and seemed as if they verily laughed with the wind that blew upon them over the lake, they looked so gay ever glancing ever changing. This wind blew directly over the lake to them. There was here and there a little knot and a few stragglers a few yards higher up but they were so few as not to disturb the simplicity and unity and life of that one busy highway . . . We put on dry clothes at Dobson's . . . We had a glass of warm rum and water. We enjoyed ourselves and wished for Mary [Wordsworth's wife]." The poem was written two years after Dorothy's journal entry. Wordsworth noted that "the two best lines in it ['They flash upon that inward eye / Which is the bliss of solitude'] are by Mary."

from THE NIGHT[1]

 Through that pure Virgin-shrine,
That sacred veil drawn o'er thy glorious noon
That men might look and live as Glow-worms shine,
  And face the Moon:
 Wise Nicodemus saw such light
 As made him know his God by night.

 Were all my loud, evil days
Calm and unhaunted as is thy dark Tent,
Whose peace but by some Angels wing or voice
  Is seldom rent;
 Then I in Heaven all the long year
 Would keep, and never wander here.

 But living where the Sun
Doth all things wake, and where all mix and tyre
Themselves and others, I consent and run
  To ev'ry myre,
 And by this world's ill-guiding light,
 Err more then I can do by night.

 There is in God (some say)
A deep, but dazzling darkness; as men here
Say it is late and dusky, because they

from THE NIGHT

See not all clear;
O for that night! where I in him
Might live invisible and dim.

Henry Vaughan
(17 April 1622 - 23 April 1695)

Henry Vaughan termed himself a "Silurist," a native of Brecon, the land of the ancient tribe of Silures. His twin brother was an alchemist whose interest in Hermeticism and magic Henry shared, although he himself was a country doctor. On the death of his wife Catherine, with whom he had four children, he married her younger sister Elizabeth and they had another four. His "profane" poetry was followed by a profoundly spiritual volume entitled *Silex Scintillans* in 1650. This new direction he attributed to a fellow poet, "the blessed man, Mr. George Herbert, whose holy life and verse gained many converts, of whom I am the least."

1. Stanzas 1, 7, 8 of this 9-stanza poem.

6 A.M. THOUGHTS

As soon as you wake they come blundering in
　　Like puppies or importunate children;
What was a landscape emerging from mist
　　Becomes at once a disordered garden.

And the mess they trail with them! Embarrassments,
　　Anger, lust, fear – in fact the whole pig-pen;
And who'll clean it up? No hope for sleep now –
　　Just heave yourself out, make the tea, and give in.

Dick Davis
(18 April 1945 -)

Dick Davis writes: "The occasion for this poem became hidden as the lines were written. It began as a poem about how children redirect a marriage from the romantic to the quotidian; that fact was represented by the rude awakenings toddlers can inflict (compared to the lying in bed together newlyweds can indulge in) and from there came the sour thoughts and self-disgust, which finally turned into the subject of the poem, the toddlers being relegated to the status of metaphor."

Dick Davis was born in Porstmouth and graduated from King's College, Cambridge. He lived for eight years in Iran, working as a teacher, and now teaches Persian at Ohio State University, Columbus. He has edited a new edition of Edward FitzGerald's *Rubáiyát of Omar Khayyám* and his own poetry has been published in London under the title *Devices and Desires*. Thom Gunn commented on his work: "It is wonderful to find a poet (English) whose poetry lives through its meter. His handling of it is masterful, and you are never aware of effort."

19 APRIL

SO WE'LL GO NO MORE A-ROVING

So we'll go no more a-roving
    So late into the night,
Though the heart be still as loving,
    And the moon be still as bright.

For the sword outwears its sheath,
    And the soul wears out the breast,
And the heart must pause to breathe,
    And Love itself have rest.

Though the night was made for loving,
    And the day returns too soon,
Yet we'll go no more a-roving
    By the light of the moon.

George Gordon, Lord Byron
(22 January 1788 - 19 April 1824)

On 19 February 1817, Byron wrote to Augusta Leigh from Venice: "The Carnival closed last night, and I have been up all night at the masked ball of the Fenice, and am rather tired or so . . . There has been the same sort of thing every night these last six weeks . . . I went out now and then, but was less dissipated than you would expect."

Writing to Thomas Moore some days later he reported that he had found " 'the sword wearing out the scabbard' though I have just turned the corner of twenty nine . . . If I live ten years longer, you will see, however, that it is not over with me – I don't mean litera-ture, for that is nothing; and it may seem odd enough to say, I do not think it my vocation. But you will see that I shall do something or other – the times and fortune per-mitting . . . But I doubt whether my constitution will hold out. I have, at intervals, exercised it most devilishly."

Byron died on 19 April 1824 of a fever contracted in a rainstorm at Missolonghi in Greece while with the insurgents fighting for their liberation from the Turkish Empire.

Leisure

What is this life if, full of care,
We have no time to stand and stare?

No time to stand beneath the boughs
And stare as long as sheep or cows.

No time to see, when woods we pass,
Where squirrels hide their nuts in grass.

No time to see, in broad daylight,
Streams full of stars, like skies at night.

No time to turn at Beauty's glance,
And watch her feet, how they can dance.

No time to wait till her mouth can
Enrich that smile her eyes began.

A poor life this if, full of care,
We have no time to stand and stare.

W. H. Davies
(20 April 1871 - 26 September 1940)

Sir John Squire writes: "Mr. Davies was born in 1871 at Newport, Monmouthshire. He wandered, as a young man, across the Atlantic. He set out with a companion for Klondyke, traveling as a stowaway on trains, missed his footing, and lost a leg." Back in England he lived in doss-houses. According to G. B. Shaw, Davies began at the age of 34 to write poems, and tried selling them door-to-door to pay to have them published: "He did not sell a single copy, though he made a house-to-house visitation in the suburbs. Most of the people he called upon were poor. They looked at the poet in amazement when he offered them a printed sheet for threepence."

LA BELLE DAME SANS MERCI

O what can ail thee, knight-at-arms,
　　Alone and palely loitering?
The sedge is wither'd from the lake,
　　And no birds sing.

O what can ail thee, knight-at-arms,
　　So haggard and so woe-begone?
The squirrel's granary is full,
　　And the harvest's done.

I see a lily on thy brow
　　With anguish moist and fever dew;
And on thy cheek a fading rose
　　Fast withereth too.

"I met a lady in the meads,
　　Full beautiful – a faery's child,
Her hair was long, her foot was light,
　　And her eyes were wild.

"I made a garland for her head,
　　And bracelets too, and fragrant zone;
She look'd at me as she did love,
　　And made sweet moan.

"I set her on my pacing steed
　　And nothing else saw all day long,
For sideways would she lean, and sing
　　A faery's song.

"She found me roots of relish sweet,
   And honey wild and manna dew,
And sure in language strange she said,
     'I love thee true !'

"She took me to her elfin grot,
   And there she wept and sigh'd full sore;
And there I shut her wild, wild eyes
     With kisses four.

"And there she lullèd me asleep,
   And there I dream'd – Ah! woe betide!
The latest dream I ever dream'd
     On the cold hill's side.

"I saw pale kings and princes too,
   Pale warriors, death-pale were they all;
Who cried – 'La belle Dame sans Merci
     Hath thee in thrall !'

"I saw their starved lips in the gloam
   With horrid warning gapèd wide,
And I awoke and found me here
     On the cold hill's side.

"And this is why I sojourn here
   Alone and palely loitering,
Though the sedge is wither'd from the lake,
     And no birds sing."

John Keats
(31 October 1795 – 23 February 1821)

143

MONEY

I was led into captivity by the bitch business
Not in love but in what seemed a physical necessity
And now I cannot even watch the spring
The itch for subsistence having become responsibility.

Money the she-devil comes to us under many veils
Tactful at first, calling herself beauty
Tear away this disguise, she proposes paternal solicitude
Assuming the dishonest face of duty.

Suddenly you are in bed with a screeching tear-sheet
This is money at last without her night-dress
Clutching you against her fallen udders and sharp bones
In an unscrupulous and deserved embrace.

C. H. Sisson
(22 April 1914 -)

C. H. Sisson gave up writing verses "at 20 because I had a great respect for poetry and did not think I could write it. The war and exile produced a few hesitant verses, wrung from me, but I stopped again without really having begun. A more productive start was about 1950, when I was already on the declining side *del cammin di nostra vita*; no wonder therefore that my themes have often been age, decline and death, with the occasional desperate hopes of the receding man." In the war, C. H. Sisson served in the British Army Intelligence Corps in India. Subsequently he worked for the Ministry of Labour and the Department of Employment, but his critical attitude to the civil service is illustrated in the couplet "Here lies a civil servant. He was civil / To everyone, servant to the devil."

from AS YOU LIKE IT

ACT II SCENE VII

Jaques. All the world's a stage,
And all the men and women merely players:
They have their exits and their entrances;
And one man in his time plays many parts,
His acts being seven ages. At first the infant,
Mewling and puking in the nurse's arms.
And then the whining school-boy, with his satchel,
And shining morning face, creeping like snail
Unwillingly to school. And then the lover,
Sighing like furnace, with a woful ballad
Made to his mistress' eyebrow. Then a soldier,
Full of strange oaths, and bearded like the pard,
Jealous in honour, sudden and quick in quarrel,
Seeking the bubble reputation
Even in the cannon's mouth. And then the justice,
In fair round belly with good capon lin'd,
With eyes severe, and beard of formal cut,
Full of wise saws and modern instances;
And so he plays his part. The sixth age shifts
Into the lean and slipper'd pantaloon,
With spectacles on nose and pouch on side,
His youthful hose well sav'd, a world too wide
For his shrunk shank; and his big manly voice,
Turning again toward childish treble, pipes
And whistles in his sound. Last scene of all,
That ends this strange eventful history,
Is second childishness and mere oblivion,
Sans teeth, sans eyes, sans taste, sans everything.

William Shakespeare
(23 April 1564 - 23 April 1616)

o sweet spontaneous

O sweet spontaneous
earth how often have
the
doting

    fingers of
prurient philosophers pinched
and
poked

thee
,has the naughty thumb
of science prodded
thy

    beauty   .how
often have religions taken
thee upon their scraggy knees
squeezing and

buffeting thee that thou mightest conceive
gods
    (but
true

o sweet spontaneous

to the incomparable
couch of death thy
rhythmic
lover

thou answerest

them only with

spring)

e.e. cummings
(14 October 1894 – 3 September 1962)

In 1930, Cummings wrote an exuberant, freewheeling letter to John Dos Passos: " . . . Q;
Whence the phrase 'virgin forest'?/ A;Only G-d can make a tree . . . . / HATS off to thea
orthodox flea, / who attempted to bugger a bee / but eamerged from thea fray/ in a
familea way . . . / which is why wea do things so fee-blea."

Nothing

I take a jewel from a junk-shop tray
And wish I had a love to buy it for.
Nothing I choose will make you turn my way.
Nothing I give will make you love me more.

I know that I've embarrassed you too long
And I'm ashamed to linger at your door.
Whatever I embark on will be wrong.
Nothing I do will make you love me more.

I cannot work. I cannot read or write.
How can I frame a letter to implore.
Eloquence is a lie. The truth is trite.
Nothing I say will make you love me more.

So I replace the jewel in the tray
And laughingly pretend I'm far too poor.
Nothing I give, nothing I do or say,
Nothing I am will make you love me more.

James Fenton
(25 April 1949 -)

Of this poem Edward Lucie-Smith wrote that it "seems to me the equal of Auden's best lyrics."

Fenton was born in Lincoln and educated at Repton School and Magdalen College, Oxford. His poetry includes *Terminal Moraine* (1972), *The Memory of War* (1982), and *Manila Envelope* (1989). His riches derive from his percentage on the profits from the musical *Les Misérables* for which he was one of the librettists.

HOME-THOUGHTS, FROM ABROAD

O to be in England
Now that April's there,
And whoever wakes in England
Sees, some morning, unaware,
That the lowest boughs and the brushwood sheaf
Round the elm-tree bole are in tiny leaf,
While the chaffinch sings on the orchard bough
In England – now!

And after April, when May follows,
And the whitethroat builds, and all the swallows!
Hark, where my blossomed pear-tree in the hedge
Leans to the field and scatters on the clover
Blossoms and dewdrops – at the bent spray's edge –
That's the wise thrush; he sings each song twice over,
Lest you should think he never could recapture
The first fine careless rapture!
And though the fields look rough with hoary dew,
All will be gay when noontide wakes anew
The buttercups, the little children's dower
– Far brighter than this gaudy melon-flower!

Robert Browning
(7 May 1812 – 12 December 1889)

This poem was probably written in England during April 1845 when Browning was recalling his second tour of Italy, and the year before he took Elizabeth Barrett there as his
wife.

BRAHMA

If the red slayer think he slays,
　Or if the slain think he is slain,
They know not well the subtle ways
　I keep, and pass, and turn again.

Far or forgot to me is near;
　Shadow and sunlight are the same;
The vanquished gods to me appear;
　And one to me are shame and fame.

They reckon ill who leave me out;
　When me they fly, I am the wings;
I am the doubter and the doubt
　And I the hymn the Brahmin sings.

The strong gods pine for my abode,
　And pine in vain the sacred Seven,
But thou, meek lover of the good!
　Find me, and turn thy back on heaven.

Ralph Waldo Emerson
(25 May 1803 - 27 April 1882)

Famed as the "God-intoxicated Yankee" with an unbending passion for independence (who still swam naked in Walden Pond daily at the age of 77), Emerson declared a credo of self-reliance: "Whoso would be a man must be a nonconformist . . . A foolish consistency is the hobgoblin of little minds." He resigned as a Unitarian minister in 1832 and helped found a Transcendentalist movement, which drew on Hinduism and a sense of the mystical oneness of the individual, nature, and God. Emerson died on this day in 1882, and he was buried in Sleepy Hollow Cemetery close to Thoreau and Hawthorne.

APRIL **28**

QUANTUM EST QUOD DESIT[1]

'Twas a new feeling – something more
Than we had dar'd to own before,
　Which then we hid not;
We saw it in each other's eye,
And wish'd in every broken sigh
　To speak, but did not!

She felt my lips' impassion'd touch;
'Twas the first time I dar'd so much,
　And yet, she chid not;
But whisper'd o'er my burning brow,
'Oh! do you doubt I love you now?'
　Sweet soul! I did not!

Warmly I felt her bosom thrill,
I prest it closer, closer still,
　Though gently bid not;
Till – oh! the world hath seldom heard
Of lovers, who so nearly err'd,
　And yet who – did not!

Thomas Moore
(28 May 1779 – 25 February 1852)

Thomas Moore has been described as "the national bard of Ireland" and his collection *Irish Melodies* was a bestseller – in his time only Byron's verse was more popular.

On this day in 1916, the Easter Rising in central Dublin was underway, led by the Irish Republican Brotherhood and Sinn Fein. The Rising was put down; 450 of the rebels died, 2,000 were injured, and the leaders were executed.

1. Roughly: 'To the brink but no further.'

WILD NIGHTS – WILD NIGHTS!

Wild Nights – Wild Nights!
Were I with thee
Wild Nights should be
Our luxury!

Futile – the Winds –
To a Heart in port –
Done with the Compass –
Done with the Chart!

Rowing in Eden –
Ah, the Sea!
Might I but moor – Tonight –
In Thee!

Emily Dickinson
(10 December 1830 – 15 May 1886)

In the "Presbyterian" for this day in 1882, there is an article by "Calvin" about the Revd. Charles Wadsworth, "a prince among preachers . . . Dr. Wadsworth was born a poet and could not cease to be one." Wadsworth has been conjectured to be the (platonically) loved one in Emily Dickinson's life who may have inspired the passion in these lines. She first met him in May 1854 when he was 40 and happily married and she was 23. Later in life she referred to him as "the beloved clergyman," "the shepherd from 'little girl'hood," "dearest earthly friend," "whom to know was life." On his deathbed Wadsworth requested that a copy of his published sermons be sent to her.

According to one critic, William H. Sinar, Emily Dickinson felt that she had undergone a form of marriage of the spirit to Wadsworth, with the lovers agreeing to a lifetime of painful separation and a subsequent marriage in heaven.

BYZANTIUM

The unpurged images of day recede;
The Emperor's drunken soldiery are abed;
Night resonance recedes, night-walkers' song
After great cathedral gong;
A starlit or a moonlit dome disdains
All that man is,
All mere complexities,
The fury and the mire of human veins.

Before me floats an image, man or shade,
Shade more than man, more image than a shade;
For Hades' bobbin bound in mummy-cloth
May unwind the winding path;
A mouth that has no moisture and no breath
Breathless mouths may summon;
I hail the superhuman;
I call it death-in-life and life-in-death.

Miracle, bird or golden handiwork,
More miracle than bird or handiwork,
Planted on the starlit golden bough,
Can like the cocks of Hades crow,
Or, by the moon embittered, scorn aloud
In glory of changeless metal
Common bird or petal
And all complexities of mire or blood.

BYZANTIUM

At midnight on the Emperor's pavement flit
Flames that no faggot feeds, nor steel has lit,
Nor storm disturbs, flames begotten of flame,
Where blood-begotten spirits come
And all complexities of fury leave,
Dying into a dance,
An agony of trance,
An agony of flame that cannot singe a sleeve.

Astraddle on the dolphin's mire and blood,
Spirit after spirit! The smithies break the flood.
The golden smithies of the Emperor!
Marbles of the dancing floor
Break bitter furies of complexity,
Those images that yet
Fresh images beget,
That dolphin-torn, that gong-tormented sea.

William Butler Yeats
(13 June 1865 – 28 January 1939)

In the spring of 1930, Yeats was at a hotel at Portofina Vetta overlooking the bay of Genoa, recovering from a vicious bout of Malta fever, which had made him ill enough to write three lines of a will witnessed by Ezra Pound and Basil Bunting. On April 30th, Yeats made a note in his diary under the heading "Subject for a Poem": "Describe Byzantium as it is in the system [ie. in Yeats' book *A Vision*] towards the end of the first Christian millennium. A walking mummy. Flames at the street corners where the soul is purified, birds of hammered gold singing in the golden trees, in the harbour dolphins, offering their backs to the wailing dead that they may carry them to Paradise."

"I think that if I could be given a month of Antiquity and leave to spend it where I chose," Yeats wrote in *A Vision*, "I would spend it in Byzantium, a little before Justinian opened St. Sophia and closed the Academy of Plato."

HAPPY THE MAN

Happy the man, and happy he alone,
  He who can call today his own:
  He who, secure within, can say,
Tomorrow do thy worst, for I have lived today.
  Be fair or foul or rain or shine
The joys I have possessed, in spite of fate, are mine.
Not Heaven itself upon the past has power,
But what has been, has been, and I have had my hour.

John Dryden
(9 August 1631 – 1 May 1700)
translating Horace (65 – 8 BC), Odes, Book III, xxix

Horace was taught in all English schools in the 17th century. Dryden was educated at Westminster School and Trinity College, Cambridge. He adapted
himself to his turbulent times, with his "Heroic Stanzas" on the death of
Cromwell soon followed by "Astrea Redux" in praise of the Restoration of
Charles II. In 1682 he wrote a poem upholding Anglicanism, and three years
later another defending his new Roman Catholicism. At the Revolution of
1688 he lost his court positions as Poet Laureate and Historiographer Royal,
returning first to the writing of plays and later to translations of Horace,
Homer, Virgil, Ovid, Boccaccio, and others.

BODY

What was so quiet a companion,
My dumb friend,
Now cries out, groans,
Swells up with noxious fluid
Clamouring for attention.
Did I neglect you,
Taking for granted
The ease with which you walked, breathed,
Ran for a bus?
We that were one, are two.
I bow before you.

Sasha Moorsom
(25 January 1931 – 22 June 1993)

Sasha's daughter, Sophie Young, was born on this day in 1961. Sophie nursed her mother during her last illness and remembers that "this poem was written towards the end of Sasha's illness, when her condition had deteriorated after a period of remission. She refused to let the pain and weakness of her body prevent her from writing poetry, and she was still able to see the beauty in everything. The week before she died, she wrote these few lines in her diary:

Skin now soft and bloated can take
Any impression like the cliffs at Lyme Regis.
On the side of my knee a beautiful shell
Fans itself out like an ammonite."

TO BE A SLAVE OF INTENSITY

Friend, hope for the Guest while you are alive.
Jump into experience while you are alive!
Think . . . and think . . . while you are alive.
What you call 'salvation' belongs to the time before death.

If you don't break your ropes while you're alive,
do you think
ghosts will do it after?

The idea that the soul will join with the ecstatic
just because the body is rotten –
that is all fantasy.
What is found now is found then.
If you find nothing now,
you will simply end up with an apartment in the City of Death.
If you make love with the divine now, in the next life you will
    have the face of satisfied desire.

So plunge into the truth, find out who the Teacher is,
    Believe in the Great Sound!

Kabir says this: When the Guest is being searched for, it is the
    intensity of the longing for the Guest that does all the work.
Look at me, and you will see a slave of that intensity.

Kabir (c. 15th Century)
Translated by Robert Bly (23 December 1926 -)

Kabir wrote in Hindi. Rabindranath Tagore and Evelyn Underhill translated him into
Victorian English, themselves working from a Bengali translation. Robert Bly, working
from the Tagore-Underhill book, has adapted the poems for today's reader.

from LOVE'S LABOUR'S LOST

ACT IV SCENE III

Berowne. A lover's eyes will gaze an eagle blind,
A lover's ear will hear the lowest sound,
When the suspicious head of theft is stopped.
Love's feeling is more soft and sensible
Than are the tender horns of cockled snails.
Love's tongue proves dainty Bacchus gross in taste.
For valour, is not Love a Hercules,
Still climbing trees in the Hesperides?
Subtle as Sphinx; as sweet and musical
As bright Apollo's lute, strung with his hair.
And when Love speaks, the voice of all the gods
Makes heaven drowsy with the harmony.
Never durst poet touch a pen to write
Until his ink were temp'red with Love's sighs;
O then his lines would ravish savage ears
And plant in tyrants mild humility,
From women's eyes this doctrine I derive.
They sparkle still the right Promethean fire;
They are the books, the arts, the academes,
That show, contain, and nourish all the world.

William Shakespeare
(23 April 1564 - 23 April 1616)

Sir Walter Cope wrote to Robert Cecil in 1604: "I have sent and bene all thys morning huntyng for players juglers and such kinde of creaturs, but finde them harde to finde, wherefore leavinge notes for them to seeke me, Burbage ys come, and sayes ther ys no new playe that the quene hath not seene, but they have reyved an olde one, Cawled Loves Labore Lost, which for wytt and mirthe he sayes will please her exceedingly."

SHE WAS A PHANTOM OF DELIGHT

She was a phantom of delight
When first she gleam'd upon my sight:
A lovely apparition, sent
To be a moment's ornament;
Her eyes as stars of twilight fair;
Like Twilight's, too, her dusky hair;
But all things else about her drawn
From May-time and the cheerful dawn;
A dancing shape, an image gay,
To haunt, to startle, and waylay.

I saw her upon nearer view,
A spirit, yet a woman too!
Her household motions light and free,
And steps of virgin-liberty;
A countenance in which did meet
Sweet records, promises as sweet;
A creature not too bright or good
For human nature's daily food,
For transient sorrows, simple wiles,
Praise, blame, love, kisses, tears, and smiles.

And now I see with eye serene
The very pulse of the machine;
A being breathing thoughtful breath,
A traveller between life and death:
The reason firm, the temperate will,
Endurance, foresight, strength, and skill;
A perfect woman, nobly plann'd

SHE WAS A PHANTOM OF DELIGHT

To warn, to comfort, and command;
And yet a Spirit still, and bright
With something of an angel-light.

William Wordsworth
(7 April 1770 - 23 April 1850)

On this day in 1805, Wordsworth told Sir George Beaumont that he had been trying to write a commemorative poem on the death of his brother John in a shipwreck, but had been too much agitated to remember what he wrote.

According to Justice Coleridge, Wordsworth said that "Phantom of Delight" "was written on 'his dear wife,' of whom he spoke in the sweetest manner; and a manner full of the warmest love and admiration, yet with delicacy and reserve," and Wordswoth noted: "It was written from my heart, as is sufficiently obvious."

from ODE TO A NIGHTINGALE[1]

My heart aches, and a drowsy numbness pains
　My sense, as though of hemlock I had drunk,
Or emptied some dull opiate to the drains
　One minute past, and Lethe-wards had sunk:
'Tis not through envy of thy happy lot,
　But being too happy in thy happiness –
　　That thou, light-wingèd Dryad of the trees,
　　　　In some melodious plot
Of beechen green, and shadows numberless,
　Singest of summer in full-throated ease.

I cannot see what flowers are at my feet,
　Nor what soft incense hangs upon the boughs,
But, in embalmèd darkness, guess each sweet
　Wherewith the seasonable month endows
The grass, the thicket, and the fruit-tree wild:
　White hawthorn, and the pastoral eglantine;
　Fast fading violets cover'd up in leaves;
　　　　And mid-May's eldest child,
The coming musk-rose, full of dewy wine,
　The murmurous haunt of flies on summer eves.

Darkling I listen; and, for many a time
　I have been half in love with easeful death,
Called him soft names in many a musèd rhyme,
　To take into the air my quiet breath;
Now more than ever seems it rich to die,
　To cease upon the midnight with no pain,
　　While thou art pouring forth thy soul abroad

from ODE TO A NIGHTINGALE

In such an ecstasy!
Still wouldst thou sing, and I have ears in vain–
To thy high requiem become a sod.

John Keats
(31 October 1795 – 23 February 1821)

This ode was written in May 1819. Charles Brown's perhaps unreliable version of the story is that "in the spring of 1819 a nightingale had built her nest near my house. Keats felt a tranquil and continual joy in her song; and one morning he took his chair from the breakfast table to the grass plot under a plum tree, where he sat for two or three hours. When he came into the house, I perceived he had some scraps of paper in his hand, and those he was quietly thrusting behind the books. On inquiry, I found these scraps, four or five in number, contained his poetic feeling on the song of our nightingale."

1. Stanzas 1, 5, and 6 of this 8-stanza poem.

THE POWER OF MAPLES

If you want to live in the country you have to understand the power
   of maples.
You have to see them sink their teeth into the roots of the old locusts.
You have to see them force the sycamores to gasp for air.
You have to see them move their thick hairs into the cellar.
   And when you cut your great green shad pole
you have to be ready for it to start sprouting in your hands;
you have to stick it in the ground like a piece of willow;
you have to plant your table under its leaves and begin eating.

Gerald Stern
(22 February 1925 -)

Gerald Stern writes: "I wrote this poem when we moved away from the crowded urban
New Jersey and New York world to the Delaware River in Pennsylvania. I suddenly became schooled in some country things, and saw the destructive as well as the gentle,
healing ornamental quality in nature. The dear maple, tree of our suburban ornament,
was, after all, a terrifying and relentless force one learned to respect."

The son of Russian immigrants, Stern was born in Pittsburgh, Pennsylvania. *Odd Mercy*
(1995) is the most recent of his eleven volumes of verse. The poet now lives in Easton,
Pennsylvania.

AT HOME FROM CHURCH

The lilacs lift in generous bloom
  Their plumes of dear old-fashioned flowers;
Their fragrance fills the still old house
  Where left alone I count the hours.

High in the apple-trees the bees
  Are humming, busy in the sun, –
An idle robin cries for rain
  But once or twice and then is done.

The Sunday-morning quiet holds
  In heavy slumber all the street,
While from the church, just out of sight
  Behind the elms, comes slow and sweet

The organ's drone, the voices faint
  That sing the quaint long-meter hymn –
I somehow feel as if shut out
  From some mysterious temple, dim

And beautiful with blue and red
  And golden lights from windows high,
Where angels in the shadows stand
  And earth seems very near the sky.

At home from church

The day-dream fades – and so I try
  Again to catch the tune that brings
No thought of temple nor of priest,
  But only of a voice that sings.

Sarah Orne Jewett
(3 September 1849 – 24 June 1909)

Jewett's success rested on her writing about characters local to coastal Maine, particularly her place of birth, Berwick. Traveling with her father, an eminent physician, on his rounds, she developed a deep familiarity with the area and the rural folk who were soon to inhabit her stories. Never marrying, she became a "New England nun," immersing herself in the lives of those she created on paper and bearing witness to the people of the Maine coast whose clipper ship trade was threatened by the railroad. Jewett's work preserves a way of life in New England that would not survive the Civil War.

In 1901, she was the first woman to receive an honorary degree from Bowdoin College. Perhaps the book most associated with Jewett's name is *The Country of the Pointed Firs*, published in 1896.

TIME

'Established' is a good word, much used in garden books,
'The plant, when established' . . .
Oh, become established quickly, quickly, garden!
For I am fugitive, I am very fugitive –

Those that come after me will gather these roses,
And watch, as I do now, the white wistaria
Burst, in the sunshine, from its pale green sheath.

Planned. Planted. Established. Then neglected,
Till at last the loiterer by the gate will wonder
At the old, old cottage, the old wooden cottage,
And say, 'One might build here, the view is glorious;
This must have been a pretty garden once.'

Mary Ursula Bethell
(6 October 1874 - 15 January 1945)

Mary Ursula Bethell was born in England but her parents soon returned to New Zealand. She herself became a social worker in Christchurch, New Zealand, and in London, returning permanently to New Zealand after the First World War. She built a house in the Cashmere Hills, with a fine view over Christchurch, and her first book of poems (in 1929) concerned her garden, where she would plant primroses to remind her of spring in England. The poet D'Arcy Cresswell wrote: "New Zealand wasn't truly discovered . . . until Ursula Bethell, 'very earnestly digging,' raised her head to look at the mountains," and Peter Simpson wrote that "Ursula Bethell felt herself to be a transplanted Englishwoman for whom her garden . . . was both a reminder of her exile and a compensation for it. To some degree, she stands for all New Zealanders, colonists all, gardening the antipodes. The garden was her pilgrimage, her way to God."

As a committed Anglican, her poetry became gradually more devotional in content and formal in style. She lived in her house with her long-term companion Effie Pollen. After Effie's death in 1934, she left the house that they had shared, and wrote little more, apart from the anguished poetry dedicated to Effie in *Six Memorials*.

Two in the campagna

I wonder do you feel to-day
  As I have felt, since, hand in hand
We sat down on the grass, to stray
  In spirit better through the land,
This morn of Rome and May?

For me, I touched a thought, I know,
  Has tantalised me many times,
(Like turns of thread the spiders throw
  Mocking across our path) for rhymes
To catch at and let go.

Help me to hold it: first it left
  The yellowing fennel, run to seed
There, branching from the brickwork's cleft
  Some old tomb's ruin: yonder weed
Took up the floating weft,

Where one small orange cup amassed
  Five beetles, – blind and green they grope
Among the honey-meal, – and last,
  Everywhere on the grassy slope
I traced it. Hold it fast!

Two in the campagna

The champaign with its endless fleece
  Of feathery grasses everywhere!
Silence and passion, joy and peace,
  An everlasting wash of air –
Rome's ghost since her decease.

Such life here, through such lengths of hours,
  Such miracles performed in play
Such primal naked forms of flowers,
  Such letting Nature have her way
While Heaven looks from its towers.

How say you? Let us, O my dove,
  Let us be unashamed of soul,
As earth lies bare to heaven above.
  How is it under our control
To love or not to love?

I would that you were all to me,
  You that are just so much, no more –
Nor yours nor mine, – nor slave nor free!
  Where does the fault lie? what the core
Of the wound, since wound must be?

I would I could adopt your will,
  See with your eyes, and set my heart
Beating by yours, and drink my fill
  At your soul's springs, – your part, my part
In life, for good and ill.

TWO IN THE CAMPAGNA

No. I yearn upward – touch you close,
   Then stand away. I kiss your cheek,
Catch your soul's warmth, – I pluck the rose
   And love it more than tongue can speak –
Then the good minute goes.

Already how am I so far
   Out of that minute? Must I go
Still like the thistle-ball, no bar,
   Onward, whenever light winds blow,
Fixed by no friendly star?

Just when I seemed about to learn!
   Where is the thread now? Off again!
The old trick! Only I discern –
   Infinite passion and the pain
Of finite hearts that yearn.

Robert Browning
(7 May 1812 – 12 December 1889)

On 10 May 1854 Mrs. Browning wrote: "The pleasantest days in Rome we have spent with the Kembles – the two sisters – who are charming and excellent both of them in different ways; and certainly they have given us some exquisite hours on the Campagna, upon picnic excursions, they and certain of their friends."

LOVE IS LOVE

The lowest trees have tops, the ant her gall,
The fly her spleen, the little spark his heat:
The slender hairs cast shadows, though but small,
And bees have stings, although they be not great;
  Seas have their source, and so have shallow springs;
  And love is love, in beggars and in kings.

Where waters smoothest run, there deepest are the fords,
The dial stirs, yet none perceives it move;
The firmest faith is found in fewest words,
The turtles do not sing, and yet they love;
  True hearts have ears and eyes, no tongues to speak;
  They hear and see, and sigh, and then they break.

Sir Edward Dyer
(ca. 1543 – May 1607)

Sir Edward Dyer, poet and diplomat, was born in Sharpham Park, Somerset. He was educated at either Broadgates Hall or Balliol College, Oxford, and then introduced at court by the Earl of Leicester. He wrote an elegy to his friend Sir Philip Sidney but the most well-known poem attributed to him, "My Mind to Me a Kingdom Is," is probably not by him. Betjeman spoke of his poetry as "easily among my favorites." In later life Dyer lived in quiet seclusion.

THE OWL AND THE PUSSY-CAT

The Owl and the Pussy-Cat went to sea
  In a beautiful pea-green boat.
They took some honey, and plenty of money,
  Wrapped up in a five-pound note.
The Owl looked up to the stars above,
  And sang to a small guitar,
'O lovely Pussy! O Pussy, my love,
  What a beautiful Pussy you are,
      You are,
      You are!
  What a beautiful Pussy you are!'

Pussy said to the Owl, 'You elegant fowl!
  How charmingly sweet you sing!
O let us be married! too long we have tarried:
  But what shall we do for a ring?'
They sailed away, for a year and a day,
  To the land where the Bong-Tree grows,
And there in a wood a Piggy-wig stood,
  With a ring at the end of his nose,
      His nose,
      His nose,
  With a ring at the end of his nose.

'Dear Pig, are you willing to sell for one shilling
  Your ring?' Said the Piggy, 'I will.'
So they took it away, and were married next day
  By the Turkey who lives on the hill.

The owl and the pussy-cat

They dinèd on mince, and slices of quince,
    Which they ate with a runcible spoon;
And hand in hand, on the edge of the sand,
    They danced by the light of the moon,
        The moon,
        The moon,
    They danced by the light of the moon.

Edward Lear
(12 May 1812 - 29 January 1888)

Born in London of Danish ancestry, Lear was forced to earn a living at age 15 when his father was imprisoned for debt. Despite suffering from epilepsy and asthma, Lear became a successful illustrator and writer of light verse. He also compiled his many wanderings in a number of travel books. "To E. L. on His Travels in Greece," written by Tennyson, praised Lear both as an artist and recorder of journeys.

THE WAY WE LIVE

Pass the tambourine, let me bash out praises
to the Lord God of movement, to Absolute
non-friction, flight, and the scarey side:
death by avalanche, birth by failed contraception.
Of chicken tandoori and reggae, loud, from tenements,
commitment, driving fast and unswerving
friendship. Of tee-shirts on pulleys, giros and Bombay,
barmen, dreaming waitresses with many fake-gold
bangles. Of airports, impulse, and waking to uncertainty,
to strip-lights, motorways, or that pantheon –
the mountains. To overdrafts and grafting

and the fit slow pulse of wipers as you're
creeping over Rannoch, while the God of moorland
walks abroad with his entourage of freezing fog,
his bodyguard of snow.
Of endless gloaming in the North, of Asiatic swelter,
to launderettes, anecdotes, passions and exhaustion,
Final Demands and dead men, the skeletal grip
of government. To misery and elation; mixed,
the sod and caprice of landlords.
To the way it fits, the way it is, the way it seems
to be: let me bash out praises – pass the tambourine.

Kathleen Jamie
(13 May 1962 -)

Kathleen Jamie's travels, mainly in the East, are reflected in her collections *The Way We Live* (1987) and *The Autonomous Region* (1993) and in her travel book *The Golden Peak* (1992). Jamie was born in Renfrewshire and now lives in Fife. Her collection *The Queen of Sheba* was published in 1994.

14 MAY

PSALM 23
A PSALM OF DAVID

The Lord is my shepherd; I shall not want.
He maketh me to lie down in green pastures;
He leadeth me beside the still waters.
He restoreth my soul;
He leadeth me in the paths of righteousness for his name's sake.
Yea, though I walk through the valley of the shadow of death,
I will fear no evil: for thou art with me;
Thy rod and thy staff they comfort me.
Thou preparest a table before me in the presence of mine enemies.
Thou anointest my head with oil; my cup runneth over.
Surely goodness and mercy shall follow me all the days of my life.
And I will dwell in the house of the Lord forever.

King David
(Died c. 990 BC)

On this day in 1948, David Ben-Gurion announced the creation of the state of Israel, following the partition of Palestine and the ending of the British Mandate. Of the *Psalms*, Donne wrote: "The songs are these, which Heaven's high Holy Muse / Whisper'd to David, David to the Jewes" and Disraeli called King David "the most popular poet in England . . . the sweet singer of Israel." Psalm 23 was written about two and a half thousand years ago, and is one of the 73 psalms (out of the 150) that have been attributed by scholars to King David himself. On Saul's death, David ruled over Judah from about 1010 BC to 990 BC, annexing Jerusalem in the process, where he built a palace on Mount Zion and installed there the Ark of the Covenant. His kingdom ranged from the Euphrates to Egypt, although his later years were troubled by civil wars in which two of his sons were involved.

The early Christians went to their death with Psalm 23 on their lips – St. Augustine chose this psalm as the Hymn of the Martyrs. E. C. D. Stanford wrote that its popularity has endured: "George Herbert paraphrased it: Ruskin learned to say it for his mother. In our day it is sung at the wedding of Queen and commoner."

Kathleen Strange associates the psalms's green pastures with the fertile Wadi Fara in Jordan, and the Valley of Death with the terrifying passage among the mountains between Jerusalem and the Dead Sea.

Because i could not stop for death

Because I could not stop for Death –
He kindly stopped for me –
The Carriage held but just Ourselves –
And Immortality.

We slowly drove – He knew no haste
And I had put away
My labor and my leisure too,
For His Civility –

We passed the School, where Children strove
At Recess – in the Ring –
We passed the Fields of Gazing Grain –
We passed the Setting Sun –

Or rather – He passed Us –
The Dews drew quivering and chill –
For only Gossamer, my Gown –
My Tippet[1] – only Tulle –

We paused before a House that seemed
A Swelling of the Ground –
The Roof was scarcely visible –
The Cornice – in the Ground –

Since then – 'tis Centuries – and yet
Feels shorter than the Day
I first surmised the Horses' Heads
Were toward Eternity –

Emily Dickinson
(10 December 1830 – 15 May 1886)

By her forties, Dickinson had completed her retreat from the outside world, refusing to leave the house. Only seven of her 1,800 poems were published in her lifetime. Discouraged the one time she actively sought publication, she appears to have accepted her "Barefoot-Rank" status. Some of her verses circulated privately in Amherst, Massachusetts, to a largely condescending group who pitied her eccentricity.

1. A tulle tippet is a neck and shoulder scarf made of fine netting.

CASABIANCA

Love's the boy stood on the burning deck
trying to recite 'The boy stood on
the burning deck.' Love's the son
    stood stammering elocution
      while the poor ship in flames went down.

Love's the obstinate boy, the ship,
even the swimming sailors, who
would like a schoolroom platform, too,
    or an excuse to stay
      on deck. And love's the burning boy.

Elizabeth Bishop
(8 February 1911 – 6 October 1979)

The publication of this poem in the August 1936 issue of *New Democracy* brought Elizabeth Bishop to an international audience. Brett C. Midler believes that the boy's love and fear in this poem stand for "Elizabeth's black conviction that love, especially parental love, is a non-negotiable trap . . . It was a long time before she could write about . . . any kind of love without screens of rhetorical statement."

OFT IN THE STILLY NIGHT

Oft in the stilly night
  Ere Slumber's chain has bound me,
Fond Memory brings the light
  Of other days around me;
    The smiles, the tears,
    Of boyhood's years,
  The words of love then spoken;
    The eyes that shone,
    Now dimmed and gone,
  The cheerful hearts now broken!
Thus, in the stilly night,
  Ere Slumber's chain has bound me,
Sad Memory brings the light
  Of other days around me.

When I remember all
  The friends so linked together,
I've seen around me fall,
  Like leaves in wintry weather:
    I feel like one
    Who treads alone
  Some banquet-hall deserted,
    Whose lights are fled,
    Whose garland's dead,
  And all but he departed!

OFT IN THE STILLY NIGHT

Thus in the stilly night,
  Ere Slumber's chain has bound me,
Fond Memory brings the light
  Of other days around me.

Thomas Moore
(28 May 1779 - 25 February 1852)

Thomas Moore was born in Dublin, the son of a Catholic grocer. His *Poems* of 1801 and his talent as a singer were his entrée into high society. He married Bessy Dyke, an actress, and they lived in Wiltshire. His *Irish Melodies* brought him an income of £500 a year. But his deputy registrar at the Admiralty Court in Bermuda defaulted with £6,000, and in 1819 Moore had to flee to the Continent to avoid arrest for this debt, returning three years later. In 1830 he published a life of Byron, despite having previously burned Byron's Memoirs.

THE EAGLE

He clasps the crag with crookèd hands;
Close to the sun in lonely lands,
Ring'd with the azure world, he stands.

The wrinkled sea beneath him crawls;
He watches from his mountain walls,
And like a thunderbolt he falls.

Alfred, Lord Tennyson
(6 August 1809 – 6 October 1892)

On this day in 1866, Tennyson told his wife that when he heard of the death of Byron, he carved Byron's name into the rectory wall at Somersby. He added that he thought Byron was popular because he wrote vulgarly and that he himself was popular because he was Poet Laureate – "something like being a Lord."

Tennyson wrote "The Eagle" into the album of Dora Wordsworth when in the Lake District in the summer of 1850.

SLOUGH

Come, friendly bombs, and fall on Slough
It isn't fit for humans now,
There isn't grass to graze a cow
  Swarm over, Death!

Come, bombs, and blow to smithereens
Those air-conditioned, bright canteens,
Tinned fruit, tinned meat, tinned milk,
      tinned beans
  Tinned minds, tinned breath.

Mess up the mess they call a town –
A house for ninety-seven down
And once a week a half-a-crown
  For twenty years,

And get that man with double chin
Who'll always cheat and always win,
Who washed his repulsive skin
  in women's tears,

And smash his desk of polished oak
And smash his hands so used to stroke
And stop his boring dirty joke
  And make him yell.

But spare the bald young clerks who add
The profits of the stinking cad;
It's not their fault that they are mad,
  They've tasted Hell.

SLOUGH

It's not their fault they do not know
The birdsong from the radio,
It's not their fault they often go
   To Maidenhead

And talk of sports and makes of cars
In various bogus Tudor bars
And daren't look up and see the stars
   But belch instead.

In labour-saving homes, with care
Their wives frizz out peroxide hair
And dry it in synthetic air
   And paint their nails.

Come, friendly bombs, and fall on Slough
To get it ready for the plough.
The cabbages are coming now;
   The earth exhales.

John Betjeman
(28 August 1906 – 19 May 1984)

John Betjeman was born in Highgate, the son of a Dutch-descended manufacturer of household objects. He was educated at Marlborough, which he disliked, and Oxford, which he left without a degree. He was a contemporary there of Louis MacNeice and W. H. Auden, who admired his verse. His range of interests as a poet, broadcaster, and writer are indicated by the following sample titles: *Ghastly Good Taste: or, A Depressing Story of the Rise and Fall of English Architecture* (1933), *Continual Dew: A Little Book of Bourgeois Verse* (1937), *English Churches* (1964), and *London's Historic Railway Stations* (1972). He was the founder of the Victorian Society and was named Poet Laureate in 1972.

MAGNIFICAT

FOR SIAN, AFTER THIRTEEN YEARS

oh this man
what a meal he made of me
how he chewed and gobbled and sucked

in the end he spat me all out

you arrived on the dot, in the nick
of time, with your red curls flying
I was about to slip down the sink like grease
I nearly collapsed, I almost
wiped myself out like a stain
I called for you, and you came, you voyaged
fierce as a small archangel with swords and breasts
you declared the birth of a new life
in my kitchen there was an annunciation
and I was still, awed by your hair's glory

you commanded me to sing of my redemption

oh my friend, how
you were mother for me, and how
I could let myself lean on you
comfortable as an old cloth, familiar as enamel saucepans
I was a child again, pyjamaed
in winceyette, my hair plaited, and you
listened, you soothed me like cakes and milk
you listened to me for three days, and I poured
it out, I flowed all over you
like wine, like oil, you touched the place where it hurt

MAGNIFICAT

at night we slept together in my big bed
your shoulder eased me towards dreams

when we met, I tell you
it was a birthday party, a funeral
it was a holy communion
between women, a Visitation

it was two old she-goats butting
and nuzzling each other in the smelly fold

Michèle Roberts
(20 May 1949 -)

Half-French novelist as well as poet, Michèle Roberts was born in England and resides in London and France. She has written three books of poems, the latest, published by Virago, is: *All the Selves I Was - New and Selected Poems* (1995). The author of six novels, Roberts was shortlisted for the Booker Prize for her *Daughters of the House* (1992) and won the W. H. Smith Literary Award in 1993.

THE WAY

My love's manners in bed
are not to be discussed by me,
as mine by her
I would not credit comment upon gracefully.

Yet I ride by the margin of that lake in
the wood, the castle,
and the excitement of strongholds,
and have a small boy's notion of doing good.

Oh well, I will say here,
knowing each man,
let you find a good wife too,
and love her as hard as you can.

Robert Creeley
(21 May 1926 -)

Robert Creeley writes: "The burden of this poem seems to remain true despite I wrote it forty or more years ago. In fact, the older one gets, the more insistent what's said here becomes. Onward!"

A NEGRO LOVE SONG

Seen my lady home las' night,
  Jump back, honey, jump back.
Hel' huh han' an' sque'z it tight,
  Jump back, honey, jump back.
Hyeahd huh sigh a little sigh,
Seen a light gleam f'om huh eye,
An' a smile go flittin' by –
  Jump back, honey, jump back.

Hyeahd de win' blow thoo de pine,
  Jump back, honey, jump back.
Mockin'-bird was singin' fine,
  Jump back, honey, jump back.
An' my hea't was beatin' so,
When I reached my lady's do',
Dat I couldn't ba' to go –
  Jump back, honey, jump back.

Put my ahm aroun' huh wais',
  Jump back, honey, jump back.
Raised huh lips an' took a tase,
  Jump back, honey, jump back.
Love me, honey, love me true?
Love me well ez I love you?
An' she answe'd, " 'Cose I do" –
  Jump back, honey, jump back.

Paul Laurence Dunbar
(27 June 1872 – 9 February 1906)

THE TABLES TURNED

Up, up! my Friend, and quit your books;
　Or surely you'll grow double:
Up, up! my Friend, and clear your looks
　Why all this toil and trouble?

The sun, above the mountain's head,
　A freshening lustre mellow
Through all the long green fields has spread,
　His first sweet evening yellow.

Books! 'tis a dull and endless strife:
　Come, hear the woodland linnet,
How sweet his music! on my life,
　There's more of wisdom in it.

And hark! how blithe the throstle sings!
　He, too, is no mean preacher:
Come forth into the light of things,
　Let Nature be your teacher.

She has a world of ready wealth,
　Our minds and hearts to bless –
Spontaneous wisdom breathed by health,
　Truth breathed by cheerfulness.

One impulse from a vernal wood
　May teach you more of man,
Of moral evil and of good,
　Than all the sages can.

Sweet is the lore which Nature brings;
  Our meddling intellect
Mis-shapes the beauteous forms of things: –
  We murder to dissect.

Enough of Science and of Art;
  Close up those barren leaves;
Come forth and bring with you a heart
  That watches and receives.

William Wordsworth
(7 April 1770 – 23 April 1850)

Composed about 23 May 1798. At the time, the Wordsworths were bringing up Basil Montagu. "We teach him nothing at present," explained Dorothy Wordsworth, "but what he learns from the evidence of his senses. He has his own insatiable curiosity which we are always careful to satisfy to the best of our ability. It is directed to everything he sees, the sky, the fields, trees, shrubs, corn, the making of tools, etc. . . . ."

from THE SONG OF SOLOMON

I am come into my garden, my sister, my spouse: I have gathered my myrrh with my spice; I have eaten my honeycomb with my honey; I have drunk my wine with my milk: eat, O friends; drink, yea, drink abundantly, O beloved.

I sleep, but my heart waketh: it is the voice of my beloved that knocketh, saying, Open to me, my sister, my love, my dove, my undefiled: for my head is filled with dew, and my locks with the drops of the night.

Behold thou art fair, my love; behold thou art fair; thou hast doves' eyes within thy locks: thy hair is as a flock of goats, that appear from mount Gilead.

Thy teeth are like a flock of sheep that are even shorn, which came up from the washing; whereof every one bear twins, and none is barren among them.

Thy lips are like a thread of scarlet, and thy speech is comely: thy temples are like a piece of pomegranate within thy locks.

My beloved is white and ruddy, the chiefest among ten thousand.

His head is as the most fine gold, his locks are bushy and black as a raven.

His eyes are as the eyes of doves by the rivers of waters, washed with milk, and fitly set.

Thy neck is like the tower of David builded for an armoury, whereon there hang a thousand bucklers, all shields of mighty men.

from THE SONG OF SOLOMON

Thy two breasts are like two young roes that are twins, which feed among the lilies.

Until the day break, and the shadows flee away, I will get me to the mountain of myrrh, and to the hill of frankincense.

Thou art all fair, my love; there is no spot in thee.

His cheeks are as a bed of spices, as sweet flowers: his lips like lilies, dropping sweet smelling myrrh.

His hands are as gold rings set with the beryl: his belly is as bright ivory overlaid with sapphires.

His legs are as pillars of mable, set upon sockets of fine gold: his countenance is as Lebanon, excellent as the cedars.

Come with me from Lebanon, my spouse, with me from Lebanon: look from the top of Amana, from the top of Shenir and Hermon, from the lions' den, from the mountains of the leopards.

Thou hast ravished my heart, my sister, my spouse: thou hast ravished my heart with one of thine eyes, with one chain of thy neck.

How fair is thy love, my sister, my spouse! how much better is thy love than wine! and the smell of thine ointments than all spices!

from THE SONG OF SOLOMON

Thy lips, O my spouse, drop as the honeycomb: honey and milk are under thy tongue; and the smell of thy garments is like the smell of Lebanon.

A garden inclosed is my sister, my spouse; a spring shut up, a fountain sealed.

His mouth is most sweet: yea, he is altogether lovely. This is my beloved, and this is my friend, O daughters of Jerusalem.

The highly erotic Song of Solomon survived in the bible under disguise as an allegory. Where the Song has, for instance, "my beloved put in his hand by the hole of the door, and my bowels were moved for him," the commentary reads "the church having a taste of Christ's love is sick of love." The Song of Solomon (at one time attributed to Solomon, but now thought to be from a later date, perhaps the 4th or 3rd century BC) is an anthology of Hebrew love poems, with two different voices – the man and the woman's voice in the version here printed represents a conflation of Chapters 4 and 5 (and was read as a dialogue by bride and groom at a recent wedding).

Rabbi Akibu wrote that "The whole world is not worth the day on which the Song of Songs was given to Israel; for all the scriptures are holy, but the Song of Songs is the Holy of Holies." How so, if it is merely sensual love poetry? Robert Davidson tells the story of a Jewish tailor talking to a Christian friend: "The real difference between a Jew and a Christian is that we Jews believe in sex."

from HAMATREYA
Ah! the hot owner sees not Death, who adds
Him to his land, a lump of mould the more.
Hear what the Earth says:

EARTH-SONG

'Mine and yours;
Mine, not yours.
Earth endures;
Stars abide –
Shine down in the old sea;
Old are the shores;
But where are old men?
I who have seen much,
Such have I never seen.

'The lawyer's deed
Ran sure,
In tail,
To them, and to their heirs
Who shall succeed,
Without fail,
Forevermore.

'Here is the land,
Shaggy with wood,
With its old valley,
Mound and flood.
But the heritors?
Fled like the flood's foam. –

EARTH-SONG

The lawyer, and the laws,
And the kingdom,
Clean swept herefrom.

'They called me theirs,
Who so controlled me;
Yet every one
Wished to stay, and is gone,
How am I theirs,
If they cannot hold me,
But I hold them?'

When I heard the Earth-song
I was no longer brave;
My avarice cooled
Like lust in the chill of the grave.

Ralph Waldo Emerson
(25 May 1803 – 27 April 1882)

"We have listened too long to the courtly muses of Europe," Emerson wrote. "The spirit of the American free man is already suspected to be timid, imitative, tame. Not so, brothers and friends, please God, ours shall be not so. We will walk on our own feet; we will work with our own hands; we will speak with our own minds."

26 MAY

POEM

And if it snowed and snow covered the drive
he took a spade and tossed it to one side.
And always tucked his daughter up at night.
And slippered her the one time that she lied.

And every week he tipped up half his wage.
And what he didn't spend each week he saved.
And praised his wife for every meal she made.
And once, for laughing, punched her in the face.

And for his mum he hired a private nurse.
And every Sunday taxied her to church.
And he blubbed when she went from bad to worse.
And twice he lifted ten quid from her purse.

Here's how they rated him when they looked back:
sometimes he did this, sometimes he did that.

Simon Armitage
(26 May 1963 -)

Simon Armitage was born in Huddersfield, West Yorkshire, and studied geography at Portsmouth Polytechnic and social work at Manchester University. He is a probation officer and lives in Marsden near Huddersfield, which has been described as Britain's "alternative poetry capital." His poetry includes *Zoom* (1989) and *Kid* (1992).

THE BATTLE HYMN OF THE REPUBLIC

Mine eyes have seen the glory of the coming of the Lord:
He is trampling out the vintage where the grapes of wrath are stored;
He hath loosed the fatal lightning of His terrible swift sword:
    His truth is marching on.

I have seen Him in the watch-fires of a hundred circling camps,
They have builded Him an altar in the evening dews and damps;
I can read His righteous sentence by the dim and flaring lamps:
    His day is marching on.

I have read a fiery gospel writ in burnished rows of steel:
'As ye deal with my contemners, so with you my grace shall deal;
Let the Hero, born of woman, crush the serpent with his heel,
    Since God is marching on.'

He has sounded forth the trumpet that shall never call retreat;
He is sifting out the hearts of men before His judgement seat:
Oh, be swift, my soul, to answer Him! Be jubilant, my feet!
    Our God is marching on.

In the beauty of the lilies Christ was born across the sea,
With a glory in his bosom that transfigures you and me:
As he died to make men holy, let us die to make men free,
    While God is marching on.

Julia Ward Howe
(27 May 1819 – 17 October 1910)

On visiting the Union Army of the Potomac, Julia Ward Howe was asked to write dignified patriotic words to the tune of "John Brown's Body." This marching song is the result.

DO NOT GO GENTLE INTO THAT
GOOD NIGHT

Do not go gentle into that good night,
Old age should burn and rave at close of day;
Rage, rage against the dying of the light.

Though wise men at their end know dark is right,
Because their words had forked no lightning they
Do not go gentle into that good night.

Good men, the last wave by, crying how bright
Their frail deeds might have danced in a green bay,
Rage, rage against the dying of the light.

Wild men who caught and sang the sun in flight,
And learn, too late, they grieved it on its way,
Do not go gentle into that good night.

Grave men, near death, who see with blinding sight
Blind eyes could blaze like meteors and be gay,
Rage, rage against the dying of the light.

And you, my father, there on the sad height,
Curse, bless, me now with your fierce tears, I pray.
Do not go gentle into that good night.
Rage, rage against the dying of the light.

Dylan Thomas
(27 October 1914 – 9 November 1953)

"Do Not Go Gentle Into That Good Night" was completed by Dylan Thomas on this day
in 1951. It was written for his agnostic father who had cancer of the throat.

To the terrestrial globe

by a miserable wretch

Roll on, thou ball, roll on!
Through pathless realms of Space
  Roll on!
What though I'm in a sorry case?
What though I cannot meet my bills?
What though I suffer toothache's ills?
What though I swallow countless pills?
    Never *you* mind!
    Roll on!

Roll on, thou ball, roll on!
Through seas of inky air
  Roll on!
It's true I've got no shirts to wear;
It's true my butcher's bill is due;
It's true my prospects all look blue –
But don't let that unsettle you!
    Never *you* mind!
    Roll on!
          [It rolls on.]

W. S. Gilbert
(18 November 1836 – 29 May 1911)

Gilbert's death on this day in 1911 seems to have resulted from an attempt to help a young friend who had got out of her depth while swimming near his home. Hearing her cries, Gilbert dived in to rescue her, but at 74 years old the exertion proved too great for him. He died of heart failure.

OF THE NATURE AND STATE OF MAN WITH RESPECT TO HIMSELF, AS AN INDIVIDUAL

from AN ESSAY ON MAN, EPISTLE II.

Know then thyself, presume not God to scan;
The proper study of mankind is Man.
Placed on this isthmus of a middle state,
A being darkly wise, and rudely great:
With too much knowledge for the skeptic side,
With too much weakness for the Stoic's pride,
He hangs between; in doubt to act, or rest,
In doubt to deem himself a god, or beast;
In doubt his mind or body to prefer,
Born but to die, and reasoning but to err;
Alike in ignorance, his reason such,
Whether he thinks too little, or too much:
Chaos of thought and passion, all confused;
Still by himself abused, or disabused;
Created half to rise, and half to fall;
Great lord of all things, yet a prey to all;
Sole judge of truth, in endless error hurled:
The glory, jest, and riddle of the world!

Alexander Pope
(21 May 1688 - 30 May 1744)

The largely self-educated son of a linen draper, Pope was a precocious poet, producing publishable work by the age of 12, the age at which a tubercular infection of his spine crippled his growth. He achieved financial independence through his translations of Homer, buying a villa in Twickenham where he lived with his mother. Many of his poems were immensely popular, ranging from his *Rape of the Lock*, a mock epic on the stealing of a lock of hair from the head of a society lady, to his mock-heroic satire *The Dunciad*. His *Essay on Man* was published in 1733-34.

from MEMORIES OF PRESIDENT LINCOLN
(in *Leaves of Grass*)

from the section WHEN LILACS LAST IN THE DOORYARD BLOOM'D[1]

Come, lovely and soothing Death,
Undulate round the world, serenely arriving, arriving,
In the day, in the night, to all, to each,
Sooner or later, delicate Death.

Praised be the fathomless universe
For life and joy, and for objects and knowledge curious;
And for love, sweet love – But praise! O praise and praise
For the sure-enwinding arms of cool-enfolding Death.

Dark Mother, always gliding near, with soft feet,
Have none chanted for thee a chant of fullest welcome?
Then I chant it for thee – I glorify thee above all;
I bring thee a song, that, when thou must indeed come, thou come
        unfalteringly.

Approach, encompassing Death – strong deliveress!
When it is so – when thou hast taken them, I joyously sing the dead
Lost in the loving, floating ocean of thee,
Laved in the flood of thy bliss, O Death.

Walt Whitman
(*31 May 1819 – 26 March 1892*)

Walt Whitman was born on this day in 1919 in West Hills, near Huntington, Long Island.

1. Lines 135 to 150 of this 206 line section.

ROUEN
PLACE DE LA PUCELLE

Here blooms the legend fed with time and chance,
Fresh as the morning, though in centuries old;
The whitest lily in the shield of France,
 With heart of virgin gold.

Along this square she moved, sweet Joan of Arc,
With face more pallid than a day-lit star,
Half seen, half doubted, while before her dark
 Stretched the array of war.

Swift furled the battle-smoke of lying breath
From off her path, as if a wind had blown,
And showed no faithless king, but righteous death
 On the low, wooden throne.

He would reward her; she who meekly wore
Alike her gilded mail and peasant gown,
Meekly received one earthly honor more, –
 The formless, fiery crown.

A white dove trembled up the heated air,
And in the opening zenith found its goal;
Soft as a downward feather fell a prayer
 For each repentant soul.

Maria White Lowell
(8 July 1821 – 27 October 1853)

Anna Maria White, a disciple of the early feminist Margaret Fuller, was a dedicated abolitionist who drew her conservative husband, James Russell Lowell, to her cause. Together, the Lowell's aided many people in their attempts to escape slavery.

A THUNDERSTORM IN TOWN

She wore a new 'terra-cotta' dress,
And we stayed, because of the pelting storm,
Within the hansom's dry recess,
Though the horse had stopped; yea, motionless
  We sat on, snug and warm.

Then the downpour ceased, to my sharp sad pain
And the glass that had screened our forms before
Flew up, and out she sprang to her door:
I should have kissed her if the rain
  Had lasted a minute more.

Thomas Hardy
(2 June 1840 – 11 January 1928)

Hardy was born in Upper Bockhampton, near Dorchester in Dorset, the son of a stone-mason. Trained as an architect, he began writing novels. He only turned his attention to poetry in his late fifties, cured of concern for the critical opinion of others by what he called the "shrill crescendo of invective" launched at his later novels. He tried to write poetry in a colloquial language that avoided "the jewelled line."

In a less than flattering tribute to his forerunner, W. H. Auden commented: "Hardy was a good poet, perhaps a great one, but not *too* good. Much as I loved him, even I could see that his diction was often clumsy and forced and that a lot of his poems were plain bad. This gave me hope, where a flawless poet might have made me despair."

3 JUNE

from AS YOU LIKE IT
ACT V SCENE III

It was a lover, and his lass,
With a hey, and a ho, and a hey nonino,
That o'er the green corn field did pass,
  In the spring time, the only pretty ring time,
  When birds do sing, hey ding a ding, ding.
  Sweet lovers love the spring.

Between the acres of the rye,
With a hey, and a ho, and a hey nonino,
Those pretty country folks would lie,
  In spring time, the only pretty ring time,
  When birds do sing, hey ding a ding, ding.
  Sweet lovers love the spring.

This carol they began that hour,
With a hey, and a ho, and a hey nonino:
How that a life was but a flower,
  In spring time, the only pretty ring time,
  When birds do sing, hey ding a ding, ding.
  Sweet lovers love the spring.

And therefore take the present time.
With a hey, and a ho, and a hey nonino,
For love is crowned with the prime.

from AS YOU LIKE IT

In spring time, the only pretty ring time,
When birds do sing, hey ding a ding, ding.
Sweet lovers love the spring.

William Shakespeare
(23 April 1564 – 23 April 1616)

Thomas Morley, who is thought to have collaborated with Shakespeare in writing this song, said of himself that he was "no professor, but like a blind man groping for my way." The song is sung by the clown Touchstone to Audrey. "Ring time" is a time for exchanging rings and a time for dancing in rings.

THE GARDEN OF LOVE

I went to the Garden of Love,
And saw what I never had seen:
A Chapel was built in the midst,
Where I used to play on the green.

And the gates of this Chapel were shut,
And 'Thou shalt not' writ over the door;
So I turn'd to the Garden of Love
That so many sweet flowers bore;

And I saw it was filled with graves,
And tomb-stones where flowers should be;
And Priests in black gowns were walking their rounds,
And binding with briars my joys & desires.

William Blake
(28 November 1757 – 12 August 1827)

For Blake, Love is innocence, spirituality released from materialism. Churches and Chapels belong to The Beast, the State and their coercive order (see E. P. Thompson's *Witness Against the Beast*).

Alexander Gilchrist, Blake's first biographer, tells the possibly apocryphal story of a visitor finding Blake and his wife naked in their garden summer house. "Come in!" said Blake, "it's only Adam and Eve you know!"

OLD IRONSIDES

Ay, tear her tattered ensign down!
  Long has it waved on high,
And many an eye has danced to see
  That banner in the sky;
Beneath it rung the battle shout,
  And burst the cannon's roar; –
The meteor of the ocean air
  Shall sweep the clouds no more!

Her deck, once red with heroes' blood
  Where knelt the vanquished foe,
When winds were hurrying o'er the flood
  And waves were white below,
No more shall feel the victor's tread,
  Or know the conquered knee; –
The harpies of the shore shall pluck
  The eagle of the sea!

O better that her shattered hulk
  Should sink beneath the wave;
Her thunders shook the mighty deep,
  And there should be her grave;
Nail to the mast her holy flag,

Old ironsides

Set every thread-bare sail,
And give her to the god of storms, –
The lightning and the gale!

Oliver Wendell Holmes
(29 August 1809 - 7 October 1894)

The *Constitution*, a 44-gun frigate launched at Boston in 1797, is the oldest and most famous vessel in U.S. history. She earned her nickname, "Old Ironsides," when cannon balls appeared to bounce off her sides during a battle in which she destroyed the *Java* off the Brazilian coast. This poem, composed in 1830 and published in the *Boston Daily Advertiser*, was written to oppose the intended dismantling of the vessel, which has been berthed in Boston as a historic relic since 1925.

DUET

1. Is it the wind of the dawn that I hear
   in the pine overhead?
2. No; but the voice of the deep as it hollows
   the cliffs of the land.
1. Is there a voice coming up with the
   voice of the deep from the strand,
   One coming up with a Song in the
   flush of the glimmering red?
2. Love that is born of the deep coming
   up with the sun from the sea.
1. Love that can shape or can shatter a
   life till the life shall have fled?
2. Nay, let us welcome him, Love that
   can lift up a life from the dead.
1. Keep him away from the lone little isle.
   Let us be, let us be.
2. Nay, let him make it his own, let him
   reign in it – he, it is he,
   Love that is born of the deep coming
   up with the sun from the sea.

Alfred, Lord Tennyson
(6 August 1809 – 6 October 1892)

On 6 June 1829, Tennyson, who was 19, was announced winner of the Chancellor's Medal at Cambridge University for his poem on the set subject of Timbuctoo.

"Duet" comes from Act 2, scene 1, of Tennyson's third play, *Beckett*, which was written in 1876-9, but only published in 1884. The actor-manager Henry Irving had been certain that the play would be a disaster theatrically and would cost £135 a night to stage. He suggested to Tennyson a shorter work in a more modern idiom.

SHE ROSE TO HIS REQUIREMENT – DROPT

She rose to His Requirement – dropt
The Playthings of Her Life
To take the honorable Work
Of Woman, and of Wife –

If aught She missed in Her new Day,
Of Amplitude, or Awe –
Or first Prospective – Or the Gold
In using, wear away,

It lay unmentioned – as the Sea
Develop Pearl, and Weed,
But only to Himself – be known
The Fathoms they abide –

Emily Dickinson
(10 December 1830 – 15 May 1886)

On this day in 1862, Emily Dickinson wrote to Thomas Wentworth Higginson that "my dying tutor [Benjamin Newton] told me he would like to live till I had been a poet." She was, however, to remain virtually unpublished in her lifetime. Earlier in spring of the same year Higginson had received a letter from Emily Dickinson containing four of her poems. He told a friend that her verses were "remarkable, though odd ... too *delicate* – not strong enough to be published." In a third letter to him, Emily Dickinson consented to his verdict:

> I smile when you suggest that I delay 'to publish' – that being foreign to my thought, as Firmament to Fin.
> If fame belonged to me, I could not escape her – if she did not, the longest day would pass me on the chase – and the approbation of my Dog, would forsake me – then. My Barefoot-Rank is better.
> The Sailor cannot see the North, but knows the Needle arm.

God's grandeur

The world is charged with the grandeur of God.
 It will flame out, like shining from shook foil[1];
 It gathers to a greatness, like the ooze of oil
Crushed. Why do men then now not reck his rod?
Generations have trod, have trod, have trod;
 And all is seared with trade; bleared, smeared with toil;
 And wears man's smudge and shares man's smell: the soil
Is bare now, nor can foot feel, being shod.

And for all this, nature is never spent;
 There lives the dearest freshness deep down things;
And though the last lights off the black West went
 Oh, morning, at the brown brink eastward, springs –
Because the Holy Ghost over the bent
 World broods with warm breast and with ah! bright wings.

Gerard Manley Hopkins
(28 July 1844 – 8 June 1889[2])

Hopkins wrote this sonnet while studying theology at St. Beuno's in the valley of the Elwy in North Wales. H. N. Fairlight suggests that Hopkins' nature poems "might not too rashly be interpreted as a deliberate campaign to Christianise the romantic cult of nature. 'God's Grandeur' may well be a direct answer to [Wordsworth's] 'The World Is Too Much with Us.'"

1. In a letter to Robert Bridges written 4 January 1883, Hopkins explained: "I mean foil in its sense of leaf or tinsel, and no other word whatever will give the effect I want. Shaken goldfoil gives off broad glares like sheet lightning and also, and this is true of nothing else, owing to its zigzag dints and crossings and network of small many cornered facets, a sort of fork lightning too."
2. Jesuits at the time lived twenty years less than other men on average. Hopkins was ill with a "sort of typhoid" for six weeks before his death in Ireland. His parents were summoned from London to visit him on his deathbed. He was heard to say "I am so happy, I am so happy" and died peacefully.

from TO A SKYLARK[1]

Hail to thee, blithe Spirit!
  Bird thou never wert,
That from Heaven, or near it,
  Pourest thy full heart
In profuse strains of unpremeditated art.

Higher still and higher
  From the earth thou springest
Like a cloud of fire;
  The blue deep thou wingest,
And singing still dost soar, and soaring ever singest.

In the golden lightning
  Of the sunken sun,
O'er which clouds are bright'ning,
  Thou dost float and run;
Like an unbodied joy whose race is just begun.

The pale purple even
  Melts around thy flight;
Like a star of Heaven,
  In the broad daylight
Thou art unseen, but yet I hear thy shrill delight,

Keen as are the arrows
  Of that silver sphere,
Whose intense lamp narrows
  In the white dawn clear
Until we hardly see – we feel that it is there.

from TO A SKYLARK

All the earth and air
    With thy voice is loud,
As, when night is bare,
    From one lonely cloud
The moon rains out her beams, and Heaven is overflowea.

What thou art we know not;
    What is most like thee?
From rainbow clouds there flow not
    Drops so bright to see
As from thy presence showers a rain of melody.

Percy Bysshe Shelley
(4 August 1792 – 8 July 1822)

In Italy, in July of 1820, Shelley received news of the death of his illegitimate daughter, Elena Shelley, and composed "To a Skylark" during this period. His wife thought highly of this poem, noting: "It was on a beautiful summer evening, while wandering among the lanes whose myrtle hedges were the bowers of the fireflies, that we heard the carolling of the skylark which inspired one of the most beautiful of his poems."

1. Stanzas 1 to 7 of this 21-stanza poem.

10 JUNE

from ALICE'S ADVENTURES IN WONDERLAND

'Will you walk a little faster?' said a whiting to a snail,
'There's a porpoise close behind us, and he's treading on my tail.
See how eagerly the lobsters and the turtles all advance!
They are waiting on the shingle – will you come and join the dance?
  Will you, wo'n't you, will you, wo'n't you, will you join the dance?
  Will you, wo'n't you, will you, wo'n't you, wo'n't you join the dance?

'You can really have no notion how delightful it will be
'When they take us up and throw us, with the lobsters, out to sea!'
But the snail replied 'Too far, too far!' and gave a look askance –
Said he thanked the whiting kindly, but he would not join the dance.
  Would not, could not, would not, could not, would not join the dance.
  Would not, could not, would not, could not, could not join the dance.

'What matters it how far we go?' his scaly friend replied.
'There is another shore, you know, upon the other side.
The further off from England the nearer is to France –
Then turn not pale, beloved snail, but come and join the dance.
  Will you, wo'n't you, will you, wo'n't you, will you join the dance?
  Will you, wo'n't you, will you, wo'n't you, wo'n't you join the dance?'

Lewis Carroll
(*27 January 1832 – 14 January 1898*)

On this day in 1864, Lewis Carroll wrote to Tom Taylor: "I should be very glad if you could help me in fixing on a name for my fairytale . . . Here are the . . . names I have thought of:

  Alice among the elves / goblins
  Alice's hours / doings / activities
  Alice in elfland / wonderland."

CONCEPTION

Death did not come to my mother
Like an old friend.
She was a mother, and she must
Conceive him.

Up and down the bed she fought crying
Help me, but death
Was a slow child
Heavy. He

Waited. When he was born
We took and tired him, now he is ready
To do his good in the world.

He has my mother's features.
He can go among strangers
To save lives.

Josephine Miles
(11 June 1911 - 1985)

Josephine Miles, poet, critic, and English professor, crippled by arthritis since childhood, was born in Chicago on this day in 1911. Her *Collected Poems* were published in 1983.

SHE WALKS IN BEAUTY

She walks in beauty, like the night
  Of cloudless climes and starry skies;
And all that's best of dark and bright
  Meet in her aspect and her eyes:
Thus mellowed to that tender light
  Which heaven to gaudy day denies.

One shade the more, one ray the less,
  Had half impaired the nameless grace
Which waves in every raven tress,
  Or softly lightens o'er her face;
Where thoughts serenely sweet express
  How pure, how dear their dwelling-place.

And on that cheek, and o'er that brow,
  So soft, so calm, yet eloquent,
The smiles that win, the tints that glow,
  But tell of days in goodness spent,
A mind at peace with all below,
  A heart whose love is innocent!

George Gordon, Lord Byron
(22 January 1788 – 19 April 1824)

On 11 June 1814, James Webster dragged Byron against his will to a party at Lady Sitwell's in Seymour Road in London. Webster recounts that "he there for the first time saw his cousin, the beautiful Mrs. Wilmot [who had appeared in mourning with numerous spangles on her dress]. When we returned to . . . the Albany, he . . . desired Fletcher to give him a tumbler of Brandy, which he drank at once to Mrs. Wilmot's health . . . The next day he wrote those charming lines upon her."

The lake isle of innisfree

I will arise and go now, and go to Innisfree,
And a small cabin build there, of clay and wattles made:
Nine bean-rows will I have there, a hive for the honey-bee,
And live alone in the bee-loud glade.

And I shall have some peace there, for peace comes dropping slow,
Dropping from the veils of the morning to where the cricket sings;
There midnight's all a-glimmer, and noon a purple glow,[1]
And evening full of the linnet's wings.

I will arise and go now, for always night and day
I hear lake water lapping with low sounds by the shore;
While I stand on the roadway, or on the pavements grey,
I hear it in the deep heart's core.

William Butler Yeats
(13 June 1865 - 28 January 1939)

Yeats was born of Irish Protestant origins, the eldest son of a painter who was married to a shopowner's daughter. This early poem of Yeats' was written in 1890. "I had still the ambition," he wrote, "formed in Sligo in my teens, of living in imitation of Thoreau on Innisfree, a little island in Lough Gill, and when walking through Fleet Street very homesick I heard a little trickle of water and saw a fountain in a shop window which balanced a little ball upon its jet, and began to remember lake water. From the sudden remembrance came my poem 'Innisfree', my first lyric with anything in its rhythm of my own music." In later life, he wrote to Miss Ruth Watt, a very young admirer of his poems: "Please don't think 'The Lake Isle of Innisfree' is better than all the rest, for I don't." Another admirer of this poem was Robert Louis Stevenson, who wrote to Yeats from Samoa to say that it had laid him under a spell, "it is so quaint and airy, simple and artful, and eloquent to the heart."

1. Yeats explained in a radio broadcast that this referred to the reflection of heather in the water. "Innisfree" means "Heather Island."

14 JUNE

from[1] THE RUBÁIYÁT[2] OF OMAR KHAYYÁM[3] OF NAISHÁPÚR

I sent my Soul through the Invisible,
Some letter of that Afterlife to spell:
   And by and by my Soul returned to me,
And answered 'I Myself am Heav'n and Hell:'

Heav'n but the Vision of fulfilled Desire,
And Hell the Shadow from a Soul on fire,
   Cast on the Darkness into which Ourselves,
So late emerged from, shall so soon expire.

We are no other than a moving row
Of Magic Shadow-shapes that come and go
   Round with the Sun-illumined Lantern held
In Midnight by the Master of the Show;

But helpless Pieces of the Game He plays
Upon his Checkerboard of Nights and Days;
   Hither and thither moves, and checks, and slays,
And one by one back in the Closet lays.

The Ball no question makes of Ayes and Noes,
But Here or There as strikes the Player goes;
   And He that tossed you down into the Field,
He knows about it all – HE knows – HE knows!

The Moving Finger writes; and, having writ,
Moves on: nor all your Piety nor Wit
   Shall lure it back to cancel half a Line,
Nor all your Tears wash out a Word of it.

from THE RUBÁIYÁT OF OMAR KHAYYÁM OF NAISHÁPÚR

And that inverted Bowl they call the Sky,
Whereunder crawling cooped we live and die
   Lift not your hands to *It* for help – for It
As impotently moves as you or I.

With Earth's first Clay They did the Last Man knead,
And there of the Last Harvest sowed the Seed:
   And the first Morning of Creation wrote
What the Last Dawn of Reckoning shall read.

YESTERDAY *This* Day's Madness did prepare;
TOMORROW's Silence, Triumph, or Despair:
   Drink! for you know not whence you came, nor why:
Drink! for you know not why you go, nor where.

Edward FitzGerald
(31 March 1809 – 14 June 1883)

This translation was first published anonymously in 1859. Edward Fitzgerald was a close friend to Thackeray, Tennyson, and Carlyle, and spent most of his life in Suffolk, often going sailing with local fishermen.

1. Stanzas 66 to 74 from the 97-stanza fourth edition.
2. Plural of "ruba'i," meaning quatrain in Arabic.
3. Persian astonomer-poet, lived in Naishápur in the eleventh century. In his translation of *The Rubáiyát*, FitzGerald made substantial alterations to the original.

15 JUNE

THE PROMISED GARDEN
FOR SUZANNE

There is a garden where our hearts converse,
At ease beside clear water, dreaming
A whole and perfect future for yourself,
Myself, our children and our friends.

And if we must rise and leave,
Put on identity and fight,
Each day more desperate than the last
And further from our future, that
Is no more than honour and respect shown
To all blocked from the garden that we own.

There is a garden at the heart of things,
Our oldest memory guards it with her strong will.
Those who by love and work attain there
Bathe in her living waters, lift up their hearts and
Turn again to share the steep privations of the hill;
They walk in the market but their feet are still.

There is a garden where our hearts converse,
At ease beside clear water, dreaming
A whole and perfect future for yourself,
Myself, our children and our friends.

Theo Dorgan
(21 September 1953 -)

Theo Dorgan writes, "In the Gaelic tradition, the Paradise Garden is a recurrent image
. . . I had in mind the need to acknowledge the privileges of love as well as the responsi-
bilities of sharing the human, everyday world."

THE PORTENT

Hanging from the beam,
 Slowly swaying (such the law),
Gaunt the shadow on your green,
 Shenandoah!

The cut is on the crown
 (Lo, John Brown),
And the stabs shall heal no more.

Hidden in the cap
 Is the anguish none can draw;
So your future veils its face,
 Shenandoah!

But the streaming beard is shown
 (Weird John Brown),
The meteor of the war.

Herman Melville
(1 August 1819 – 28 September 1891)

John Brown, a militant abolitionist, was hanged in Virginia in 1859 for his thwarted mission to destroy slavery in America by force of arms. Thoreau called him "an angel of light"; Emerson, a hero of "simple, artless goodness." But it was perhaps Melville who, with the last image of this poem, came closest to describing Brown's fiery, magnetic personality. The title, too, is significant, for the emotions that Brown incited would not dissipate. His death seemed an omen of the greater violence that was to come with the start of the Civil War.

from IN A GONDOLA

The moth's kiss first!
Kiss me as if you made believe
You were not sure, this eve,
How my face, your flower, had pursed
Its petals up; so, here and there
You brush it, till I grow aware
Who wants me, and wide ope I burst.

The bee's kiss, now!
Kiss me as if you entered gay
My heart at some noonday,
A bud that dares not disallow
The claim, so all is rendered up,
And passively its shattered cup
Over your head to sleep I bow.

Robert Browning
(7 May 1812 - 12 December 1889)

Robert Browning never went to school, his education coming from the 6,000 volumes in his father's library and the occasional tutor. He dropped out of London University in his second term and began traveling – "Italy was my university." His poem *Sordello*, published when he was 28, was widely ridiculed for its obscurity. Tennyson said that of its 5,800 lines there were just two he could comprehend, the first "Who will may hear Sordello's story told" and the last "Who would has heard Sordello's story told" – and that both these lines were lies.

At the age of 33, Browning began a romance with Elizabeth Barrett, who inspired his love poems. Among his most popular poetry in his lifetime were *Men and Women* and *The Ring and the Book*. His last poems, *Asolando*, were published on the day of his death. He was buried on 31 December 1889 in Westminster Abbey.

To Jane: the keen stars were twinkling

The keen stars were twinkling,
And the fair moon was rising among them,
  Dear Jane!
  The guitar was tinkling,
But the notes were not sweet till you sung them
  Again.

As the moon's soft splendour
O'er the faint cold starlight of Heaven
  Is thrown,
  So your voice most tender
To the strings without soul had then given
  Its own.

The stars will awaken,
Though the moon sleep a full hour later,
  Tonight;
  No leaf will be shaken
Whilst the dews of your melody scatter
  Delight.

Though the sound overpowers,
Sing again, with your dear voice revealing
  A tone

To Jane: The Keen Stars Were Twinkling

Of some world far from ours,
Where music and moonlight and feeling
Are one.

Percy Bysshe Shelley
(4 August 1792 – 8 July 1822)

This poem was written for Jane Williams, with whom Shelley became increasingly infatuated. She and her husband lived with Shelley and his wife Mary in Italy at the Casa Magni in Lerici in the summer of 1822. Shelley was unable to borrow 70 to 80 guineas to buy Jane a harp from Paris, and gave her a guitar instead. On this day in 1822, three weeks before his death by drowning, Shelley wrote to John Gisborne: "I like Jane more and more, and I find Williams the most amiable of companions. She has a taste for music, and an elegance of form and motions that compensates in some degree for the lack of literary refinement . . . I listen the whole evening on our terrace to the simple melodies with excessive delight. I have a boat here . . . Williams is captain, and we drive along this delightful bay in the evening wind, under the summer moon, until earth appears another world. Jane brings her guitar, and if the past and future could be obliterated, the present would content me so well that I could say with Faust to the passing moment 'Remain, thou, thou art so beautiful.'"

This particular poem Shelley left in Jane's room with a note:"I commend [it] to your secrecy and your mercy, and will try to do better another time."

from THE BROOK

I come from haunts of coot[1] and hern,°   *heron*
  I make a sudden sally
And sparkle out among the fern,
  To bicker° down a valley.   *to flow noisily*

By thirty hills I hurry down,
  Or slip between the ridges,
By twenty thorps,° a little town,   *hamlets*
  And half a hundred bridges.

Till last by Philip's farm I flow
  To join the brimming river,
For men may come and men may go,
  But I go on for ever.

I chatter over stony ways,
  In little sharps and trebles,
I bubble into eddying bays,
  I babble on the pebbles.

With many a curve my banks I fret
  By many a field and fallow,
And many a fairy foreland set
  With willow-weed and mallow.

from THE BROOK

I chatter, chatter, as I flow
  To join the brimming river,
For men may come and men may go
  But I go on for ever.

Alfred, Lord Tennyson
(6 August 1809 – 6 October 1892)

A map in Bag Enderby church in Lincolnshire (near to Somersby where Tennyson was born) claims to show places referred to in this poem, but, according to Peter Levi, Tennyson in his old age denied that there were these links.

1. A water fowl with a distinctive white spot on its forehead, an extension of the beak, suggesting baldness and giving us the phrase "bald as a coot."

ALL YOU WHO SLEEP TONIGHT

All you who sleep tonight
Far from the ones you love,
No hand to left or right,
And emptiness above –

Know that you aren't alone.
The whole world shares your tears,
Some for two nights or one,
And some for all their years.

Vikram Seth
(20 June 1952 -)

Vikram Seth was born in Calcutta and educated at Oxford, Stanford, and Nanjing universities, training as an economist.

This poem comes from *All You Who Sleep Tonight*, a slim collection of his short poems from the previous seven years that was published in 1990. His other work includes *The Golden Gate*, a novel in verse published in 1986, and *A Suitable Boy* (1993), a novel (in prose) of 1,349 pages, that was judged by Lord Gowrie to be too long to deserve the Booker prize.

from THE TEMPEST
ACT V SCENE I

Ariel. Where the bee sucks, there suck I:
In a cowslip's bell I lie;
There I couch when owls do cry;
On the bat's back I do fly
After summer merrily:
Merrily, merrily shall I live now
Under the blossom that hangs on the bough.

William Shakespeare
(23 April 1564 – 23 April 1616)

Ariel's song is placed here in celebration of the summer solstice, 21 June.

Hazlitt observes that "there is a peculiar charm in the songs introduced in Shakespeare, which, without conveying any distinct images, seem to recall all the feelings connected with them, like snatches of half-gotten music heard indistinctly and at intervals. This is the effect produced by Ariel's songs, which seem to sound in the air, and as if the person playing them were invisible."

It has been pointed out that if Shakespeare is implying here that bats migrate, they do not, but Elizabethans thought that they did.

The company of the birds

Ah the company of the birds
I loved and cherished on earth
Now, freed of flesh we fly
Together, a flock of beating wings,
I am as light, as feathery,
As gone from gravity we soar
In endless circles.

Sasha Moorsom
(25 January 1931 - 22 June 1993)

Sasha's daughter, Sophie Young, writes: "Sasha loved birds. They seemed to represent the freedom of spirit that soared in her own heart. She would delight in watching them from the kitchen window, splashing in the bird bath she had sculpted, and always making sure they had enough food in the winter. This poem was read at the end of Sasha's funeral, a sad but beautiful reminder of immortality. As she said herself not long before she died, 'My spirit is strong, it's just the body that's collapsing.'"

from THE VOYAGE
for T. S. Eliot

We imitate, oh horror! tops and bowls
in their eternal waltzing marathon;
even in sleep, our fever whips and rolls –
like a black angel flogging the brute sun.
Strange sport! where destination has no place
or name, and may be anywhere we choose –
where man, committed to his endless race,
runs like a madman diving for repose!
Our soul is a three-master seeking port:
a voice from starboard shouts, 'We're at the dock!'
Another, more elated, cries from port,
'Here's dancing, gin and girls!' Balls! it's a rock!
The islands sighted by the lookout seem
the El Dorados promised us last night;
imagination wakes from its drugged dream,
sees only ledges in the morning light.

Robert Lowell
(1 March 1917 – 12 September 1977)
based on a French poem by Charles Baudelaire
(9 April 1821 – 31 August 1867)

A ceaseless innovator, Lowell collected his translations in the volume *Imitations*, containing many purposeful inaccuracies. The adaptations thus produced give many clues to the way Lowell approached poetic sources.
  "I belong to no 'school' of poetry," he claimed, "but various living or once-living poets have fascinated me – W. C. Williams, Pound, Tate, Ransom, Eliot, and Yeats. And many, many others, though perhaps I've tried to be a chameleon in vain."

DIFFERENT

Not to say what everyone else was saying
not to believe what everyone else believed
not to do what everybody did,
then to refute what everyone else was saying
then to disprove what everyone else believed
then to deprecate what everybody did,

was his way to come by understanding

how everyone else was saying the same as he was saying
believing what he believed
and did what doing.

Clere Parsons
(1908 – 1931)

Clere Parsons died at the age of 23 from pneumonia and a severe form of diabetes. Louis MacNeice thought of Clere Parsons as different from the norm, describing him from his Oxford days as "a bleached frail little man, who brought special bread with him to lunch because he had diabetes" and who had "an invalid's fanaticism" in politics, though sensitive to the "melody of words." Grigson described him as "young, thin, tall, white face under pale hair." At Oxford, he helped found a poetry society by involving MacNeice, Stephen Spender, and others.

He was born in India, where his father worked in the Indian Civil Service.

JOHN ANDERSON MY JO

John Anderson my jo,° John,   *darling*
   When we were first acquent;
Your locks were like the raven,
   Your bony brow was brent;[1]
But now your brow is bald, John,
   Your locks are like the snaw;
But blessings on your frosty pow,°   *head*
John Anderson my Jo.

John Anderson my jo, John,
   We clamb the hill the gither,°   *together*
And mony a canty,° day, John,   *merry*
   We've had wi' ane anither:
Now we maun totter down, John,
   And hand in hand we'll go;
And sleep the gither at the foot,
   John Anderson my Jo.

Robert Burns
(25 January 1759 – 21 July 1796)

Burns has here metamorphosed a bawdy version of this song. In the original (he was not above writing bawdy verses himself, and this version has been attributed to him in some collections): "When first that ye began / Ye had as good a tail-tree / As any ither man; / But now its waxen wan, John, / And wrinkles to and fro; / I've twa gae-ups for one gae-down, / John Anderson, my jo . . ."

   Burns himself did not live to an old age, dying of rheumatic heart disease in his 37th year. Ten thousand people followed his coffin to the grave.

1. High and straight (because of a thick head of hair).

HOME FROM ABROAD

Far-fetched with tales of other worlds and ways,
My skin well-oiled with wines of the Levant,
I set my face into a filial smile
To greet the pale, domestic kiss of Kent.

But shall I never learn? That gawky girl,
Recalled so primly in my foreign thoughts,
Becomes again the green-haired queen of love
Whose wanton form dilates as it delights.

Her rolling tidal landscape floods the eye
And drowns Chianti in a dusky stream;
The flower-flecked grasses swim with simple horses,
The hedges choke with roses fat as cream.

So do I breathe the hayblown airs of home,
And watch the sea-green elms drip birds and shadows,
And as the twilight nets the plunging sun
My heart's keel slides to rest among the meadows.

Laurie Lee
(26 June 1914 - 13 May 1997)

Laurie Lee described his childhood in *Cider with Rosie* (1959), which has now sold over two million copies. He was born in Stroud, Gloucestershire, and educated at Slad village school and at Stroud Central School. In June 1934, at the age of 19, he left home and walked to London where he worked as a laborer. His travels through Spain in 1935 and 1936 are recounted in *As I Walked Out One Midsummer Morning* (1969). In 1936, "June came in full blast, with the heat bouncing off the sea as from a buckled sheet of tin"; he witnessed the first stirrings of the Spanish Civil War in Castillo: a Falangist boy of about twenty had been shot through the head and his body left sprawled on the riverbank.

Laurie Lee married Catherine Francesca Polge in 1950 and they have a daughter. His *Selected Poems* were published in 1983.

ADLESTROP

Yes. I remember Adlestrop –
The name, because one afternoon
Of heat the express-train drew up there
Unwontedly. It was late June.

The steam hissed. Someone cleared his throat.
No one left and no one came
On the bare platform. What I saw
Was Adlestrop – only the name

And willows, willow-herb, and grass,
And meadowsweet, and haycocks dry,
No whit less still and lonely fair
Than the high cloudlets in the sky.

And for that minute a blackbird sang
Close by, and round him, mistier,
Farther and farther, all the birds
Of Oxfordshire and Gloucestershire.

Edward Thomas
(3 March 1878 – 9 April 1917)

Edward Thomas only started to write poetry at the age of 36, encouraged by Robert Frost, and with a sense of urgency brought on by the start of the First World War. Up until then, he had been struggling to support a family by churning out books, anthologies, and reviews. He had become depressed and at times suicidal, "so confoundedly busy I feel as if the back of my head would come out." He was killed at Aras in 1917, having written his 143rd poem, but before his first collection was published.

BERMUDAS

Where the remote Bermudas ride
In th' ocean's bosom unespied,
From a small boat, that rowed along,
The list'ning winds received this song.
   "What should we do but sing His praise
That led us through the wat'ry maze,
Unto an isle so long unknown,
And yet far kinder than our own?
Where he the huge sea-monsters wracks,°   *wrecks*
That lift the deep upon their backs.
He lands us on a grassy stage,
Safe from the storms' and prelates' rage;
He gave us this eternal Spring
Which here enamels every thing,
And sends the fowls to us in care,
On daily visits through the air;
He hangs in shades the orange bright,
Like golden lamps in a green night,
And does in the pomegranates close
Jewels more rich than Ormus° shows;   *Hormuz (diamond market)*
He makes the figs our mouths to meet,
And throws the melons at our feet,
But apples° plants of such a price,   *pineapples*
No tree could ever bear them twice;
With cedars, chosen by his hand,
From Lebanon, he stores the land;
And makes the hollow seas, that roar,
Proclaim the ambergris on shore;
He cast (of which we rather boast)
The Gospel's pearl upon our coast,

BERMUDAS

And in these rocks for us did frame
A temple, where to sound His name.
Oh, let our voice his praise exalt
Till it arrive at Heaven's vault,
Which thence (perhaps) rebounding, may
Echo beyond the Mexique Bay."
    Thus sung they, in the English boat,
An holy and a cheerful note,
And all the way, to guide their chime,
With falling oars they kept the time.

Andrew Marvell
(31 March 1621 - 16 or 18 August 1678)

Born in Yorkshire, the son of a vicar, Marvell was an ardent satirist of the political scene. One of his scathing attacks on Charles II resulted in a one hundred pounds price on his head. Yet Marvell was also one of the first English poets to praise nature for itself without feeling the need to draw any moral conclusions.
    In 1653, Marvell became tutor to Oliver Cromwell's ward, William Dutton, and moved to Eton, where he is thought to have written "Bermudas."

I REMEMBER CLIFFORD

Wakening in a small room,
the walls high and blue, one high window
through which the morning enters,
I turn to the table beside me
painted a thick white. There instead
of a clock is a tumbler of water,
clear and cold, that wasn't there
last night. Someone quietly entered,
and now I see the white door
slightly ajar and around three sides
the light on fire. I remember once
twenty-seven years ago walking
the darkened streets
of my home town when up ahead
on Joy Road at the Bluebird of Happiness
I heard over the rumble of my own head
for the first time the high clear trumpet
of Clifford Brown calling us all
to the dance he shared with us
such a short time. My heart quickened
and in my long coat, breathless
and stumbling, I ran

I REMEMBER CLIFFORD

through the swirling snow
to the familiar sequined door
knowing it would open on something new.

Philip Levine
(10 January 1928 -)

Philip Levine writes: "The title comes from a fabulous melody written by the saxophon-ist Benny Golson as a tribute to his departed friend, the astonishing jazz trumpeter Clifford Brown, who died at the age of twenty-six in an auto accident.

"Where do such talents come from, such musicians as Clifford, and how do we come to deserve such gifts? The poem is concerned with the sudden generosity of the world, the unexplainable giving that occurs in the midst of deprivation, for I discovered the mo-ment of Clifford deep in the misery of one of the hardest years of my life. A door opened, and his music – unexpected and unearned by me was – suddenly mine, pure, clear, and free, as water was in my first years."

Born in Detroit, Philip Levine, the author of a book of essays, two books of transla-tions, and 18 volumes of poetry, most recently *The Simple Truth* (1994), makes his home in Fresno, California.

SONG

And when our streets are green again
When metalled roads are green
And girls walk barefoot through the weeds
Of Regent Street, Saint Martin's Lane

And children hide in factories
Where burdock blooms and vetch and rust,
And elms and oaks and chestnut trees
Are tall again and hope is lost

When up the Strand the foxes glide
And hedgehogs sniff and wildcats yell
And golden orioles come back
To flash through Barnes and Clerkenwell

When governments and industries
Lie choked by weeds in fertile rain
For sure the few who stay alive
Will laugh and grow to love again

John McGrath
(*1 June 1935 –*)

John McGrath was the founder-director of the radical popular theater company 7:84, taking theater to working class audiences. His *A Good Night Out* is a statement of the aims of the counter-theater movement, and his plays include *Events While Guarding the Bofors Gun* and *Yobbo Nowt*.

Angry at the "cultural terrorism" of the Thatcher years, he dedicated his book *The Bone Won't Break* to "The Resistance, to those who have had their lives distorted or destroyed so others could consume; to those who insist that co-operation rather than individual possessiveness is the better principle for the future happiness of humanity; may they survive, and that principle bring more joy to the lives of more people."

from HOLY SONNETS

14

Batter my heart, three-person'd God; for, you
As yet but knock, breathe, shine, and seek to mend;
That I may rise, and stand, o'erthrow me, and bend
Your force, to break, blow, burn and make me new.
I, like an usurp'd town, to another due,
Labour to admit you, but Oh, to no end,
Reason your viceroy in me, me should defend,
But is captiv'd, and proves weak or untrue.
Yet dearly I love you, and would be loved fain,
But am betroth'd unto your enemy:
Divorce me, untie, or break that knot again,
Take me to you, imprison me, for I
Except you enthral me, never shall be free,
Nor ever chaste, except you ravish me.

John Donne
(c. June 1572 ‒ 31 March 1631)

On this day in 1627, Donne gave a sermon at the funeral of Lady Danvers, George
Herbert's mother. It was to Lady Danvers that Donne had sent his *Divine Poems* twenty
years before.
   Donne was brought up a Catholic and thus was debarred from taking a university degree. His brother Henry died in prison having harbored a Catholic suspected of being a
priest (the latter was hanged, cut down, and disembowelled). John Donne about that
time renounced his Catholicism.
   This sonnet reflects the Protestant belief that faith is entirely in God's gift, and that
man as a fallen creature is incapable of good works.
   John Carey writes that Donne's "love poems display, in their obsession with woman's in-
constancy, a profound anxiety about his own ability to attract or merit stable affection.
His fear of damnation and of exclusion from God's love in the 'Holy Sonnets' reflects the
same anxiety, transposed to the religious sphere."

NOBODY KNOWS THE TROUBLE I'VE HAD

Nobody Knows de Trouble I've had,
Nobody knows but Jesus,
Nobody knows de trouble I've had,
Glory hallelu!

One morning I was a walking down, O yes, Lord!
I saw some berries a-hanging down, O yes, Lord!

I pick de berry and I suck de juice, O yes, Lord!
Just as sweet as the honey in de comb, O yes, Lord!

Sometimes I'm up, sometimes I'm down, O yes, Lord!
Sometimes I'm almost on de groun', O yes, Lord!

What make ole Satan hate me so? O yes, Lord!
Because he got me once and he let me go, O yes, Lord!

Anonymous

In 1867, the first important collection of spirituals, *Slave Songs of the United States*, was published. In his *A Narrative of the Life of Frederick Douglass, an American Slave, Written by Himself* (1845), Douglass states: "The singing of a man cast away upon a desolate island might be as appropriately considered as evidence of contentment and happiness, as the singing of a slave; the songs of the one and of the other are prompted by the same emotion."

THE AUTHOR TO HER BOOK

Thou ill-formed offspring of my feeble brain,
Who after birth did'st by my side remain,
Till snatched from thence by friends, less wise than true,
Who thee abroad exposed to public view;
Made thee in rags, halting, to the press to trudge,
Where errors were not lessened, all my judge.
At thy return my blushing was not small,
My rambling brat (in print) should mother call;
I cast thee by as one unfit for light,
Thy visage was so irksome in my sight;
Yet being mine own, at length affection would
Thy blemishes amend, if so I could:
I washed thy face, but more defects I saw,
And rubbing off a spot, still made a flaw.
I stretched thy joints to make thee even feet,
Yet still thou run'st more hobbling than is meet;
In better dress to trim thee was my mind,
But nought save homespun cloth in the house I find.
In this array, 'mongst vulgars may'st thou roam;
In critics' hands beware thou dost not come;
And take thy way where yet thou are not known.
If for thy Father asked, say thou had'st none;
And for thy Mother, she alas is poor,
Which caused her thus to send thee out of door.

Anne Bradstreet
(c. 1612 - 16 September 1672)

Bradstreet sailed from England to America on board the *Arabella* in 1630. She bore eight children, and was arguably the first significant woman poet in America despite her aversion to having her work published.

THE NEW COLOSSUS

Not like the brazen giant of Greek fame,
With conquering limbs astride from land to land;
Here at our sea-washed, sunset gates shall stand
A mighty woman with a torch, whose flame
Is the imprisoned lightning, and her name
Mother of Exiles. From her beacon-hand
Glows world-wide welcome; her mild eyes command
The air-bridged harbor that twin cities frame.
"Keep, ancient lands, your storied pomp!" cries she
With silent lips. "Give me your tired, your poor,
Your huddled masses yearning to breathe free,
The wretched refuse of your teeming shore.
Send these, the homeless, tempest-tost to me,
I lift my lamp beside the golden door!"

Emma Lazarus
(22 July 1849 – 19 November 1887)

On this day in 1886, a year before her death at 38, Emma Lazarus recited her sonnet, "The New Colossus," at the dedication of the Statue of Liberty, a gift from the French people to commemorate the centennial of American independence. Lazarus, herself a Sephardic Jew, was prominent in her role as head of an organization providing relief for Jewish immigrants. The closing lines of the poem, carved at the base of the statue, express her position that America continue to be "Mother of Exiles."

At 305 feet from base to torch, the Statue of Liberty is the largest statue ever made.

THE CLOD AND THE PEBBLE

'Love seeketh not Itself to please,
'Nor for itself hath any care,
'But for another gives its ease,
'And builds a Heaven in Hell's despair.'

So sung a little Clod of Clay
Trodden with the cattle's feet,
But a Pebble of the brook
Warbled out these metres meet:

'Love seeketh only Self to please,
'To bind another to Its delight,
'Joys in another's loss of ease,
'And builds a Hell in Heaven's despite.'

William Blake
(28 November 1757 – 12 August 1827)

On this day in 1826 Blake wrote to Mr. Linnell: "I thank you for the receipt of five pounds this morning, and compliment you on the receipt of another fine boy . . . I am getting better every hour. My plan is diet only; but if the machine is capable of it, shall make an old man yet . . . These paroxysms . . . I now believe will never more return."

For Blake in this poem, the Clod of Clay represents unselfish love and innocence. The hard Pebble is materialism. These are the contraries we live with. To transcend them calls for "the annihilation of selfhood" and the release of the poetic genius.

from SONG OF MYSELF (in *Leaves of Grass*)

5

I believe in you my soul, the other I am must not abase itself to you,
And you must not be abased to the other.

Loafe with me on the grass, loose the stop from your throat,
Not words, not music or rhyme I want, not custom or lecture, not even the
       best,
Only the lull I like, the hum of your valvèd voice.

I mind how once we lay such a transparent summer morning,
How you settled your head athwart my hips and gently turn'd over upon me,
And parted the shirt from my bosom-bone, and plunged your tongue to my
       bare-stript heart,
And reach'd till you felt my beard, and reach'd till you held my feet.

Swiftly arose and spread around me the peace and knowledge that pass all the
       argument of the earth,
And I know that the hand of God is the promise of my own,
And I know that the spirit of God is the brother of my own,
And that all the men ever born are also my brothers, and the women my
       sisters and lovers,
And that a kelson[1] of the creation is love,

from SONG OF MYSELF

And limitless are leaves stiff or drooping in the fields,
And brown ants in the little wells beneath them,
And mossy scabs of the worm fence, heap'd stones, elder, mullein² and
    poke-weed.³

Walt Whitman
(31 May 1819 – 26 March 1892)

Whitman was renowned as a "loafer." "What was Adam, I should like to know, but a loafer?" he asked. "Of all human beings, none equals your genuine, inbred, unvarying loafer." He finished the first edition of his *Leaves of Grass* at the age of 36. His aim was for a "Divine Style": "Make no quotations and no references to any other writers. Lumber the writing with nothing – let it go as lightly as a bird flies in the air, or a fish swims in the sea . . . Clearness, simplicity, no twistified or foggy sentences at all – the most translucid clearness without variation."

Expanded editions of *Leaves of Grass* were published throughout Whitman's lifetime, with the last in the year of his death. He had hoped to produce an edition with one poem for every day of the year, a scripture of everyday life, "the latest construction of the New Bible . . . this main life work – the three hundred and sixty five."

1. In shipbuilding, a beam used to stiffen and strengthen the keel structures.
2. Erect plant with sharp yellow flowers.
3. Plant with poisonous, deep red or black berries – also known as Virginian poke or poke-berry.

MY OWN HEART LET ME MORE HAVE PITY ON

My own heart let me more have pity on; let
Me live to my sad self hereafter kind,
Charitable; not live this tormented mind
With this tormented mind tormenting yet.
    I cast for comfort I can no more get
By groping round my comfortless, than blind
Eyes in their dark can day or thirst can find
Thirst's all-in-all in all a world of wet.

Soul, self; come, poor Jackself,[1] I do advise
You, jaded, let be; call off thoughts awhile
Elsewhere; leave comfort root-room; let joy size
At God knows when to God knows what; whose smile
's not wrung, see you; unforeseen times rather – as skies
Betweenpie[2] mountains – lights a lovely mile.

Gerard Manley Hopkins
(28 July 1844 – 8 June 1889)

This was probably one of the sonnets to which Hopkins referred in his letter to Robert Bridges of 1 September 1885: "I shall shortly have some sonnets to send you, five or more. Four of these came like inspirations unbidden and against my will. And in the life I lead now, which is one of a continually jaded and harassed mind, if in any leisure I try to do anything I make no way – nor with my work, alas! but so it must be." At the time he was professor of Greek at University College, Dublin, overworked and ill.

1. Workaday, humble self.
2. Verb coined from "pied": checkers, dapples.

OZYMANDIAS

I met a traveller from an antique land
Who said: Two vast and trunkless legs of stone
Stand in the desert. Near them, on the sand,
Half sunk, a shattered visage lies, whose frown,
And wrinkled lip, and sneer of cold command,
Tell that its sculptor well those passions read
Which yet survive, stamped on these lifeless things,
The hand that mocked them, and the heart that fed:
And on the pedestal these words appear:
'My name is Ozymandias, king of kings:
Look on my works, ye Mighty, and despair!'
Nothing beside remains. Round the decay
Of that colossal wreck, boundless and bare
The lone and level sands stretch far away.

Percy Bysshe Shelley
(4 August 1792 – 8 July 1822)

Shelley visited the British Museum in 1817 with a fellow-poet Horace Smith and suggested that they should both produce a sonnet on the subject of the recent Egyptian finds. Shelley's sonnet, "Ozymandias," reflects his lifelong hatred of tyranny. In a book by the ancient Greek historian Diodorus, Shelley had read an inscription to an Egyptian monarch's monument similar to that quoted here. The sonnet was first published on 11 January 1818 attributed to "Glirastes" (from the Latin for dormouse, Mary Shelley's pet name for her husband).

On this day in 1822, Shelley, Edward Williams, and Charles Vian, their boat boy, set off from Livorne in their 18-foot sailing boat, the Bon Juan. A storm came up rapidly and the boat went down in the Gulf of Spezia under full sail. Shelley's body was recovered ten days later.

from THE TEMPEST
ACT III SCENE II

Caliban. Be not afeard: the isle is full of noises,
Sounds and sweet airs, that give delight, and hurt not.
Sometimes a thousand twangling instruments
Will hum about mine ears; and sometime voices,
That, if I then had wak'd after a long sleep,
Will make me sleep again: and then, in dreaming,
The clouds methought would open and show riches
Ready to drop upon me; that, when I wak'd
I cried to dream again.

William Shakespeare
(23 April 1564 - 23 April 1616)

Of this speech, Hazlitt wrote in 1817: "This is not more beautiful than it is true. The poet here shows us the savage with the simplicity of a child, and makes the strange monster amiable. Shakespeare had to paint the human animal rude and without choice in its pleasures, but not without the sense of pleasure or some germ of the affections."

RENDEZVOUS

I have a rendezvous with Death
At some disputed barricade,
When Spring comes back with rustling shade
And apple-blossoms fill the air –
I have a rendezvous with Death
When Spring brings back blue days and fair.

It may be he shall take my hand
And lead me into his dark land
And close my eyes and quench my breath –
It may be I shall pass him still.
I have a rendezvous with Death
On some scarred slope of battered hill,
When Spring comes round again this year
And the first meadow-flowers appear.

God knows 'twere better to be deep
Pillowed in silk and scented down,
Where love throbs out in blissful sleep,
Pulse nigh to pulse, and breath to breath,
Where hushed awakenings are dear . . .
But I've a rendezvous with Death
At midnight in some flaming town,

RENDEZVOUS

When Spring trips north again this year,
And I to my pledged word am true,
I shall not fail that rendezvous.

Alan Seeger
(22 June 1888 – 4 July 1916)

Alan Seeger was born in New York, educated at Harvard, and lived in the Latin Quarter of Paris. In World War I he enlisted in the French Foreign Legion. In 1916, his company went into attack near Belloy-en-Santerre, and, though wounded, he continued urging his men on. His body was found in a shell hole the next day. He was awarded the Croix de Guerre posthumously.

Code poem for the french resistance

The life that I have is all that I have,
And the life that I have is yours.
The love that I have of the life that I have
Is yours and yours and yours.

A sleep I shall have
A rest I shall have,
Yet death will be but a pause,
For the peace of my years in the long green grass
Will be yours and yours and yours.

Leo Marks
(1920 -)

On this day in 1940, Marshal Pétain, at the spa town of Vichy, became head of a collaborationist "French State," despite General de Gaulle's appeal to the French people the previous month. Pétain was sentenced to death for treason after the war, a sentence commuted to imprisonment on the Ile d'Yeu, where he subsequently died.

PROTOCOLS

What can I say to you? How can I now retract
  All that that fool, my voice, has spoken –
Now that the facts are plain, the placid surface cracked,
  The protocols of friendship broken?

I cannot walk by day as now I walk at dawn
  Past the still house where you lie sleeping.
May the sun burn away these footprints on the lawn
  And hold you in its warmth and keeping.

Vikram Seth
(20 June 1952 –)

This poem comes from Vikram Seth's collection *All You Who Sleep Tonight*, published in 1990. Seth has homes in both California and New Delhi and is the author of the best-selling novel *A Suitable Boy*.

I AM

I am: yet what I am none cares or knows,
  My friends forsake me like a memory lost;
I am the self-consumer of my woes,
  They rise and vanish in oblivious host,
Like shades in love and death's oblivion lost;
And yet I am, and live with shadows tost

Into the nothingness of scorn and noise,
  Into the living sea of waking dreams,
Where there is neither sense of life nor joys,
  But the vast shipwreck of my life's esteems;
And een the dearest – that I loved the best –
Are strange – nay, rather stranger than the rest.

I long for scenes where man has never trod;
  A place where woman never smiled or wept;
There to abide with my Creator, GOD,
  And sleep as I in childhood sweetly slept:
Untroubling and untroubled where I lie;
The grass below – above the vaulted sky.

John Clare
· (13 July 1793 – 20 May 1864)

"If life had a second edition," wrote Clare, "how I would correct the proofs." He spent the last 22 years of his life in a lunatic asylum in Northampton, forsaken by his former friends and family. He had wished to be buried at his birthplace in Helpstone, and despite the refusal of his former patron to supply the necessary money, enough was raised to enable Clare's wish to be fulfilled. He was buried there on 25 May 1864.

ON A FLY DRINKING OUT OF HIS CUP

Busy, curious, thirsty fly!
Drink with me and drink as I:
Freely welcome to my cup,
Couldst thou sip and sip it up:
Make the most of life you may,
Life is short and wears away.

Both alike are mine and thine
Hastening quick to their decline:
Thine's a summer, mine's no more,
Though repeated to threescore.
Threescore summers, when they're gone,
Will appear as short as one!

William Oldys
(14 July 1696 – 15 April 1761)

William Oldys was the illegitimate son of the chancellor of Lincoln. He collected rare books and manuscripts, and sold his collection to the Earl of Oxford, who made him his librarian. He wrote a *Life of Sir Walter Raleigh*. Being appointed Norroy king-at-arms for the last six years of his life saved him from poverty and the Fleet prison.
   This poem was first published in 1732.

15 J U L Y

THE SONG OF A MAN WHO HAS COME THROUGH

Not I, not I, but the wind that blows through me!
A fine wind is blowing the new direction of Time.
If only I let it bear me, carry me, if only it carry me!
If only I am sensitive, subtle, oh, delicate, a winged gift!
If only, most lovely of all, I yield myself and am borrowed
By the fine, fine wind that takes its course through the chaos of the world
Like a fine, an exquisite chisel, a wedge-blade inserted;
If only I am keen and hard like the sheer tip of a wedge
Driven by invisible blows,
The rock will split, we shall come at the wonder, we shall find the Hesperides.[1]

Oh, for the wonder that bubbles into my soul,
I would be a good fountain, a good well-head,
Would blur no whisper, spoil no expression.

What is the knocking?
What is the knocking at the door in the night?
It is somebody wants to do us harm.

No, no, it is the three strange angels.[2]
Admit them, admit them.

D. H. Lawrence
(11 September 1885 - 2 March 1930)

This poem was written on or very shortly after the day of Lawrence's marriage to Frieda, July 13th, 1914.

1. The sisters who guarded the garden where the golden apples of Hera, queen of the gods, grew. Also the delightful garden itself, a place of fulfillment.
2. Possibly the three angels who appeared to Abraham in Genesis 18 to announce that Abraham and Sarah had been chosen to bear the seed of the future.

from MILTON

And did those feet in ancient time
Walk upon England's mountains green?
And was the holy lamb of God
On England's pleasant pastures seen?

And did the countenance divine
Shine forth upon our clouded hills?
And was Jerusalem builded here
Among those dark satanic mills?

Bring me my bow of burning gold:
Bring me my arrows of desire:
Bring me my spear: O clouds unfold!
Bring me my chariot of fire.

I will not cease from mental fight,
Nor shall my sword sleep in my hand
Till we have built Jerusalem
In England's green and pleasant land.

William Blake
(28 November 1757 - 12 August 1827)

Blake gave this poem no name. His prose *Introduction to Milton* concludes with this poem, now best known as a hymn. There was a popular eighteenth-century belief that Joseph of Arimethea brought the boy Jesus to Britain – thus the first verse. The dark satanic mills refer first and foremost to Oxford and Cambridge and the rigidity of classics and mathematics. The third verse treats of the poetic genius, humanity's bottom line and the foundation of all religions."'Jerusalem" is the name of his greatest epic poem, engraved on a hundred copper plates, of which he finished only a single copy. He wrote of this magnum opus:"I may praise it since I dare not pretend to be any other than the secretary; the authors are in Eternity. I consider it as the grandest poem that the world contains."

from MUCH ADO ABOUT NOTHING
ACT II SCENE III

Sigh no more, ladies, sigh no more,
  Men were deceivers ever,
One foot in sea and one on shore,
  To one thing constant never:
Then sigh not so, but let them go,
  And be you blithe and bonny,
Converting all your sounds of woe
  Into Hey nonny, nonny.

Sing no more ditties, sing no more,
  Of dumps so dull and heavy;
The fraud of men was ever so,
  Since summer first was leafy:
Then sigh not so, but let them go,
  And be you blithe and bonny,
Converting all your sounds of woe
  Into Hey nonny, nonny.

William Shakespeare
(23 April 1564 – 23 April 1616)

In Shakespeare's time, pronunciation of the word "nothing" is thought to have been more like "noting." The play abounds in puns on notes and noting. Deception and disguise are major themes.

SCOTTSBORO

Paper come out – done strewed de news
Seven po' chillun moan deat' house blues,
Seven po' chillun moanin' deat' house blues.
Seven nappy heads wit' big shiny eye
All bound' in jail and framed to die,
All bound' in jail and framed to die.

Messin' white woman – snake lyin' tale
Hang and burn and jail wit' no bail.
Dat hang and burn and jail wit' no bail.
Worse ol' crime in white folks' lan'
Black skin coverin' po' working' man,
Black skin coverin' po' workin' man.

Judge and jury – all in de stan'
Lawd, biggety name for same lynchin' ban',
Lawd, biggety name for same lynchin' ban'.
White folks and nigger in great co't house
Like cat down cellar wit' nohole mouse.
Like cat down cellar wit' nohole mouse.

Anonymous

In 1931 nine young black men in Scottsboro, Alabama were charged with raping two white women. This folk blues was written during the initial trials (later the men were found not guilty) after a death sentence had been handed down.

NOT LOVE PERHAPS

This is not Love perhaps – Love that lays down
Its life, that many waters cannot quench, nor the floods drown –
But something written in lighter ink, said in a lower tone:
Something perhaps especially our own:
A need at times to be together and talk –
And then the finding we can walk
More firmly through dark narrow places
And meet more easily nightmare faces:
A need to reach out sometimes hand to hand –
And then find Earth less like an alien land:
A need for alliance to defeat
The whisperers at the corner of the street:
A need for inns on roads, islands in seas, halts for discoveries to be shared,
Maps checked and notes compared:
A need at times of each for each
Direct as the need of throat and tongue for speech.

A. S. J. Tessimond
(19 July 1902 – 13 May 1962)

Arthur Seymour John Tessimond was born in Birkenhead, the only child of a bank inspector. He felt warmth in his childhood from an aunt, but felt unloved by his parents. At 16 he ran away from Charterhouse School (for a fortnight) to London. In 1925, he sent his poems to Ezra Pound, who wrote back biliously: "Can't see that yr. work has any marked individuality, or as yet any character to distinguish it from anyone elses. England has gone to hell, and if you are determined you had better go somewhere else, as you will get nothing but carion and pus from your surroundings." "Not hopeless," Pound added as an afterthought on the envelope, "if you are less than 21." He was 23.

WHOSO LIST TO HUNT

Whoso list° to hunt, I know where is an hind,°   *wishes; female deer*
But as for me, helas,° I may no more.   *alas*
The vain travail hath wearied me so sore,
I am of them that farthest cometh behind.
Yet may I by no means my wearied mind
Draw from the deer, but as she fleeth afore
Fainting I follow. I leave off therefore
Since in a net I seek to hold the wind.
Who list her hunt, I put him out of doubt,
As well as I may spend his time in vain.
And graven with diamonds in letters plain
There is written her fair neck round about:
"*Noli me tangere*° for Caesar's I am,   *Touch me not*
And wild for to hold though I seem tame."

Sir Thomas Wyatt
(1503 – 11 October 1542)
based on a sonnet by Petrarch
(20 July 1304 – 19 July 1374)

This sonnet has echoes of Wyatt's relationship with Anne Boleyn in about 1527. Antonio Bonvisi claims that Wyatt went to King Henry VIII to warn him against marrying Anne Boleyn: "She is not meet to be copled with your grace, her conversation hath been so loose and base; which thing I know not so much by hear-say as by my own experience as one that have had my carnal pleasure with her."

Anne Gainsforth, one of Anne Boleyn's maids, gave this account of Wyatt's falling in love: "The knight in the beginning coming to be holden and surprised somewhat with the sight thereof, after much more with her witty and graceful speech, his ear also had him charmed unto her, so as finally his heart seemed to say, 'I could gladly yield to be tied for ever with the knot of her love.'"

Anne Boleyn's other lovers were executed. Wyatt was merely imprisoned in the Tower of London for a time, later returning to favor as ambassador to the court of Charles V in Spain.

from FROM JUNE TO DECEMBER
SUMMER VILLANELLE

You know exactly what to do –
Your kiss, your fingers on my thigh –
I think of little else but you.

It's bliss to have a lover who,
Touching one shoulder, makes me sigh –
You know exactly what to do.

You make me happy through and through,
The way the sun lights up the sky –
I think of little else but you.

I hardly sleep – an hour or two;
I can't eat much and this is why –
You know exactly what to do.

The movie in my mind is blue –
As June runs into warm July
I think of little else but you.

But is it love? And is it true?
Who cares? This much I can't deny:
You know exactly what to do;
I think of little else but you.

Wendy Cope
(21 July 1945 –)

Wendy Cope recalls: "I wrote this one hot Saturday morning in 1984 when I had been planning to go to Sainsburys. I felt guilty about lazing around writing a poem instead."

from A DIALOGUE OF SELF AND SOUL[1]

I am content to follow to its source
Every event in action or in thought;
Measure the lot; forgive myself the lot!
When such as I cast out remorse
So great a sweetness flows into the breast
We must laugh and we must sing,
We are blest by everything,
Everything we look upon is blest.

William Butler Yeats
(13 June 1865 – 28 January 1939)

On this day in 1921 the president of Sinn Fein, Eamon De Valera, agreed a truce with the British government. Yeats had been impressed by a saying attributed to De Valera after the failed Easter Rising of 1916: "If the people had only come out with knives and forks."

"A Dialogue of Self and Soul" was written in 1928, Yeats notes, "during a long illness and indeed finished the day before a Cannes doctor told me to stop writing."

Yeats commented in an essay that "there is in the creative joy an acceptance of what life brings, because we have understood the beauty of what it brings, or a hatred of death for what it takes away, which arouses within us, through some sympathy perhaps with all other men, an energy so noble, so powerful, that we laugh aloud and mock, in the terror or the sweetness of our exultation, at death and oblivion."

1. The final stanza of section II, spoken by "My Self."

WOODNICHE

The dragonflies were here before us, friend:
Cupboard of branch and bramble, woodniche
Where the sun tumbles, foxgloves are gorgeous.
Children tore their knees among these thorns,

Fleshed their pullovers with raspberries.
Orange peel made ripples in the brown water,
Pebbles explored beyond our peering. I
Chewed dandelions and the sun brothered me.
Huge as policemen, sombre as soutanes,

The kind trees whispered in the long watch
And I used wonder in tremendous shadow
And be afraid of where the wonder led.

Summer was wealthy with a daze of suntraps,
Daffodil-spitting, sumptuous. Everywhere
Ours for the taking. Whoever has said
It is time to go home is an adult.

Aidan Carl Mathews
(16 January 1956 -)

Aidan Carl Mathews was educated at Gonzaga College, University College, Dublin, Trinity College, Dublin, and Stanford University in California. He is the winner of several poetry prizes among them the Irish Times Award for 1974 and the Patrick Kavanagh Award for 1976. His collections of poems include *Windfalls* (1977) and *Minding Ruth* (Gallery Books, Dublin, 1983). He is married and lives in Dublin.

JULY

The air without has taken fever;
Fast I feel the beating of its pulse.
The leaves are twisted on the maple,
In the corn the autumn's premature;
The weary butterfly hangs waiting
For a breath to waft him thither at
The touch, but falls, like truth unheeded,
Into dust-blown grass and hollyhocks.

The air without is blinding dusty;
Cool I feel the breezes blow; I see
The sunlight, crowded on the porch, grow
Smaller till absorbed in shadow; and
The far blue hills are changed to gray, and
Twilight lingers in the woods between;
And now I hear the shower dancing
In the cornfield and the thirsty grass.

Alexander L. Posey
(3 August 1873 - 27 May 1908)

Posey was one of twelve children born in Oklahoma to a Chickasaw-Creek woman and her husband, a rancher and later a lawman. According to Posey, before his fourteenth year he rarely spoke English. Posey drowned while attempting to cross the Oktahutche River in Oklahoma by boat. In 1910, his poems were published posthumously by his wife.

from THE TEMPEST
ACT I SCENE II

Ariel. Full fathom five thy father lies;
  Of his bones are coral made:
Those are pearls that were his eyes:
  Nothing of him that doth fade,
But doth suffer a sea-change
Into something rich and strange.
Sea-nymphs hourly ring his knell:

[Burden¹: ding-dong.

Hark! now I hear them, – ding-dong, bell.

William Shakespeare
(23 April 1564 – 23 April 1616)

Shakespeare is thought to have derived some of the inspiration for *The Tempest* from a shipwreck that began on this day in 1609, as described by Silvester Jourdan in *A Discovery of the Barmudas, Otherwise called the Ile of Divels*, published in 1610: "I being in ship called the Sea-venture, with Sir Thomas Gates . . . bound for Virginia . . . we were taken with a most sharpe and cruell storme upon the five and twentieth day of July, Anno 1609, which did separate us from the residue of our fleete . . . It pleased God to send her within halfe an English mile of . . . the Ilandes of the Barmudas, . . . ever esteemed, and reputed, a most prodigious and inchanted place . . . Yet did we finde there the ayre so temperate and the Country so abundantly fruitful of all fit necessaries . . . that we were there for the space of nine moneths . . . well refreshed."

1. Refrain.

THE WIND, ONE BRILLIANT DAY

The wind, one brilliant day, called
to my soul with an odor of jasmine.

'In return for the odor of my jasmine,
I'd like all the odor of your roses.'

'I have no roses; all the flowers
in my garden are dead.'

'Well then, I'll take the withered petals
and the yellow leaves and the waters of the fountain.'

The wind left. And I wept. And I said to myself:
'What have you done with the garden that was entrusted to you?'

Antonio Machado
(26 July 1875 - 22 February 1939)
translated by Robert Bly
(23 December 1926 -)

Antonio Machado was born in Seville and wrote books of spirited if often melancholic
poetry, such as *Campos de Castilla*, and collaborated on plays with his brother.
   Robert Bly includes Machado's work in his collection of "poems for men," *The Rag and
Bone Shop of the Heart* (published by HarperPerennial).

TARANTELLA

Do you remember an Inn,
Miranda?
Do you remember an Inn?
And the tedding and the spreading
Of the straw for a bedding,
And the fleas that tease in the High Pyrenees,
And the wine that tasted of the tar?
And the cheers and the jeers of the young muleteers
(Under the vine of the dark verandah)?
Do you remember an Inn, Miranda,
Do you remember an Inn?
And the cheers and the jeers of the young muleteers
Who hadn't got a penny,
And who weren't paying any,
And the hammer at the doors and the Din?
And the Hip! Hop! Hap!
Of the clap
Of the hands to the twirl and the swirl
Of the girl gone chancing,
Glancing,
Dancing,
Backing and advancing,
Snapping of a clapper to the spin
Out and in –
And the Ting, Tong, Tang of the Guitar!
Do you remember an Inn,
Miranda?
Do you remember an Inn?

TARANTELLA

Never more;
Miranda,
Never more.
Only the high peaks hoar:
And Aragon a torrent at the door.
No sound
In the walls of the Halls where falls
The tread
Of the feet of the dead to the ground
No sound:
But the boom
Of the far Waterfall like Doom.

Hilaire Belloc
(27 July 1870 – 16 July 1953)

Hilaire Belloc was born in St. Cloud near Paris, the son of a French barrister. He did French military service, became an English Liberal MP, was an outspoken Catholic and friend of G.K. Chesterton. His book *The Servile State* advocated a return to the medieval guilds.

28 J U L Y

THE WINDHOVER[1]
TO CHRIST OUR LORD

I caught this morning morning's minion,[2] king-
   dom of daylight's dauphin, dapple-dawn-drawn Falcon, in his riding
  Of the rolling level underneath him steady air, and striding
High there, how he rung upon the rein of a wimpling[3] wing
In his ecstasy! then off, off forth on swing,
   As a skate's heel sweeps smooth on a bow-bend: the hurl and gliding
  Rebuffed the big wind. My heart in hiding
Stirred for a bird, – the achieve of, the mastery of the thing!

Brute beauty and valour and act, oh, air, pride, plume, here
   Buckle! AND the fire that breaks from thee then, a billion
Times told lovelier, more dangerous, O my chevalier![4]

   No wonder of it: shéer plód makes plough down sillion[5]
Shine, and blue-bleak embers, ah my dear,
   Fall, gall themselves, and gash gold-vermilion.

Gerard Manley Hopkins
(28 July 1844 – 8 June 1889)

Hopkins composed this sonnet on 30 May 1877. On 22 June 1879 he wrote to Robert Bridges that this poem was "the best thing I ever wrote." In the last part of the poem Hopkins the Jesuit may be associating the "fire" that shines from the bird with the fire that comes from Christ, his "chevalier" – a fire that is hardly surprising, he says, given that even a mere plough can make the earth shine, and that embers when they break open, glow golden within.

1. "A name for the kestrel, from its habit of hovering or hanging with its head to the wind" (O. E. D.).
2. favorite.
3. rippling.
4. knight/champion.
5. furrow.

MILKMAID

The girl's far treble, muted to the heat,
calls like a fainting bird across the fields
to where her flock lies panting for her voice,
their black horns buried deep in marigolds.

They climb awake, like drowsy butterflies,
and press their red flanks through the tall branched grass,
and as they go their wandering tongues embrace
the vacant summer mirrored in their eyes.

Led to the limestone shadows of a barn
they snuff their past embalmed in the hay,
while her cool hand, cupped to the udder's fount,
distils the brimming harvest of their day.

Look what a cloudy cream the earth gives out,
fat juice of buttercups and meadow-rye;
the girl dreams milk within her body's field
and hears, far off, her muted children cry.

Laurie Lee
(26 June 1914 – 13 May 1997)

At about this time of year in 1936, Laurie Lee was "rescued" from Spain and the Spanish Civil War by a British destroyer sent from Gibraltar to pick up marooned British subjects. He describes the scene in *As I Walked Out One Midsummer Morning:* " 'Hurry!' cried [Emilia]. 'Leaving everything – you are saved! Your king has sent you a ship. They are waiting for you on the beach and have come to take you home. Before God, who more fortunate than you?' "

Elegy written in a country churchyard

The curfew tolls the knell of parting day,
  The lowing herd wind slowly o'er the lea,
The plowman homeward plods his weary way,
  And leaves the world to darkness and to me.

Now fades the glimmering landscape on the sight,
  And all the air a solemn stillness holds,
Save where the beetle wheels his droning flight,
  And drowsy tinklings lull the distant folds;

Save that from yonder ivy-mantled tower
  The moping owl does to the moon complain
Of such as, wand'ring near her secret bower,
  Molest her ancient solitary reign.

Beneath those rugged elms, that yew-tree's shade,
  Where heaves the turf in many a mould'ring heap,
Each in his narrow cell for ever laid,
  The rude forefathers of the hamlet sleep.

The breezy call of incense-breathing morn,
  The swallow twitt'ring from the straw-built shed,
The cock's shrill clarion, or the echoing horn,
  No more shall rouse them from their lowly bed.

For them no more the blazing hearth shall burn,
  Or busy housewife ply her evening care:
No children run to lisp their sire's return,
  Or climb his knees the envied kiss to share.

Oft did the harvest to their sickle yield,
  Their furrow oft the stubborn glebe has broke:
How jocund did they drive their team afield!
  How bowed the woods beneath their sturdy stroke!

Let not Ambition mock their useful toil,
  Their homely joys, and destiny obscure;
Nor Grandeur hear with a disdainful smile
  The short and simple annals of the poor.

The boast of heraldry, the pomp of power,
  And all that beauty, all that wealth e'er gave,
Awaits alike th' inevitable hour:
  The paths of glory lead but to the grave.

Nor you, ye proud, impute to These the fault,
  If Memory o'er their tomb no trophies raise,
Where through the long-drawn aisle and fretted vault
  The pealing anthem swells the note of praise.

Can storied urn or animated bust
  Back to its mansion call the fleeting breath?
Can Honour's voice provoke the silent dust,
  Or Flatt'ry soothe the dull cold ear of death?

Perhaps in this neglected spot is laid
  Some heart once pregnant with celestial fire;
Hands, that the rod of empire might have swayed,
  Or waked to ecstasy the living lyre.

But Knowledge to their eyes her ample page
  Rich with the spoils of time did ne'er unroll;
Chill Penury repressed their noble rage,
  And froze the genial current of the soul.

Full many a gem of purest ray serene
  The dark unfathomed caves of ocean bear:
Full many a flower is born to blush unseen,
  And waste its sweetness on the desert air.

Some village Hampden that with dauntless breast
  The little tyrant of his fields withstood,
Some mute inglorious Milton here may rest,
  Some Cromwell guiltless of his country's blood.

Th' applause of list'ning senates to command,
  The threats of pain and ruin to despise,
To scatter plenty o'er a smiling land,
  And read their history in a nation's eyes,

Their lot forbade: nor circumscribed alone
  Their growing virtues, but their crimes confined;
Forbade to wade through slaughter to a throne.
  And shut the gates of mercy on mankind,

The struggling pangs of conscious truth to hide,
  To quench the blushes of ingenuous shame,
Or heap the shrine of Luxury and Pride
  With incense kindled at the Muse's flame.

ELEGY WRITTEN IN A COUNTRY CHURCHYARD

Far from the madding crowd's ignoble strife
  Their sober wishes never learned to stray;
Along the cool sequestered vale of life
  They kept the noiseless tenor of their way.

Yet ev'n these bones from insult to protect
  Some frail memorial still erected nigh,
With uncouth rhymes and shapeless sculpture decked,
  Implores the passing tribute of a sigh.

Their name, their years, spelt by th' unlettered Muse,
  The place of fame and elegy supply:
And many a holy text around she strews,
  That teach the rustic moralist to die.

For who, to dumb Forgetfulness a prey,
  This pleasing anxious being e'er resigned,
Left the warm precincts of the cheerful day,
  Nor cast one longing ling'ring look behind?

On some fond breast the parting soul relies,
  Some pious drops the closing eye requires;
E'en from the tomb the voice of Nature cries,
  E'en in our Ashes live their wonted fires.

For thee, who, mindful of th' unhonoured dead,
  Dost in these lines their artless tale relate;
If chance, by lonely contemplation led,
  Some kindred spirit shall inquire thy fate,

Haply some hoary-headed Swain may say,
  'Oft have we seen him at the peep of dawn
Brushing with hasty steps the dews away
  To meet the sun upon the upland lawn.

'There at the foot of yonder nodding beech
  That wreathes its old fantastic roots so high,
His listless length at noontide would he stretch,
  And pore upon the brook that babbles by.

'Hard by yon wood, now smiling as in scorn,
  Mutt'ring his wayward fancies he would rove,
Now drooping, woeful wan, like one forlorn,
  Or crazed with care, or crossed in hopeless love.

'One morn I missed him on the customed hill,
  Along the heath and near his fav'rite tree;
Another came; nor yet beside the rill,
  Nor up the lawn, nor at the wood was he;

'The next with dirges due in sad array
  Slow through the church-way path we saw him borne.
Approach and read (for thou canst read) the lay
  Graved on the stone beneath yon aged thorn:'

Here rests his head upon the lap of Earth
  A Youth to Fortune and to Fame unknown.
Fair Science frowned not on his humble birth,
  And Melancholy marked him for her own.

ELEGY WRITTEN IN A COUNTRY CHURCHYARD

THE EPITAPH

Here rests his head upon the lap of Earth
  A Youth to Fortune and to Fame unknown.
Fair Science frowned not on his humble birth,
  And Melancholy marked him for her own.

Large was his bounty, and his soul sincere,
  Heaven did a recompense as largely send:
He gave to Mis'ry all he had, a tear,
  He gained from Heaven ('twas all he wished) a friend.

No further seek his merits to disclose,
  Or draw his frailties from their dread abode,
(There they alike in trembling hope repose,)
  The bosom of his Father and his God.

Thomas Gray
(26 December 1716 – 30 July 1771)

Though well-to-do, Gray's father refused to support his son's education. This was left to his mother whose wages as a milliner paid for her son's years at Eton and Cambridge. Gray became a professor of history and modern languages at Cambridge. Painstaking in his writing, Gray published the "Elegy Written in a Country Churchyard" after seven years of revision, when he was thirty-five. Though offered the laureateship after Southey's death, Gray refused. He was buried at Stoke Poges in Buckinghamshire, the village which inspired his "Elegy."

A POISON TREE

I was angry with my friend:
I told my wrath, my wrath did end.
I was angry with my foe:
I told it not, my wrath did grow.

And I water'd it in fears,
Night & morning with my tears;
And I sunned it with smiles,
And with soft deceitful wiles.

And it grew both day and night,
Till it bore an apple bright;
And my foe beheld it shine,
And he knew that it was mine,

And into my garden stole
When the night had veil'd the pole:
In the morning glad I see
My foe outstretch'd beneath the tree.

William Blake
(28 November 1757 - 12 August 1827)

Blake's notebook from 1793 comments on the Poison Tree: "There is just such a tree at
Java Found." The tree is the *upas*, which legend has endowed with the power to kill creatures for many miles around; its native name means "poison."
  The theme of the poem is the nature of violence seen in terms of its origins. The last
verse is utterly realistic. People do exult in the defeat of their enemies, but this is written
not in exultation but as a warning. To Blake "Mutual forgiveness of each vice / Such are
the gates of Paradise." This mutuality is new to Christian doctrine.

JACOB

He dwelt among 'apartments let,'
  About five stories high;
A man I thought that none would get,
  And very few would try.

A boulder, by a larger stone
  Half hidden in the mud,
Fair as a man when only one
  Is in the neighborhood.

He lived unknown, and few could tell
  When Jacob was not free;
But he has got a wife, – and O!
  The difference to me!

Phoebe Cary
(4 September 1824 – 31 July 1871)

Phoebe Cary took charge of the household when she and her sisters, Alice and Elmina, moved to New York City from Ohio. Together they hosted a weekly salon where writers mixed with at least one businessman, P. T. Barnum, who gave a prize for the poem chosen to be sung by Jenny Lind, the popular Swedish soprano.

Cary's "Jacob" is a rather arch parody of one of Wordsworth's five "Lucy lyrics." The identity of Lucy remains a mystery, assuming she even existed.

LATE FRAGMENT

And did you get what
you wanted from this life, even so?
I did.
And what did you want?
To call myself beloved, to feel myself
beloved on the earth.

Raymond Carver
(25 May 1938 - 2 August 1988)

Raymond Carver, poet and short-story writer ("the American Chekhov") died aged 50 from cancer. This poem is the last in the book of poems *A New Path to the Waterfall*, published by The Atlantic Monthly Press. He prepared them while facing his death, with the help of his long-time partner Tess Gallagher, whom he married in June 1988. In her introduction she comments about this poem that "for a recovering alcoholic, this self-recognition and more generalized feeling of love he was allowing himself was no small accomplishment. Ray knew he had been graced and blessed and that his writing had enabled him to reach far beyond the often mean circumstances from which he and those he wrote about had come, and also that through his writing those working-class lives had become part of literature. On a piece of scrap paper near his typewriter he had written: 'Forgive me if I'm thrilled with the idea, but just now I thought that every poem I write ought to be called Happiness.'"

from THE OLD VICARAGE, GRANTCHESTER
(CAFÉ DES WESTENS, BERLIN, MAY 1912)

Ah God! to see the branches stir
Across the moon at Grantchester!
To smell the thrilling-sweet and rotten
Unforgettable, unforgotten
River-smell and hear the breeze
Sobbing in the little trees.
Say, do the elm-clumps greatly stand
Still guardians of that holy land?
The chestnut shade, in reverend dream,
The yet unacademic stream?
Is dawn a secret shy and cold
Anadyomene,[1] silver-gold?
And sunset still a golden sea
From Haslingfield to Madingley?
And after, ere the night is born,
Do hares come out about the corn?
Oh, is the water sweet and cool,
Gentle and brown, above the pool?
And laughs the immortal river still
Under the mill, under the mill?
Say, is there Beauty yet to find?
And Certainty? and Quiet kind?
Deep meadows yet, for to forget

from THE OLD VICARAGE, GRANTCHESTER

The lies, and truths, and pain? . . . Oh! yet
Stands the Church clock at ten to three?
And is there honey still for tea?

Rupert Brooke

(3 August 1887 – 23 April 1915)

Rupert Brooke was born on this day in 1887 at Rugby School where his father was an assistant master and where he was educated. In 1909, whilst up at Cambridge University, he took up lodgings in Grantchester. On 25 April 1912, Brooke wrote to Ka Cox: "I'm just passing through Potsdam. I've a fancy you may be, just now, in Grantchester. I envy you frightfully. That river and the chestnuts – come back to me a lot. Tea on the lawn. Just wire to me and we'll spend the summer there; with Eddie to tea every Saturday and a fancy dress ball on Midsummer night." In the first draft, the clock stood at half past three (the actual time it had been stuck during most of 1911); the poem was entitled "Home" – and in the next draft "The Sentimental Exile." He sent his editor a telegram : "A masterpiece on its way"; but to Mrs Cornford he merely wrote that he had "scrawled in a café a very long poem about Grantchester, that seemed to me to have pleasant silly passages."

1. A painting of Venus rising from the sea and wringing her hair, which adorned the sanctuary of Aesculapius.

from PROMETHEUS UNBOUND

To suffer woes which Hope thinks infinite;
To forgive wrongs darker than death or nights;
To defy Power, which seems omnipotent;
To love, and bear; to Hope till Hope creates
From its own wreck the thing it contemplates;
Neither to change, nor falter, nor repent;
This, like thy glory, Titan, is to be
Good, great and joyous, beautiful and free;
This is alone Life, Joy, Empire, and Victory.

Percy Bysshe Shelley
(4 August 1792 – 8 July 1822)

As a child Shelley was idolized by his younger sisters, hated the bullying at his boarding schools (Syon House and Eton), and was expelled from Oxford for refusing to acknowledge having published a pamphlet entitled *The Necessity of Atheism*. Shelley eloped with 16-year-old Harriet Westbrook and was expelled from Field Place, the family seat, by his father, Sir Timothy Shelley, so that he would not corrupt his sisters, and was cut off from his inheritance. Eventually, Sir Timothy and Harriet's father felt obliged to give Shelley an annuity of £400 a year, to prevent him "cheating strangers" and leaving a trail of unpaid debts behind him – which Shelley did, nevertheless, escaping to Italy and being a total of some £25,000 in debt by the time of his death.

In Rome, on 25 May 1819, Shelley gave his second wife, Mary, the completed manuscript of his long poem "Prometheus Unbound" to read. In his preface he commented: "This poem was chiefly written upon the mountainous ruins of the Baths of Caracalla among the flowery glades, and the thickets of odoriferous blossoming trees, which are extended in ever winding labyrinths upon its immense platforms and dizzy arches suspended in the air. The bright blue sky of Rome, and the effect of the vigorous awakening spring in that divinest climate, and the new life with which it drenches the spirits even to intoxication, were the inspiration of this drama." Of Prometheus, the fire bringer and liberator of mankind, he wrote: "The only imaginary being resembling in any degree Prometheus, is Satan; and Prometheus is, in my judgement, a more poetical character than Satan, because, in addition to courage, and majesty, and firm and patient opposition to omnipotent force, he is susceptible of being described as exempt from the taints of ambition, envy, revenge and a desire for personal aggrandisement . . . [he] is, as it were, the type of the highest perfection of moral and intellectual nature."

5 AUGUST

MEMORY

One had a lovely face,
And two or three had charm,
But charm and face were in vain
Because the mountain grass
Cannot but keep the form
Where the mountain hare has lain.

William Butler Yeats
(13 June 1865 – 28 January 1939)

Editors have associated the "lovely face" of the first line with Olivia Shakespear ("the centre of my life in London," wrote Yeats, "when first I met her, she was in her late twenties but in looks a lovely young girl"). The association for the "mountain hare" is with Iseult Gonne (who refused Yeats' proposal of marriage, as her mother, Maud Gonne, had before her).

SONG: TO CELIA

Drink to me, only, with thine eyes,
  And I will pledge with mine;
Or leave a kiss but in the cup,
  And I'll not look for wine.
The thirst, that from the soul doth rise,
  Doth ask a drink divine:
But might I of Jove's nectar sup,
  I would not change for thine.
I sent thee, late, a rosy wreath,
  Not so much honouring thee,
As giving it a hope, that there
  It could not withered be.
But thou thereon did'st only breathe,
  And sent'st it back to me:
Since when it grows, and smells, I swear,
  Not of itself, but thee.

Ben Jonson
(11 June 1572 - 6 August 1637)

The end of Jonson's life was marked by poverty. The story goes that Jonson arranged with the Dean of Westminster to be buried upright, as he could not afford the six feet of earth necessary for being buried lying down. The famous inscription on his tomb, "O Rare Ben Jonson," was carved by a mason who had been paid eighteen pence to inscribe the unmarked grave by a passer-by at Jonson's funeral.

7 AUGUST

PARTING IN WARTIME

How long ago Hector took off his plume,
Not wanting that his little son should cry,
Then kissed his sad Andromache goodbye –
And now we three in Euston waiting-room.

Frances Cornford
(30 March 1886 – 19 August 1960)

On this day in 1914, the first units of the British Expeditionary Force were sent across to France to reinforce the left wing of the French army.

Frances Cornford's son, the poet John Cornford, was killed in the Spanish Civil War.

The dead at clonmacnois

In a quiet water'd land, a land of roses,
 Stands Saint Kieran's city fair;
And the Warriors of Erin in their famous generations
 Slumber there.

There beneath the dewy hillside sleep the noblest
 Of the clan of Conn,
Each below his stone with name in branching Ogham
 And the sacred knot thereon.

There they laid to rest the seven Kings of Tara,
 There the sons of Cairbrè sleep –
Battle-banners of the Gael that in Kieran's plain of crosses
 Now their final hosting keep.

And in Clonmacnois they laid the men of Teffia,
 And right many a lord of Breagh;
Deep the sod above Clan Creidè and Clan Conaill,
 Kind in hall and fierce in fray.

THE DEAD AT CLONMACNOIS

Many and many a son of Conn the Hundred-Fighter
   In the red earth lies at rest;
Many a blue eye of Clan Colman the turf covers,
   Many a swan-white breast.

Thomas William Rolleston
(1 May 1857 – 5 December 1920)
based on an original poem in Irish by Angus O'Gillan

Rolleston's son, C. H. Rolleston, wrote that "these lovely lines first appeared in *Poems and Ballads of Young Ireland* in 1888. Clonmacnois, on the bank of the Shannon in King's Country, was the burial place of the ancient Kings of Ireland – a spot as sacred to the Irish people as the Holy Hill of Tara itself."

T. W. Rolleston was the co-founder with Yeats and Ernest Rhys of the Rhymers' Club that met at the Cheshire Cheese in London during the early 1890s – Ernest Dowson was a member too. Rolleston was also the founder of the Irish Literary Society of London and author of *Myths and Legends of the Celtic Race*. One of his friends was the Irish poet George Russell. In his diary for this day in 1898, Rolleston wrote:

"George Russell came in to dine. And he talked – opalescently, about his spiritualistic experiences, his visions, dreams, and phantasms. Everything he saw was either opalescent or iridescent, and I wished at times he would opalesce himself into an iridescent vision. At last I could stand it no longer, and I went to bed, and read his poetry."

The heart

In the desert
I saw a creature, naked, bestial,
Who, squatting upon the ground,
Held his heart in his hands,
And ate of it.

I said, 'Is it good, friend?'
'It is bitter – bitter,' he answered;
'But I like it
Because it is bitter,
And because it is my heart.'

Stephen Crane
(1 November 1871 – 5 June 1900)

In ill health, having survived a shipwreck en route from Cuba, Crane was recuperating in Jacksonville, Florida when he met Cora Taylor, an older woman and proprietress of a brothel, Hotel de Dream. Sensitive to what people might say of her, Crane decided they should move to England. However, it was Crane himself who was to become the object of unfounded gossip in America. Called a seducer, a morphine addict, and a drunk, Crane avoided returning to his homeland. At twenty-eight and a half years of age, Crane was hurriedly sent to the Black Forest with the hope that his tuberculosis would be cured. He died in Germany.

Crane's two books of poems grew out of his enthusiasm for the then few published poems of Emily Dickinson.

ARS POETICA

A poem should be palpable and mute
As a globed fruit

Dumb
As old medallions to the thumb

Silent as the sleeve-worn stone
Of casement ledges where the moss has grown –

A poem should be wordless
As the flight of birds

A poem should be motionless in time
As the moon climbs

Leaving, as the moon releases
Twig by twig the night-entangled trees,

Leaving, as the moon behind the winter leaves,
Memory by memory the mind –

A poem should be motionless in time
As the moon climbs

A poem should be equal to:
Not true

ARS POETICA

For all the history of grief
An empty doorway and a maple leaf

For love
The leaning grasses and two lights above the sea –

A poem should not mean
But be.

Archibald MacLeish
(7 May 1892 - 20 April 1982)

MacLeish was born in Illinois, the son of a Chicago merchant born in Scotland. At 24 he married, at 25 he joined a hospital ship, went to France, transferred to an artillery unit, and was a captain by the end of the First World War. At 31, he gave up his job as a lawyer, to focus on his poetry, traveling abroad with his wife and two children. During World War II he was one of President Roosevelt's advisers.

SONNET 18

Shall I compare thee to a summer's day?
Thou art more lovely and more temperate:
Rough winds do shake the darling buds of May,
And summer's lease hath all too short a date:
Sometime too hot the eye of heaven shines,
And often is his gold complexion dimm'd:
And every fair from fair sometime declines,
By chance, or nature's changing course untrimm'd;
But thy eternal summer shall not fade,
Nor lose possession of that fair thou ow'st,
Nor shall death brag thou wander'st in his shade,
When in eternal lines to time thou grow'st;
  So long as men can breathe, or eyes can see,
  So long lives this, and this gives life to thee.

William Shakespeare
(23 April 1564 – 23 April 1616)

On this day in 1596, Shakespeare buried his only son Hamnet in Stratford-on-Avon parish church.

LONDON

I wander through each chartered street,
Near where the chartered Thames does flow,
And mark in every face I meet
Marks of weakness, marks of woe.

In every cry of every man,
In every infant's cry of fear,
In every voice, in every ban,
The mind-forged manacles I hear.

How the chimney-sweeper's cry
Every blackening church appals;
And the hapless soldier's sigh
Runs in blood down palace walls.

But most through midnight streets I hear
How the youthful harlot's curse
Blasts the new-born infant's tear,
And blights with plagues the marriage hearse.

William Blake
(28 November 1757 – 12 August 1827)

Blake loved preindustrial London and its rural hinterland. But also in London he found the things he hated: poverty, tyranny, violence, and manacles in the mind. He indicted every degradation of the human spirit.

William Blake died 12 August 1827. His attitude to death is captured in his comment on the death of his friend Flaxman: "I cannot think of death as more than going out of one room into another." Blake died on a Sunday evening. Earlier in the day, so the story goes, he told his wife: "Kate, you have been a good Wife. I will draw your portrait." He sketched her at the bedside, then threw the paper down and sang "Hallelujahs & songs of Joy & Triumph ..."

CREATION MYTH HAIKU

After the First Night
the Sun kissed the Moon
'Darling, you were wonderful!'

HAIKU: AFTER THE ORGIES

All the Maenads had
terrible hangovers and
unwanted babies.

HAIKU: THE SEASON OF CELEBRITY

With summer comes the
bluebottle; with pleasant fame
comes the Journalist.

NORTH AMERICAN HAIKU

Hail, tribes of Outer
Alcoholia – the Rednose
and Goutfoot Indians!

Gavin Ewart
(4 February 1916 – 23 October 1995)

Gavin Ewart once wrote that "Good light verse is better than bad heavy verse / any day of the week." He was the editor of the *Penguin Book of Light Verse* (1980) and *Other People's Clerihews* (1983). His poems were first published when he was still a 17-year-old pupil at Wellington College.

Non sum qualis eram bonae sub regno Cynarae[1]

Last night, ah, yesternight, betwixt her lips and mine
There fell thy shadow, Cynara! thy breath was shed
Upon my soul between the kisses and the wine;
And I was desolate and sick of an old passion,
　Yea, I was desolate and bowed my head:
I have been faithful to thee, Cynara! in my fashion.

All night upon mine heart I felt her warm heart beat,
Night-long within mine arms in love and sleep she lay;
Surely the kisses of her bought red mouth were sweet;
But I was desolate and sick of an old passion,
　When I awoke and found the dawn was gray:
I have been faithful to thee, Cynara! in my fashion.

I have forgot much, Cynara! gone with the wind,
Flung roses, roses riotously with the throng,
Dancing, to put thy pale, lost lilies out of mind;
But I was desolate and sick of an old passion,
　Yea, all the time, because the dance was long:
I have been faithful to thee, Cynara! in my fashion.

I cried for madder music and for stronger wine,
But when the feast is finished and the lamps expire,
Then falls thy shadow, Cynara! the night is thine;
And I am desolate and sick of an old passion,
   Yea hungry for the lips of my desire:
I have been faithful to thee, Cynara! in my fashion.

Ernest Dowson
(2 August 1867 – 23 February 1900)

After the death of his father and the suicide of his mother, Dowson lived an intemperate life in France, England, and Ireland. In his world-weariness he remembered nostalgically the innocent Adelaide Foltinowicz (Millie), who was a girl of twelve when he met her in 1891.

1. "I am not as I was under the reign of the good Cynara" (from Horace, *Odes*, IV. i. The poet asks Venus to excuse him from further efforts in her service).

from MACBETH
ACT V SCENE V

Macbeth. Tomorrow, and tomorrow, and tomorrow,
Creeps in this petty pace from day to day,
To the last syllable of recorded time;
And all our yesterdays have lighted fools
The way to dusty death. Out, out, brief candle!
Life's but a walking shadow, a poor player
That struts and frets his hour upon the stage
And then is heard no more: it is a tale
Told by an idiot, full of sound and fury,
Signifying nothing.

William Shakespeare
(23 April 1564 - 23 April 1616)

On 15 August 1057, Macbeth was killed by Malcolm at Lumphanan in Mar. He was buried on Iona.

from THOUGHTS IN A GARDEN[1]

What wondrous life is this I lead!
Ripe apples drop about my head;
The luscious clusters of the vine
Upon my mouth do crush their wine;
The nectarine and curious peach
Into my hands themselves do reach;
Stumbling on melons, as I pass,
Ensnared with flowers, I fall on grass.

Meanwhile the mind from pleasure less
Withdraws into its happiness;
The mind, that Ocean where each kind
Does straight its own resemblance find;
Yet it creates, transcending these,
Far other worlds, and other seas;
Annihilating all that's made
To a green thought in a green shade.

Andrew Marvell
(31 March 1621 – 16 or 18 August 1678)

Marvell's editors comment that "like Adam, the poet is placed . . . in a paradise of delights, and like him he has a duty to contemplate them." Elsewhere in this poem Marvell contrasts the garden to the artificial life of courts and towns.

1. Stanzas 5 and 6 of this 9-stanza poem.

Thistles

Against the rubber tongues of cows and the hoeing hands of men
Thistles spike the summer air
And crackle open under a blue-black pressure.

Every one a revengeful burst
Of resurrection, a grasped fistful
Of splintered weapons and Icelandic frost thrust up

From the underground stain of a decayed Viking.
They are like pale hair and the gutterals of dialects.
Every one manages a plume of blood.

Then they grow grey like men.
Mown down, it is a feud. Their sons appear
Stiff with weapons, fighting back over the same ground.

Ted Hughes
(17 August 1930 -)

Looking back, Ted Hughes writes: "In 1961 I was living in London, close to Primrose Hill. I had a season ticket for the zoo, and most mornings I would take my baby daughter to see the owls, lions and the rest. This meant passing the SE corner of Primrose Hill itself. As that year developed, so did a clump of thistles – just inside the railings there, on that corner. I watched them, day by day. It seems to me now that they became a focus, of a kind, for what I was thinking about certain things – about that ideal possibility, a durable, undating poetic language, for instance. An essential sort of language – not linked too closely to what changes with every decade and century, everliving yet solid with living stuff, like the pattern of lines on the human hand. At least, that is what I see behind these verses now – that preoccupation. At the time, I was aware of using those thistles, behind the railings there, in that dusty corner by the traffic lights, to prompt a little poem about my liking for thistles in general."

from A U G U R I E S   O F   I N N O C E N C E

To see a World in a grain of sand,
And a Heaven in a wild flower,
Hold Infinity in the palm of your hand,
And Eternity in an hour.

A robin redbreast in a cage
Puts all Heaven in a rage.
A dove-house filled with doves and pigeons
Shudders Hell thro' all its regions.
A dog starved at his master's gate
Predicts the ruin of the State.
A horse misused upon the road
Calls to Heaven for human blood.

Each outcry of the hunted hare
A fibre from the brain does tear.
A skylark wounded in the wing,
A cherubim does cease to sing.

William Blake
(28 November 1757 - 12 August 1827)

All 128 lines of this poem constitute a great manifesto of eco-philosophy two hundred years ahead of its time. Central to "Auguries" is Blake's lifelong struggle against both Platonic and Cartesian dualism, the artificial division between the head and the heart, the sciences and the arts.

Aged 25 and recovering from being jilted, William Blake met Catherine Boucher, age 21. Their initial courtship was exceptionally brief: he asked her, "Do you pity me?" She replied, "Indeed I do," and he declared, "Then I love you." One year later they were married. Of their time spent together she was to explain, "I have very little of Mr. Blake's company. He is always in Paradise."

YEROKASTRINOS

On a stony hill
above the Cretan sea
a heart hangs, still
watching from an olive tree.

Blue boat loved:
toward Libya last
the white wake curved.
Ten years have passed.

Wind sighs.
Bees dance the air
round the heart. It dries
sweet, a dark red pear.

Karen Chamberlain
(1 December 1942 –)

Karen Chamberlain works in many genres: poetry, the novel, essay, memoir, and nature writing. She was honored with a "Poet of the Year" award from Poets & Writers and the Poetry Society of America. She lives in Aspen, Colorado.

She writes: "I believe it was Robert Pinsky (a superb memorizer of poetry) who explained that the only way to know something is 'by heart.' If you can hold a poem or a song in your heart, it is truly yours. Imagine Nadezda Mandelstam walking the cold roads, memorizing the bits of poems tucked between the pots and pans she carried. Imagine Mandelstam in the camps, speaking to himself the gifts he had made, the poems no one could pluck from his heart."

LAST LINES

No coward soul is mine,
No trembler in the world's storm-troubled sphere!
I see Heaven's glories shine,
And Faith shines equal, arming me from Fear.

O God within my breast,
Almighty ever-present Deity!
Life, that in me hast rest
As I, undying Life, have power in thee!

Vain are the thousand creeds
That move men's hearts, unutterably vain;
Worthless as withered weeds,
Or idlest froth, amid the boundless main

To waken doubt in one
Holding so fast by thy infinity,
So surely anchored on
The steadfast rock of Immortality.

With wide-embracing love
Thy spirit animates eternal years,
Pervades and broods above,
Changes, sustains, dissolves, creates and rears.

Last lines

Though earth and moon were gone,
And suns and universes ceased to be,
And thou were left alone,
Every Existence would exist in thee.

There is not room for Death,
Nor atom that his might could render void,
Since thou art Being and Breath,
And what thou art may never be destroyed.

Emily Brontë
(30 July 1818 – 19 December 1848)

Emily Brontë was christened on this day in St. James' church, Thornton, Yorkshire, in 1818. She died aged 30 at her family home in Haworth, having refused all medical care and believing doctors "poisonous." Her life was, in the words of her poem "The Death of A.G.A.," "stormy and brief."

NUDE DESCENDING A STAIRCASE

Toe upon toe, a snowing flesh,
A gold of lemon, root and rind,
She sifts in sunlight down the stairs
With nothing on. Nor on her mind.

We spy beneath the banister
A constant thresh of thigh on thigh –
Her lips imprint the swinging air
That parts to let her parts go by.

One-woman waterfall, she wears
Her slow descent like a long cape
And pausing, on the final stair
Collects her motions into shape.

X. J. Kennedy
(21 August 1929 -)

X. J. Kennedy comments: "To have this particular poem assigned to my birthday seems fitting. Like most of us, I descended into this world quite as nude as a jaybird. The poem was inspired by Marcel Duchamp's painting of the same title, but describes that work only with very rough fidelity."

X. J. Kennedy was born in Dover, New Jersey. He was raised as a Roman Catholic, although his poetry expresses an often irreverent view of religion. His first volume of poetry, *Nude Descending a Staircase*, won the 1961 Lamont Award. Of late, Kennedy has written mostly verse for children.

ONE PERFECT ROSE

A single flow'r he sent me, since we met.
  All tenderly his messenger he chose;
Deep-hearted, pure, with scented dew still wet –
  One perfect rose.

I knew the language of the floweret;
  'My fragile leaves,' it said, 'his heart enclose.'
Love long has taken for his amulet
  One perfect rose.

Why is it no one ever sent me yet
  One perfect limousine, do you suppose?
Ah no, it's always just my luck to get
  One perfect rose.

Dorothy Parker
(22 August 1893 – 7 June 1967)

Dorothy Parker was born in West End, New Jersey, the daughter of a cloth salesman. Her mother died when she was five. Of her poetic influences Dorothy Parker once remarked: "I was following in the exquisite footsteps of Miss Edna St. Vincent Millay, unhappily in my own horrible sneakers." Renowned for the acerbity with which she commented on the vanity and foolishness of others, she could turn her wit on herself almost as easily. At her 70th birthday party she remarked: "If I had any decency, I'd be dead. Most of my friends are."

MADAM LIFE'S A PIECE IN BLOOM

Madam Life's a piece in bloom
  Death goes dogging everywhere:
She's the tenant of the room,
  He's the ruffian on the stair.

You shall see her as a friend,
  You shall bilk him once or twice;
But he'll trap you in the end,
  And he'll stick you for her price.

With his kneebones at your chest,
  And his knuckles in your throat,
You would reason – plead – protest!
  Clutching at her petticoat;

But she's heard it all before,
  Well she knows you've had your fun,
Gingerly she gains the door,
  And your little job is done.

W. E. Henley
(23 August 1849 - 11 June 1903)

W. E. Henley was born in Gloucester and educated at the Crypt Grammar School, Gloucester. He was crippled by tubercular arthritis as a boy, had a foot amputated, and was in pain most of his life. In the hospital for two years (1873 to 1875), he met R. L. Stevenson, who became a close friend and described him later as burly, boisterous, and piratic. Stevenson used him as his inspiration for his Long John Silver character in *Treasure Island*.

THE BRACELET: TO JULIA

Why I tie about thy wrist,
Julia, this silken twist;
For what other reason is't
But to show thee how, in part,
Thou my pretty captive art?
But thy bond-slave is my heart:
'Tis but silk that bindeth thee,
Knap the thread and thou art free;
But 'tis otherwise with me:
– I am bound and fast bound, so
That from thee I cannot go;
If I could, I would not so.

Robert Herrick
(24 August 1591 – 15 October 1674)

Born into a prosperous family of jewelers, Robert Herrick was sixteen months old when his father died falling from a fourth-floor window in his London home. In due course Robert was apprenticed into the family firm under the (frequently neglectful) eye of his uncle, before going on to St. John's College, Cambridge. Back in London he became one of Ben Jonson's circle and trained as a minister.

Age 38, Herrick was made vicar of Dean Prior in Devon. Though later he became attached to the place, at first he pined from his rural living for the delights of the city. For a time he left without permission from his bishop to live in London with Tomasin Parsons, who was 27 years younger than he.

As a Royalist, he was deprived of his living at Dean Prior by Parliament in 1647. He swore he would revisit the place only when "Rocks turn to rivers, rivers turn to men," but in the event spent the last twelve years of his life there following the Restoration.

SWEET CONTENT

Art thou poor, yet hast thou golden slumbers,
        O sweet content!
Art thou rich, yet is thy mind perplexed?
        O punishment!
Dost thou laugh to see how fools are vexed
To add to golden numbers, golden numbers?
O sweet content! O sweet, O sweet content!
  Work apace, apace, apace, apace;
  Honest labour bears a lovely face;
Then hey nonny nonny, hey nonny nonny!

Canst drink the waters of the crispèd spring?
        O sweet content!
Swimm'st thou in wealth, yet sink'st in thine own tears?
        O punishment!
Then he that patiently want's burden bears
No burden bears, but is a king, a king!
O sweet content! O sweet, O sweet content!
  Work apace, apace, apace, apace;
  Honest labour bears a lovely face;
Then hey nonny nonny, hey nonny nonny!

Thomas Dekker
(?1570 – 25 August 1632)

Thomas Dekker could have done with some "golden numbers," since he went to prison for debt on two occasions, the second time for nearly seven years (from 1612). Nevertheless he is said to have retained a sunny disposition and to have developed a strong sympathy for oppressed people and animals. "Sweet Content," composed some time after his first spell in prison, is the basket maker's song from his play *Patient Grissill* (1603), which was written in collaboration with Chettle and Haughton. In the same year he published a graphic description of the plague in London, *The Wonderful Year*.

The ninth secret poem

I worship your fleece which is the perfect triangle
    Of the Goddess
I am the lumberjack of the only virgin forest
    O my Eldorado
I am the only fish in your voluptuous ocean
    You my lovely Siren
I am the climber on your snowy mountains
    O my whitest Alp
I am the heavenly archer of your beautiful mouth
    O my darling quiver
I am the hauler of your midnight hair
    O lovely ship on the canal of my kisses
And the lilies of your arms are beckoning me
    O my summer garden
The fruits of your breast are ripening their honey for me
    O my sweet-smelling orchard
And I am raising you O Madeleine O my beauty above the earth
    Like the torch of all light

Guillaume Apollinaire
(26 August 1880 – 9 November 1918)
translated by Oliver Bernard

Apollinaire was the illegitimate son of Angelica Kostrowitzky and a Swiss Italian noble-man, Francesco Flugi D'Aspermont, who disappeared very early on from Apollinaire's life. His mother tended to disappear too, once leaving him for the holidays at a hotel in the Ardennes with his younger brother, and at the end of the holidays sending them the rail fare so that they could abscond to Paris without paying the hotel bill.

In Paris Apollinaire became friendly with painters such as Picasso and Braque, brought out a selection of erotic literature, and spent a period in jail on suspicion of having stolen statuettes from the Louvre. His poetry collection *Alcools* came out in 1913. He was wounded in the head by a shell splinter in March 1916 and died in the 1918 influenza epidemic.

from THE PRINCESS

Now sleeps the crimson petal, now the white;
Nor waves the cypress in the palace walk;
Nor winks the gold fin in the porphyry font:
The fire-fly wakens: waken thou with me.

Now droops the milkwhite peacock like a ghost,
And like a ghost she glimmers on to me.

Now lies the Earth all Danae to the stars,
And all thy heart lies open unto me.

Now slides the silent meteor on, and leaves
A shining furrow, as thy thoughts in me.

Now folds the lily all her sweetness up,
And slips into the bosom of the lake:
So fold thyself, my dearest, thou, and slip
Into my bosom and be lost in me.

Alfred, Lord Tennyson
(*6 August 1809 – 6 October 1892*)

Tennyson was fond of declaiming his poetry to a receptive audience. Montague Eliot told how Tennyson used to visit their house in Cornwall. He reckoned it put him off poetry for life – he and the younger children would be sat in the front row for Tennyson's recitals, and they would dread the occurrence of words with *p*'s or *b*'s in them, because then "we children were regaled with a shower of spittle."

A SUBALTERN'S LOVE-SONG

Miss J. Hunter Dunn, Miss J. Hunter Dunn,
Furnish'd and burnish'd by Aldershot sun,
What strenuous singles we played after tea,
We in the tournament – you against me!

Love-thirty, love-forty, oh! weakness of joy,
The speed of a swallow, the grace of a boy,
With carefullest carelessness, gaily you won,
I am weak from your loveliness, Joan Hunter Dunn.

Miss Joan Hunter Dunn, Miss Joan Hunter Dunn
How mad I am, sad I am, glad that you won.
The warm-handled racket is back in its press,
But my shock-headed victor, she loves me no less.

Her father's euonymus° shines as we walk,   *Spindle-tree shrub*
And swing past the summer-house, buried in talk
And cool the verandah that welcomes us in
To the six-o'clock news and a limejuice and gin.

The scent of the conifers, sound of the bath,
The view from my bedroom of moss-dappled path,
As I struggle with double-end evening tie,
For we dance at the Golf Club, my victor and I.

On the floor of her bedroom lie blazer and shorts
And the cream-coloured walls are be-trophied with sports,
And westering, questioning settles the sun
On your low-leaded window, Miss Joan Hunter Dunn.

A SUBALTERN'S LOVE-SONG

The Hillman is waiting, the light's in the hall,
The pictures of Egypt are bright on the wall,
My sweet, I am standing beside the oak stair
And there on the landing's the light on your hair.

By roads 'not adopted,' by woodlanded ways,
She drove to the club in the late summer haze,
Into nine-o'clock Camberley, heavy with bells
And mushroomy, pine-woody, evergreen smells.

Miss Joan Hunter Dunn, Miss Joan Hunter Dunn,
I can hear from the car-park the dance has begun.
Oh! full Surrey twilight! importunate band!
Oh! strongly adorable tennis-girl's hand!

Around us are Rovers and Austins afar,
Above us, the intimate roof of the car,
And here on my right is the girl of my choice,
With the tilt of her nose and the chime of her voice,

And the scent of her wrap, and the words never said,
And the ominous, ominous dancing ahead.
We sat in the car park till twenty to one
And now I'm engaged to Miss Joan Hunter Dunn.

Sir John Betjeman
(28 August 1906 – 19 May 1984)

William Plomer on Sir John Betjeman: "His lifelong love-affair with Edwardian England has included old churches, old railways, old gaslit streets, old country-towns, old dons, and old invalids; it has also given him a distaste for much of what is supposed to represent progress."

TAMER AND HAWK

I thought I was so tough,
But gentled at your hands
Cannot be quick enough
To fly for you and show
That when I go I go
At your commands.

Even in flight above
I am no longer free:
You seeled me with your love,
I am blind to other birds –
The habit of your words
Has hooded me.

As formerly, I wheel
I hover and I twist,
But only want the feel,
In my possessive thought,
Of catcher and of caught
Upon your wrist.

You but half-civilize,
Taming me in this way.
Through having only eyes

Tamer and Hawk

For you I fear to lose,
I lose to keep, and choose
Tamer as prey.

Thom Gunn
(29 August 1929 -)

Thom Gunn was born in Gravesend and raised in Hampstead. After two years National Service, Gunn in 1950 went to Trinity College, Cambridge.

Timothy Steele comments that Donne and Shakespeare "contributed to the formation of his early style, which is exemplified in 'Tamer and Hawk.'"

Thom Gunn settled in San Francisco in 1961, and his poetry since has covered themes from psychedelic drugs (in *Moly*, 1971) to AIDS (in *The Man with Night Sweats*, 1992).

RECENSION DAY

Unburn the boat, rebuild the bridge,
Reconsecrate the sacrilege,
Unspill the milk, decry the tears,
Turn back the clock, relive the years
Replace the smoke inside the fire,
Unite fulfilment with desire,
Undo the done, gainsay the said,
Revitalise the buried dead,
Revoke the penalty and clause,
Reconstitute unwritten laws,
Repair the heart, untie the tongue,
Change faithless old to hopeful young,
Inure the body to disease
And help me to forget you please.

Duncan Forbes
(17 September 1947 -)

Duncan Forbes read English at Corpus Christi College, Oxford, and has worked as a teacher. He is married with a son and daughter. His poetry collections include *August Autumn* (1984), *Public Confidential* (1989), and *Taking Liberties* (1993).

Gavin Ewart has commended him as a poet: "Duncan Forbes has a good sense of reality, and of what Thomas Hardy called 'life's little ironies.'" U. A. Fanthorpe considers his poems "densely written and disturbing"; and in Anthony Thwaite's assessment Forbes is "a poet of many moods, hedonistic, flippant, caustic, comically fanciful, and wistfully puzzled."

VALIANT-FOR-TRUTH'S SONG

Who would true Valour see
Let him come hither;
One here will Constant be,
Come Wind, come Weather.
There's no Discouragement
Shall make him once Relent,
His first avow'd Intent,
To be a Pilgrim.

Who so beset him round,
With dismal Stories,
Do but themselves Confound;
His Strength the more is.
No Lyon can him fright,
He'll with a Giant Fight,
But he will have a right,
To be a Pilgrim.

Hobgoblin, nor foul Fiend,
Can daunt his Spirit:
He knows, he at the end,
Shall Life Inherit.

Then Fancies fly away,
He'll fear not what men say,
He'll labour Night and Day,
To be a Pilgrim.

John Bunyan
(Baptized 30 November 1628 - 31 August 1688)

John Bunyan was born in Elstow, near Bedford, the son of a tinker. He was drafted into the parliamentary army in 1644, and about 1649 married his first wife, a poor woman who brought with her two religious books that had belonged to her father. These books, and Bunyan's own religious experiences, led him in due course to start preaching without a license in the villages around Bedford. He was arrested in November 1660 and spent most of the next twelve years completing the writing of more than nine books in jail. He also began to write *The Pilgrim's Progress*. He was released after the Declaration of Indulgence in 1672, under which he became a licensed preacher, but was rearrested in 1673 when this declaration was canceled. The first part of *The Pilgrim's Progress* was finished during this renewed period of imprisonment. Bunyan died after riding through the rain from Reading to London and was buried in Bunhill Fields.

HURRAHING IN HARVEST

Summer ends now; now, barbarous in beauty, the stooks arise
  Around; up above, what wind-walks! what lovely behaviour
  Of silk-sack clouds! has wilder, wilful-wavier
Meal-drift moulded ever and melted across skies?

I walk, I lift up, I lift up heart, eyes,
  Down all that glory in the heavens to glean our Saviour;[1]
  And, éyes, heárt, what looks, what lips yet gave you a
Rapturous love's greeting of realer, of rounder replies?

And the azurous hung hills are his world-wielding shoulder
  Majestic – as a stallion stalwart, very-violet-sweet! –
These things, these things were here and but the beholder
  Wanting; which two when they once meet,
The heart réars wíngs bold and bolder
  And hurls for him, O half hurls earth for him off under his feet.

Gerard Manley Hopkins
(28 July 1844 – 8 June 1889)

Hopkins wrote this sonnet on this day in 1877, whilst in the Vale of Clwyd in Wales. He
noted that "The Hurrahing sonnet was the outcome of half an hour of extreme enthusiasm as I walked home alone one day from fishing in the Elwy."

1. To gather the knowledge of Christ as gleaners gather corn during the harvest.

AT PARTING

Since we through war awhile must part
Sweetheart, and learn to lose
Daily use
Of all that satisfied our heart:
Lay up those secrets and those powers
Wherewith you pleased and cherished me these two years.

Now we must draw, as plants would,
On tubers stored in a better season,
Our honey and heaven;
Only our love can store such food.
Is this to make a god of absence?
A new-born monster to steal our sustenance?

We cannot quite cast out lack and pain.
Let him remain – what he may devour
We can well spare:
He never can tap this, the true vein.
I have no words to tell you what you were,
But when you are sad, think, Heaven could give no more.

Anne Ridler
(30 July 1912 -)

On this day in 1939, the day after Britain demanded that Germany halt its invasion of Poland, all places of entertainment in London were closed in case of bombing.
Anne Ridler writes: "The parting was not to be a final one, for we have lived to celebrate our Golden Wedding. But it was hard enough to bear: we had only been married two years, and our first child was on the way. My husband was posted to the RAF base in Scapa Flow, Orkney, and I was able to join him there for a few months before he was sent to West Africa."
Her *Collected Poems* are published by Carcanet Press, Manchester (October 1994).

COMPOSED UPON WESTMINSTER BRIDGE

3 SEPTEMBER 1802

Earth has not anything to show more fair:
Dull would he be of soul who could pass by
A sight so touching in its majesty:
This city now doth, like a garment, wear
The beauty of the morning; silent, bare,
Ships, towers, domes, theatres, and temples lie
Open unto the fields, and to the sky;
All bright and glittering in the smokeless air.
Never did sun more beautifully steep
In his first splendour, valley, rock, or hill;
Ne'er saw I, never felt, a calm so deep!
The river glideth at his own sweet will:
Dear God! the very houses seem asleep;
And all that mighty heart is lying still!

William Wordsworth
(7 April 1770 – 23 April 1850)

Wordsworth completed this sonnet on this day in 1802. William's sister Dorothy wrote in her Grasmere Journal for 1802: "After various troubles and disasters we left London at half past 5 or 6 (I have forgot which). We mounted the Dover coach at Charing Cross. It was a beautiful morning. The City, St. Paul's, with the River and a multitude of little Boats, made a beautiful sight as we crossed Westminster Bridge. The houses were not overhung by their cloud of smoke and they were spread out endlessly, yet the sun shone so brightly with such a pure light that there was even something like the purity of one of nature's own good spectacles."

THE FASCINATION OF WHAT'S DIFFICULT

The fascination of what's difficult
Has dried the sap out of my veins, and rent
Spontaneous joy and natural content
Out of my heart. There's something ails our colt
That must, as if it had not holy blood
Nor on Olympus leaped from cloud to cloud,
Shiver under the lash, strain, sweat and jolt
As though it dragged road-metal. My curse on plays
That have to be set up in fifty ways,
On the day's war with every knave and dolt,
Theatre business, management of men.
I swear before the dawn comes round again
I'll find the stable and pull out the bolt.

William Butler Yeats
(13 June 1865 - 28 January 1939)

In September 1909, Yeats wrote an outline of this poem in his diary: "Subject. To complain at the fascination of what's difficult. It spoils spontaneity and pleasure, and wastes time." Daniel Albright believes that this poem "anticipates Yeats' surrender, eight years later, to his wife's trances of automatic writing, and other strategies of self-liberation."

from AS YOU LIKE IT
ACT II SCENE V

Amiens. Under the greenwood tree,
  Who loves to lie with me,
  And turn his merry note
  Unto the sweet bird's throat,
Come hither, come hither, come hither:
    Here shall he see
    No enemy
But winter and rough weather.

Amiens, Jaques and others.
  Who doth ambition shun,
  And loves to live i' the sun,
  Seeking the food he eats,
  And pleased with what he gets,
Come hither, come hither, come hither:
    Here shall he see
    No enemy
But winter and rough weather.

William Shakespeare
(23 April 1564 – 23 April 1616)

On this day in 1571, Shakespeare's father John was appointed chief alderman for Stratford.

"Greenwood tree" songs were a familiar genre in Shakespeare's time. It has been suggested that it is used here partly to suggest scenery where perhaps there was none. (Thomas Hardy's novel *Under the Greeenwood Tree* came out in 1872.)

IN DEATH VALLEY

There came gray stretches of volcanic plains,
Bare, lone and treeless, then a bleak lone hill,
Like to the dolorous hill that Dobell saw.
Around were heaps of ruins piled between
The Burn 'o Sorrow and the Water o' Care;
And from the stillness of the down-crushed walls
One pillar rose up dark against the moon.
There was a nameless Presence everywhere;
In the gray soil there was a purple stain,
And the gray reticent rocks were dyed with blood –
Blood of a vast unknown Calamity.
It was the mark of some ancestral grief –
Grief that began before the ancient Flood.

Edwin Markham
(23 April 1852 – 7 March 1940)

In California, Markham was a schoolteacher, superintendent of schools, and principal. When the *San Francisco Examiner* published "The Man with the Hoe" in 1899, Markham gained immediate celebrity and moved to New York City where he entertained numerous literary figures during his Sunday salons. Such was his popularity that Carnegie Hall was the venue for marking the occasion of eightieth birthday.

FALL

So it's today, and in the chokecherry this year:
the first leaves turn ochre, there, by the open gate.

I grab the sweater you left on a chair, wrap it
around my shoulders, and – as I did for days last year

until I couldn't keep up with the season – I pick
every single rusting leaf, each fading flower

and hide them in my apron pocket: their crush
clandestine against my belly. It's a simple gift

for you – for us – such an easy thing to do
for a few more days of summer.

Laure-Anne Bosselaar
(17 November 1943 –)

Belgian-born, Laure-Anne Bosselaar comments: "The day I wrote this poem, our two children had just left for their second year in college. Our garden and house were eerily still. Suddenly, a most ordinary fact struck me with extraordinary force: I was aging and my child-bearing years were over. The poem's central metaphor describes an ultimately useless act against the usual encroachments of time."

Laure-Anne Bosselaar's first book of verse in English will be published in 1997 by BOA Editions, Ltd. The poet makes her home in Cambridge, Massachusetts with her husband Kurt Brown.

EVERYONE SANG

Everyone suddenly burst out singing;
And I was filled with such delight
As prisoned birds must find in freedom,
Winging wildly across the white
Orchards and dark-green fields; on – on – and out of sight.

Everyone's voice was suddenly lifted;
And beauty came like the setting sun:
My heart was shaken with tears; and horror
Drifted away ... O, but Everyone
Was a bird; and the song was wordless; the singing will never
be done.

Siegfried Sassoon
(8 September 1886 – 1 September 1967)

Siegfried Sassoon was born in Kent into a privileged, artistic family of Persian-Jewish origin. His parents divorced, his father died early, he was sickly as a child, and he failed to take a degree at Clare College, Cambridge. He volunteered on the first day of the Great War, won the MC for bringing back a wounded lance-corporal under heavy fire, and was recommended, unsuccessfully, for a VC, after capturing a German trench single-handed. Agonized by the horrors of the trenches, he threw his MC into the Mersey, and his letter protesting the war was read out in the House of Commons. He attempted to have himself court-martialed for desertion, but was rescued by his friend Robert Graves who wangled him a place in the hospital at Craiglockhart under a diagnosis of shellshock. Here he met Wilfred Owen, who greeted him "as a man; as a friend and a poet":
"Know that since mid-September, when you still regarded me as a tiresome little knocker on your door, I hold you as Keats + Christ + Elijah + my Colonel + my father-confessor + Amenophis IV in profile."
Sasson was discharged and eventually rejoined his former battalion in France. He was wounded in the head on 13 July 1918 and spent the remainder of the war on sick leave.
In 1957 he became a Roman Catholic. Some of his devotional poems remain unpublished. He himself preferred his later poetry to his war poems, which were, he claimed, "improvised by an impulsive, intolerant, immature young creature under the extreme stress of experience" – ingredients that could be deemed, however, to constitute a near-perfect recipe for interesting and unusual poetry.

GUNGA DIN

You may talk o' gin and beer
When you're quartered safe out 'ere,
An' you're sent to penny-fights an' Aldershot it;
But when it comes to slaughter
You will do your work on water,
An' you'll lick the bloomin' boots of 'im that's got it.
Now in Injia's sunny clime,
Where I used to spend my time
A-servin' of 'Er Majesty the Queen,
Of all them blackfaced crew
The finest man I knew
Was our regimental *bhisti*, Gunga Din.
     He was 'Din! Din! Din!
  You limpin' lump o' brick-dust, Gunga Din!
    Hi! Slippy *hitherao!*
    Water, get it! *Panee lao,*
  You squidgy-nosed old idol, Gunga Din.'

The uniform 'e wore
Was nothin' much before,
An' rather less than 'arf o' that be'ind,
For a piece o' twisty rag
An' a goatskin water-bag
Was all the field-equipment 'e could find.
When the sweatin' troop-train lay
In a sidin' through the day,
Where the 'eat would make your bloomin' eyebrows crawl,
We shouted 'Harry By!'
Till our throats were bricky-dry,
Then we wopped 'im 'cause 'e couldn't serve us all.

It was 'Din! Din! Din!
You 'eathen, where the mischief 'ave you been?
    You put some juldee in it
    Or I'll marrow you this minute
If you don't fill up my helmet, Gunga Din!'

'E would dot an' carry one
Till the longest day was done;
An' 'e didn't seem to know the use o' fear.
If we charged or broke or cut,
You could bet your bloomin' nut,
'E'd be waitin' fifty paces right flank rear.
With 'is *mussick* on 'is back,
'E would skip with our attack,
An' watch us till the bugles made 'Retire',
An' for all 'is dirty 'ide
'E was white, clear white, inside
When 'e went to tend the wounded under fire!
    It was 'Din! Din! Din!'
  With the bullets kickin' dust-spots on the green.
    When the cartridges ran out,
    You could hear the front-ranks shout,
  'Hi! ammunition-mules an' Gunga Din!'

I shan't forgit the night
When I dropped be'ind the fight
With a bullet where my belt-plate should'a' been.
I was chokin' mad with thirst,
An' the man that spied me first
Was our good old grinnin', gruntin' Gunga Din.

E lifted up my 'ead,
   An' he plugged me where I bled,
   An' 'e guv me 'arf-a-pint o' water green.
It was crawlin' and it stunk,
But of all the drinks I've drunk,
I'm gratefullest to one from Gunga Din.
      It was 'Din! Din! Din!
   'Ere's a beggar with a bullet through 'is spleen;
      'E's chawin' up the ground,
      An' 'e's kickin' all around:
   For Gawd's sake git the water, Gunga Din!'

'E carried me away
To where a *dooli* lay,
An' a bullet come an' drilled the beggar clean.
'E put me safe inside,
An' just before 'e died,
'I 'ope you liked your drink,' sez Gunga Din.
So I'll meet 'im later on
At the place where 'e is gone –
Where it's always double drill and no canteen.
'E'll be squattin' on the coals
Givin' drink to poor damned souls
An' I'll get a swig in hell from Gunga Din!
      Yes, Din! Din! Din!
   You Lazarushian-leather Gunga Din!
      Though I've belted you and flayed you,
      By the livin' Gawd that made you,
   You're a better man than I am, Gunga Din!

Rudyard Kipling
(30 December 1865 – 18 January 1936)

Pied beauty

Glory be to God for dappled things –
  For skies of couple-colour as a brinded[1] cow;
    For rose-moles all in stipple upon trout that swim;
Fresh fire-coal chestnut-falls; finches' wings;
  Landscape plotted and pieced – fold, fallow, and plough;
    And áll trádes, their gear and tackle and trim.

All things counter, original, spare, strange;
  Whatever is fickle, freckled (who knows how?)
    With swift, slow; sweet, sour; adazzle, dim;
He fathers-forth whose beauty is past change:
                    Praise him.

Gerard Manley Hopkins
(28 July 1844 – 8 June 1889)

On this day in 1864, Hopkins in a letter to A. W. M. Baillie derided Tennyson's Parnassian style – the way the poet saw and described things "without further effort of inspiration."

1. Streaked.

PIANO

Softly, in the dusk, a woman is singing to me;
Taking me back down the vista of years, till I see
A child sitting under the piano, in the boom of the tingling strings
And pressing the small, poised feet of a mother who smiles as she sings.

In spite of myself, the insidious mastery of song
Betrays me back, till the heart of me weeps to belong
To the old Sunday evenings at home, with winter outside
And hymns in the cozy parlour, the tinkling piano our guide.

So now it is vain for the singer to burst into clamour
With the great black piano appassionato. The glamour
Of childish days is upon me, my manhood is cast
Down in the flood of remembrance, I weep like a child for the past.

D. H. Lawrence
(11 September 1885 - 2 March 1930)

Lawrence, whose early universe was passionately centered on his mother, remembered
asking himself as a child, "why God was a man, not a woman. In heaven, God was the
fount of right and wrong, and on earth, woman. Woman knows best. Man didn't care.
God knows best of all – That was my childish argument of the moral scheme." Lawrence
was the son of a Nottingham miner, who drank and bullied him, and his mother encouraged the boy to escape the mines through an education. When he was 26, his mother
died and he became seriously ill, but recovered sufficiently to elope with Frieda Weekley,
a mother of three children and six years his senior.

PEOPLE LIKE US

When the ox was the gray enemy
of the forest and engine of the plow,
the poor drifted across the fields,
through the sweet grasses and the vile,
and tendered bare bowls at our doors.
We hoarded and they begged. We stacked
our hayricks high and they slept there
like barncats or cuckoos.

When we sluiced the maculate streets
with fermenting slops, and strode to our jobs
furred by coaldust, didn't the poor
punctuate our routines with cries
for alms? Our sclerotic rivers
turned the color of old leather
and the poor fished them anyway
and slept under their bridges.

Now they come flaring up the stairs
and up the fire escapes. Open our door
to them and then they're us,
and if we don't we're trapped inside
with only us for company
while in the hall they pray and sing
their lilting anthems of reproach
while we bite our poor tongues.

William Matthews
(11 November 1942 -)

THE SOLITARY REAPER

Behold her, single in the field,
Yon solitary Highland lass,
Reaping and singing by herself,
Stop here, or gently pass.
Alone she cuts and binds the grain,
And sings a melancholy strain;
O listen, for the vale profound
Is overflowing with the sound.

No Nightingale did ever chaunt
More welcome notes to weary bands
Of travellers in some shady haunt,
Among Arabian sands;
A voice so thrilling ne'er was heard
In spring-time from the Cuckoo-bird,
Breaking the silence of the seas
Among the farthest Hebrides.

Will no one tell me what she sings? –
Perhaps the plaintive numbers flow
For old unhappy far-off things
And battles long ago;
Or is it some more humble lay,
Familiar matter of to-day?
Some natural sorrow, loss or pain,
That has been and may be again?

THE SOLITARY REAPER

Whate'er the theme, the Maiden sang
As if her song could have no ending;
I saw her singing at her work,
And o'er the sickle bending; –
I listened, motionless and still;
And, as I mounted up the hill,
The music in my heart I bore,
Long after it was heard no more.

William Wordsworth
(7 April 1770 – 23 April 1850)

Dorothy Wordsworth wrote in her journal for 13 September 1803 (during a tour that she and her brother made in Scotland): "It was harvest-time and the fields were quietly (might I be allowed to say passively?) enlivened by small companies of reapers. It is not uncommon in the more lonely parts of the Highlands to see a single person so employed."

THE SICK ROSE

O rose, thou art sick!
The invisible worm
That flies in the night,
In the howling storm,

Has found out thy bed
Of crimson joy:
And his dark secret love
Does thy life destroy.

William Blake
(28 November 1757 - 12 August 1827)

Blake's design for this poem has a rose drooping around the text, with a caterpillar eating one of its leaves, and a spirit expelled from the flower's closed center.

The theme is erotic love. The merely sensuous worm enters the rose and drives out the spirit of joy, of authentic love. The caterpillar is the Church, with its sick preoccupation with sex as sin, eating away a life-giving leaf. Blake's pictures are not just visual representations of his text. They tell different parts of the story in visual counterpoint.

from IN MEMORIAM A. H. H.

XXVII

I envy not in any moods
   The captive void of noble rage,
   The linnet born within the cage,
That never knew the summer woods:

I envy not the beast that takes
   His license in the field of time,
   Unfetter'd by the sense of crime,
To whom a conscience never wakes;

Nor, what may count itself as blest,
   The heart that never plighted troth
   But stagnates in the weeds of sloth,
Nor any want-begotten rest.

I hold it true, whate'er befall;
   I feel it when I sorrow most;
   'Tis better to have loved and lost
Than never to have loved at all.

Alfred, Lord Tennyson
(6 August 1809 – 6 October 1892)

Tennyson started writing this poem in 1833, and dedicated it to the memory of Arthur Henry Hallam who died in Vienna on 15 September 1833, while traveling with his father. Hallam had been Tennyson's close friend at Cambridge, and the previous year, with both still in their early twenties, they had traveled together on the Continent. Tennyson said of *In Memoriam* that "it must be remembered that this is a poem, *not* an actual biography. It is founded on our friendship, on the engagement of Arthur Hallam to my sister, on his sudden death at Vienna, just before the time fixed for their marriage, and on his burial at Clevedon Church."

THE EMBANKMENT
(THE FANTASIA OF A FALLEN GENTLEMAN ON A COLD, BITTER NIGHT)

Once, in finesse of fiddles found I ecstasy,
In a flash of gold heels on the hard pavement.
Now see I
That warmth's the very stuff of poesy.
Oh, God, make small
The old star-eaten blanket of the sky,
That I may fold it round me and in comfort lie.

T. E. Hulme

(16 September 1883 - 28 September 1917)

T. E. Hulme is yet another poet to have been killed in World War I – serving with the Royal Marine Artillery. His *Complete Poetical Works* (five poems, the longest being of nine lines) were printed in admiration by Ezra Pound as an addendum to the latter's *Ripostes* (1912). Eliot said of Hulme that he was "classical, reactionary, and revolutionary . . . the antipodes of the eccentric, tolerant, and democratic mind of the end of the century."

Hulme was born in Endon, Staffordshire, and was expelled from St. John's College, Cambridge, possibly for brawling (he is said to have carried a knuckle-duster around with him). In 1908, while living in London, he joined the "experimental" Poets' Club.

THE DIRGE OF ST. MALO

Alas! young men, come, make lament
For poor St. Malo in distress!
They chased, they hunted him with dogs,
They fired at him with a gun,

They hauled him from the cypress swamp.
His arms they tied behind his back,
They tied his hands in front of him;
They tied him to a horse's tail,
They dragged him up into the town.
Before those grand Cabildo men
They charged that he had made a plot
To cut the throats of all the whites.
They asked him who his comrades were,
Poor St. Malo said not a word!
The judge his sentence read to him,
And then they raised the gallows-tree.
They drew the horse – the cart moved off –
And left St. Malo hanging there.
The sun was up an hour high
When on the Levee he was hung;
They left his body swinging there,
For carrion crows to feed upon.

George Washington Cable
(12 October 1844 - 31 January 1925)

Born in New Orleans, Cable was a self-educated man. In his attempts to further his
learning, he discovered the records of the French speaking natives of Louisiana. A series
of novels which addressed the issue of slavery in the South resulted from the mining of
these archives. In 1886, he published translations of Creole slave songs.

335

18 SEPTEMBER

No worst, there is none

No worst, there is none. Pitched past pitch of grief,
More pangs will, schooled at forepangs, wilder wring.
Comforter, where, where is your comforting?
Mary, mother of us, where is your relief?
My cries heave, herds-long; huddle in a main, a chief
Woe, world-sorrow; on an age-old anvil wince and sing –
Then lull, then leave off. Fury had shrieked 'No ling-
ering! Let me be fell: force I must be brief.'

O the mind, mind has mountains; cliffs of fall
Frightful, sheer, no-man-fathomed. Hold them cheap
May who ne'er hung there. Nor does long our small
Durance deal with that steep or deep. Here! creep,
Wretch, under a comfort serves in a whirlwind: all
Life death does end and each day dies with sleep.

Gerard Manley Hopkins
(28 July 1844 - 8 June 1889)

On this day in 1873 Hopkins wrote: "I had a nightmare last night. I thought something or someone leapt on me and held me quite fast: this I think woke me . . . so that I could speak, whispering at first, then louder . . . thinking I could recover myself if I could move my finger . . . and then the arm and so the whole body. The feeling is terrible . . . I cried on the holy name and by degrees recovered myself . . . It made me think that this was how the souls in hell would be imprisoned in their bodies."

This sonnet was probably one of the ones Hopkins referred to in his letter of 1 September 1885 to Robert Bridges in which he wrote, "Four of these [sonnets] came like inspiration unbidden and against my will." Previously he had written to Bridges: "I think that my fits of sadness, though they do not affect my judgment, resemble madness . . . I must absolutely have encouragement as much as crops rain."

To autumn

Season of mists and mellow fruitfulness,
  Close bosom-friend of the maturing sun;
Conspiring with him how to load and bless
  With fruit the vines that round the thatch-eaves run;
To bend with apples the mossed cottage-trees,
  And fill all fruit with ripeness to the core;
    To swell the gourd, and plump the hazel shells
  With a sweet kernel; to set budding more,
And still more, later flowers for the bees,
Until they think warm days will never cease,
    For Summer has o'er-brimmed their clammy cells.

Who hath not seen thee oft amid thy store?
  Sometimes whoever seeks abroad may find
Thee sitting careless on a granary floor,
  Thy hair soft-lifted by the winnowing wind;
Or on a half-reaped furrow sound asleep,
  Drowsed with the fume of poppies, while thy hook°   *sickle*
    Spares the next swath and all its twinèd flowers:
And sometimes like a gleaner° thou dost keep   *corn gatherer*
  Steady thy laden head across a brook;
Or by a cider-press, with patient look,
    Thou watchest the last oozings hours by hours.

Where are the songs of Spring? Aye, where are they?
  Think not of them, thou hast thy music too –
While barrèd clouds bloom the soft-dying day,
  And touch the stubble-plains with rosy hue;

To autumn

Then in a wailful choir the small gnats mourn
  Among the river sallows,° borne aloft   *willows*
    Or sinking as the light wind lives or dies;
And full-grown lambs loud bleat from hilly bourn;
  Hedge crickets sing; and now with treble soft
  The redbreast whistles from a garden-croft;
    And gathering swallows twitter in the skies.

John Keats
(31 October 1795 - 23 February 1821)

Keats wrote "To Autumn" on this day in 1819. That month he wrote: "I 'kepen in solitari-
ness' for Brown has gone a-visiting. I am surprised myself at the pleasure I live alone in.
How beautiful the season is now – how fine the air. A temperate sharpness about it – I
never liked stubble fields so much as now – Aye better than the chilly green of the
Spring. Somehow a stubble field looks warm – in the same way that some pictures look
warm. This struck me so much on my Sunday's walk that I composed upon it . . . Oh how
I admire the middlesized delicate Devonshire girls of about fifteen. There was one at the
inn door holding a quatern of brandy – the very thought of her kept me warm a whole
stage – and a 16 miler too."

THE HEAVENLY CITY

I sigh for the heavenly country,
Where the heavenly people pass,
And the sea is as quiet as a mirror
Of beautiful, beautiful glass.

I walk in the heavenly field,
With lilies and poppies bright,
I am dressed in a heavenly coat
Of polished white.

When I walk in the heavenly parkland
My feet on the pastures are bare,
Tall waves the grass, but no harmful
Creature is there.

At night I fly over the housetops,
And stand on the bright moony beams;
Gold are all heaven's rivers,
And silver her streams.

Stevie Smith
(20 September 1902 – 7 March 1971)

"I can't make up my mind," Stevie Smith once wrote, "if God is good, impotent, or unkind." In this untypically positive poem she could be Blake reincarnated as Emily Dickinson.

SUZANNE TAKES YOU DOWN

Suzanne takes you down to her place near the river,
You can hear the boats go by
You can spend the night beside her.
And you know that she's half crazy
But that's why you want to be there
And she feeds you tea and oranges
That come all the way from China.
And just when you mean to tell her
That you have no love to give her,
Then she gets you on her wavelength
And she lets the river answer
That you've always been her lover.
And you want to travel with her,
And you want to travel blind
And you know that she will trust you
For you've touched her perfect body with your mind.

And Jesus was a sailor
When he walked upon the water
And he spent a long time watching
From his lonely wooden tower
And when he knew for certain
Only drowning men could see him
He said 'All men will be sailors then
Until the sea shall free them,'
But he himself was broken
Long before the sky would open,
Forsaken, almost human,
He sank beneath your wisdom like a stone.
And you want to travel with him,

Suzanne takes you down

And you want to travel blind
And you think maybe you'll trust him
For he's touched your perfect body with his mind.

Now Suzanne takes your hand,
And she leads you to the river,
She is wearing rags and feathers
From Salvation Army counters.
And the sun pours down like honey
on our lady of the harbour
And she shows you where to look
Among the garbage and the flowers
There are heroes in the seaweed
There are children in the morning
They are leaning out for love
And they will lean that way forever
While Suzanne holds the mirror.
And you want to travel with her
And you want to travel blind
And you know you can trust her
For she's touched your perfect body with her mind.

Leonard Cohen
(*21 September 1934 -*)

Over two decades since the composition of this song, Cohen, on tour as the dark guru of the disaffected and despondent, is as popular as ever. Of his gifts as a poet, D. D. C. Chambers has written: "The figures in Leonard Cohen's poems rise like figures in Chagall, transformed from the ordinary, surprised into a world of visionary experience. Out of the junk of the everyday – the 'garbage and the flowers' – the magical world of the imaginative is created. There is a strong sense in which his poetry is a prodigious search of experience for the exit from the ordinary."

ROSALYNDE'S MADRIGAL

Love in my bosome like a Bee
   doth sucke his sweete:
Now with his wings he playes with me,
   now with his feete.
  Within mine eyes he makes his nest,
  His bed amidst my tender breast,
  My kisses are his daily feast;
  And yet he robs me of my rest.
    Ah wanton, will ye?

And if I sleepe, then pearcheth he
   with prettie flight,
And makes his pillow of my knee
   the livelong night.
  Strike I my lute, he tunes the string;
  He musicke playes if so I sing,
  He lends me everie lovelie thing,
  Yet cruell he my heart doth sting.
    Whist wanton, still ye.

Else I with roses everie day
   will whip you hence;
And binde you when you long to play,
   for your offence.
  Ile shut mine eyes to keepe you in,
  Ile make you fast it for your sinne,
  Ile count your power not worth a pinne;
  Alas what hereby shall I winne
    If he gainsay me?

ROSALYNDE'S MADRIGAL

What if I beate the wanton boy
   with manie a rod?
He will repay me with annoy,
   because a God.
  Then sit thou safely on my knee,
  Then let thy bowre my bosome be:
  Lurke in mine eyes I like of thee;
  Oh Cupid so thou pitie me.
    Spare not but play thee.

Thomas Lodge
(ca. 1556 - September 1625)

On this day in 1589, Thomas Lodge's first volume of verse, *Romance Rosa*, was licensed for the press. "Rosalynde" ("in tedious prose enlivened by lyrics") was written on his voyage to the Canaries and published in 1850. Thomas Lodge was born in Lincolnshire. His father became Lord Mayor of London, but went bankrupt while Lodge was a student. After 1596, no longer wishing "to ravel out his wits in rhyme," Lodge's writing was primarily religious and scientific treatises, having converted to Roman Catholicism and taken his M.D. from Oxford in 1602.

EGYPT'S MIGHT IS TUMBLED DOWN

Egypt's might is tumbled down
  Down a-down the deeps of thought;
Greece is fallen and Troy town,
Glorious Rome hath lost her crown,
  Venice' pride is nought.

But the dreams their children dreamed
  Fleeting, unsubstantial, vain.
Shadowy as the shadows seemed
Airy nothing, as they deemed,
  These remain.

Mary Coleridge
(23 September 1861 – 25 August 1907)

Mary Coleridge was born in London and educated at home. She was the great-great grandaughter of Samuel Taylor Coleridge's elder brother. Her family were on visiting terms with Browning, Tennyson, Millais, and Robert Bridges, and it was the latter who encouraged her to publish her first poetry collection, *Fanny's Following*, in 1896.

After the death of her mother in 1898, she stayed at home to help her sister look after their father, publishing novels, essays, and further poetry.

from[1] JUBILATE AGNO[2]

For I will consider my Cat Jeoffry.

For he is the servant of the Living God duly and daily serving him.

For at the first glance of the glory of God in the East he worships in his way.

For this done by wreathing his body seven times round with elegant
quickness.

For then he leaps up to catch the musk, which is the blessing of God upon his
prayer.

For he rolls upon prank to work it in.

For having done duty and received blessing he begins to consider himself.

For this he performs in ten degrees.

For first he looks upon his fore-paws to see if they are clean.

For secondly he kicks up behind to clear away there.

For thirdly he works it upon stretch with the fore paws extended.

For fourthly he sharpens his paws by wood.

For fifthly he washes himself.

For Sixthly he rolls upon wash.

For Seventhly he fleas himself, that he may not be interrupted upon the beat.

For Eighthly he rubs himself against a post.

For Ninthly he looks up for his instructions.

For Tenthly he goes in quest of food.

For having consider'd God and himself he will consider his neighbour.

For if he meets another cat he will kiss her in kindness.

For when he takes his prey he plays with it to give it a chance.

For one mouse in seven escapes by his dallying.

For when his day's work is done his business more properly begins.

For he keeps the Lord's watch in the night against the adversary.

For he counteracts the powers of darkness by his electrical skin & glaring eyes.

For he counteracts the Devil, who is death, by brisking about the life.

For in his morning orisons he loves the sun and the sun loves him.

For he is of the tribe of Tiger.

from JUBILATE AGNO

For the Cherub Cat is a term of the Angel Tiger.
For he has the subtlety and hissing of a serpent, which in goodness he
        suppresses.
For he will not do destruction if he is well-fed, neither will he spit without
        provocation.
For he purrs in thankfulness, when God tells him he's a good Cat.
For he is an instrument for the children to learn benevolence upon.
For every house is incompleat without him & a blessing is lacking in the spirit.
For the Lord commanded Moses concerning the cats at the departure of the
        Children of Israel from Egypt.
For every family had one cat at least in the bag.
For the English Cats are the best in Europe.
For he is the cleanest in the use of his fore-paws of any quadrupede.
For the dexterity of his defence is an instance of the love of God to him
        exceedingly.
For he is the quickest to his mark of any creature.
For he is tenacious of his point.
For he is a mixture of gravity and waggery.
For he knows that God is his Saviour.
For there is nothing sweeter than his peace when at rest.
For there is nothing brisker than his life when in motion.
For he is of the Lord's poor and so indeed is he called by benevolence
        perpetually – Poor Jeoffry! poor Jeoffry! the rat has bit thy throat.
For I bless the name of the Lord Jesus that Jeoffry is better.
For the divine spirit comes about his body to sustain it in compleat cat.
For his tongue is exceeding pure so that it has in purity what it wants in
        musick.
For he is docile and can learn certain things.
For he can set up with gravity which is patience upon approbation.
For he can fetch and carry, which is patience in employment.

from JUBILATE AGNO

For he can jump over a stick which is patience upon proof positive.

For he can spraggle upon waggle at the word of command.

For he can jump from an eminence into his master's bosom.

For he can catch the cork and toss it again.

For he is hated by the hypocrite and miser.

For the former is afraid of detection.

For the latter refuses the charge.

For he camels his back to bear the first notion of business.

For he is good to think on, if a man would express himself neatly.

For he made a great figure in Egypt for his signal services.

For he killed the Icneumon-rat very pernicious by land.

For his ears are so acute that they sting again.

For from this proceeds the passing quickness of his attention.

For by stroaking of him I have found out electricity.

For I have perceived God's light about him both wax and fire.

For the Electrical fire is the spiritual substance, which God sends from heaven
     to sustain the bodies both of man and beast.

For God has blessed him in the variety of his movements.

For, tho he cannot fly, he is an excellent clamberer.

For his motions upon the face of the earth are more than any other
     quadrupede.

For he can tread to all measures upon the musick.

For he can swim for life.

For he can creep.

Christopher Smart
(11 April 1722 - 21 May 1771)

1. Lines 697 to 770. Half a dozen fragments of the poem survive, 1,575 lines in total.
2. "Rejoice in the Lamb" (Jesus, the Lamb of God). Smart wrote "Jubilate Agno" while he
was confined in an asylum for the insane. He described it as "my Magnificat."

ANTHEM FOR DOOMED YOUTH

What passing-bells for these who die as cattle?
  Only the monstrous anger of the guns.
  Only the stuttering rifles' rapid rattle
Can patter out their hasty orisons.
No mockeries for them from prayers or bells,
  Nor any voice of mourning save the choirs, –
The shrill, demented choirs of wailing shells;
  And bugles calling for them from sad shires.

What candles may be held to speed them all?
Not in the hands of boys, but in their eyes
Shall shine the holy glimmers of good-byes.
  The pallor of girls' brows shall be their pall;
Their flowers the tenderness of silent minds,
And each slow dusk a drawing-down of blinds.

Wilfred Owen
(18 March 1893 – 4 November 1918)

Owen sent this poem to his mother on 25 September 1917 from the Craiglockhart War Hospital in Edinburgh where he was recovering from shell shock. Here he met the poet Siegfried Sassoon, an army officer and war protester whom the authorities preferred to treat as shell-shocked. The poem was provoked by remarks in *Poems of Today* about a poet who had supposedly gone "singing to lay down his life for his country's cause." The poem's first draft was largely unrhymed. Sassoon suggested "Anthem for Dead Youth" as a title, which Owen changed to "Doomed Youth." On reading the fifth and final draft, Sassoon realized "that my little friend was much more than the promising minor poet I had hitherto acknowledged him to be. I now realized that his verse, with its sumptuous epithets and large-scale imagery, its noble naturalness and the depth of meaning, had impressive affinities with Keats, whom he took as his supreme exemplar. This new sonnet was a revelation . . . It confronted me with classic and imaginative serenity."

from YESTERDAY HE STILL LOOKED IN MY EYES

Yesterday he still looked in my eyes, yet
　　today　his looks are bent aside.　Yesterday
he sat here until the birds began, but
　　today,　all those larks are　ravens.

Yesterday he lay at my feet. He even
　　compared me with the Chinese Empire! Then
suddenly he let his hands fall open, and
　　my life fell out like　a rusty kopek.

I know everything, don't argue with me!
　　I can see now, I'm a lover no longer.
And now I know wherever love holds power
　　Death approaches soon　like a gardener.

It is almost like shaking a tree, in time
　　some ripe apple comes falling down. So
for everything, for everything　forgive me,
　　– my love　whatever it was I did to you.

Marina Tsvetayeva
(26 September 1892 – 31 August 1941)
translated by Elaine Feinstein
(14 October 1930 –)

Marina Tsvetayeva was born in Moscow, her father a professor of fine arts. Her mother, a gifted pianist, died of tuberculosis when Marina was 14. During the Moscow famine, Marina was forced to put her younger daughter in an orphanage, where she died of hunger in 1919. In 1939, her daughter Adriana was arrested and shot and her husband, Sergei Efron, was arrested. Marina was evacuated to Elabuga in the Tatar Autonomous Republic, where she hanged herself.

MY BOY JACK

'Have you news of my boy Jack?'
  Not this tide.
'When d'you think that he'll come back?'
  Not with this wind blowing, and this tide.

'Has anyone else had word of him?'
  Not this tide.
For what is sunk will hardly swim,
  Not with this wind blowing and this tide.

'Oh, dear, what comfort can I find?'
  None this tide,
  Nor any tide,
Except he did not shame his kind –
  Not even with that wind blowing, and that tide.

Then hold your head up all the more,
  This tide,
  And every tide;
Because he was the son you bore,
  And gave to that wind blowing and that tide!

Rudyard Kipling
(30 December 1865 – 18 January 1936)

Kipling's son John was killed in the Battle of Loos on 27 September 1915. Kipling conducted a two-year search in vain for news of his son. His grief may be reflected not only in this poem but also in this couplet from a poem with many voices:

My son died laughing at some jest, I would I knew
What it were, and it might serve me at a time when jests are few.

INVERSNAID

This darksome burn,° horseback brown,   *stream*
His rollrock highroad roaring down,
In coop° and in comb° the fleece of his foam   *hollow; crest*
Flutes and low to the lake falls home.

A windpuff-bonnet of fáwn-fróth
Turns and twindles over the broth
Of a pool so pitchblack, féll-frówning,
It rounds and rounds Despair to drowning.

Degged° with dew, dappled with dew   *sprinkled*
Are the groins of the braes° that the brook treads through,   *steep banks*
Wiry heathpacks,° flitches of fern,   *heather*
And the beadbonny ash that sits over the burn.

What would the world be, once bereft
Of wet and of wildness? Let them be left,
O let them be left, wildness and wet;
Long live the weeds and the wilderness yet.

Gerard Manley Hopkins
(28 July 1844 – 8 June 1889)

Never a town lover, Hopkins's patience had been greatly tried in the summer of 1881 when an unexpected extension of his work at St. Joseph's in Glasgow left him without the regenerative holiday he needed before taking up his next post near London. Instead he was given "two days to see something of the Highlands," time that, he commented, would afford him nothing more than "a glimpse of their skirts." On 28 September he headed for Inversnaid on Loch Lomond: "The day was dark and partly hid the lake, yet it did not altogether disfigure it but gave it a pensive or solemn beauty which left a deep impression on me." The poem travels the course of the stream, Arklet Water, in reverse, taking us back to its source in Loch Arklet. Inversnaid is also the scene of Wordsworth's poem "To a Highland Girl."

FRIENDSHIP AFTER LOVE

After the fierce midsummer all ablaze
  Has burned itself to ashes, and expires
  In the intensity of its own fires,
There come the mellow, mild, St. Martin days
Crowned with the calm of peace, but sad with haze.
  So after Love has led us, till he tires
  Of his own throes, and torments, and desires,
Comes large-eyed friendship: with a restful gaze,
He beckons us to follow, and across
  Cool verdant vales we wander free from care.
  Is it a touch of frost lies in the air?
Why are we haunted with a sense of loss?
We do not wish the pain back, or the heat;
And yet, and yet, these days are incomplete.

Ella Wheeler Wilcox
(5 November 1850 – 31 October 1919)

By the age of eighteen, Wilcox was earning a fair income from her writing. Her parents sent her to the University of Wisconsin, but Wilcox left after one semester, feeling she had nothing to learn there. She continued writing her two poems a day, essays and stories, her work was published and she received various prizes. However, she became a national sensation when *Poems of Passion* (1883) was published, having been rejected by Jansen & McClurg of Chicago on the basis that the book was immoral.

THE ROAD NOT TAKEN

Two roads diverged in a yellow wood,
And sorry I could not travel both
And be one traveler, long I stood
And looked down one as far as I could
To where it bent in the undergrowth;

Then took the other, as just as fair,
And having perhaps the better claim,
Because it was grassy and wanted wear;
Though as for that, the passing there
Had worn them really about the same,

And both that morning equally lay
In leaves no step had trodden black.
Oh, I kept the first for another day!
Yet knowing how way leads on to way,
I doubted if I should ever come back.

I shall be telling this with a sigh
Somewhere ages and ages hence:
Two roads diverged in a wood, and I –
I took the one less traveled by,
And that has made all the difference.

Robert Frost
(26 March 1874 – 29 January 1963)

"The Road Not Taken" was inspired by Frost's friend, the poet Edward Thomas, and was intended to be gently ironic of the habit of regret. Frost said of Thomas, "He more than anyone else was accessory to what I had done and was doing."

THE METRONOMIC MOON

In other years I would say, how pretty they are,
The cherries outside our house.
This autumn I see the first leaves
Writhe from the green into the yellow and
From the yellow into what seems a frantic red
Before they corkscrew to their conclusion
When the morning wipers scrape them from the windscreens
To drop them in the dog shit on the pavement.
Their beauty has not brought them mercy.

The cherry flaunting first and shedding fastest
Flies a few prayer flags in tatters.
When the time is ripe (soon now)
The metronomic moon on cue will let slip
The north wind to bite the branches bare and
Lay out the bony tree against the back-lit tombgrey sky.
In other years I would say, how lucky we are,
The people inside our house.
But the luck has not brought us mercy.

Michael Young
(9 August 1915 -)

This poem was occasioned by the illness of Michael Young's second wife, Sasha Moorsom, who died in 1994. Their poems are published by Carcanet. A social innovator, Michael Young has helped found the Consumers' Association and *Which?* magazine, the Open University, the Institute of Community Studies in Bethnal Green, the College of Health, the Family Covenant Association, and many other organizations. He is the author of a number of books, of which perhaps the best known are *Family and Kinship in East London* and *The Rise of the Meritocracy*. He was created a life peer in 1973.

HOPE

Old spirit, in and beyond me,
keep, and extend me. Amid strangers,
friends, great trees and big seas breaking,
let love move me. Let me hear the whole music,
see clear, reach deep. Open me to find due words,
that I may shape them to ploughshares of my own making.
After such luck, however late, give me to give to
the oldest dance .... Then to good sleep,
and – if it happens – glad waking.

Philip Booth
(8 October 1925 –)

Philip Booth comments: "Looking back into notebooks, I find that 'Hope' was written at the beginning and end of the first March of the century's final decade. The first sentence had long been in my head; the next two words, however they may have come to me (likely in the dark before dawn), surely catalyzed my four days of handwritten, then typed, drafts. I trust that the structure of the poem is self-evident; within its structure, I could hope that one or another reader might sense the poem countering a dreadful children's prayer, and even Joel 3:10. The poem, as I now reenter it, reminds the New Englander in me of how deeply I know that October-November and March-April are my most creative seasons. And how the turn of the decade must have reminded me that I was already half into my 65th year."

Booth is a resident of Castine, Maine, and the author of nine books of poetry. He has received numerous awards for his work, among them the Lamont Prize, and the Maurice English Poetry Award.

Last poems

XL

Tell me not here, it needs not saying,
  What tune the enchantress plays
In aftermaths of soft September
  Or under blanching mays,
For she and I were long acquainted
  And I knew all her ways.

On russet floors, by waters idle,
  The pine lets fall its cone;
The cuckoo shouts all day at nothing
  In leafy dells alone;
And traveller's joy beguiles in autumn
  Hearts that have lost their own.

On acres of the seeded grasses
  The changing burnish heaves;
Or marshalled under moons of harvest
  Stand still all night the sheaves;
Or beeches strip in storms for winter
  And stain the wind with leaves.

Possess, as I possessed a season,
  The countries I resign,
Where over elmy plains the highway
  Would mount the hills and shine,
And full of shade the pillared forest
  Would murmur and be mine.

LAST POEMS

For nature, heartless, witless nature,
    Will neither care nor know
What stranger's feet may find the meadow
    And trespass there and go,
Nor ask amid the dews of morning
    If they are mine or no.

A. E. Housman
(26 March 1859 – 30 April 1936)

"I am not a poet by trade; I am a professor of Latin." There was a 36-year gap between Housman's first and second collections (*Last Poems* was this second, and, in the event, penultimate, volume). "In barrenness," Housman admitted, "I hold a high place among English poets, excelling even Gray."

THE LEAVING

My father said I could not do it,
but all night I picked the peaches.
The orchard was still, the canals ran steadily.
I was a girl then, my chest its own walled garden.
How many ladders to gather an orchard?
I had only one and a long patience with lit hands
and the looking of the stars which moved right through me
the way the water moved through the canals with a voice
that seemed to speak of this moonless gathering
and those who had gathered before me.
I put the peaches in the pond's cold water,
all night up the ladder and down, all night my hands
twisting fruit as if I were entering a thousand doors,
all night my back a straight road to the sky.
And then out of its own goodness, out
of the far fields of the stars, the morning came,
and inside me was the stillness a bell possesses
just after it has been rung, before the metal
begins to long again for the clapper's stroke.
The light came over the orchard.
The canals were silver and then were not,
and the pond was – I could see as I laid
the last peach in the water – full of fish and eyes.

Brigit Pegeen Kelly
(21 April 1951 –)

Born in Palo Alto, California, Brigit Pegeen Kelly lives in Urbana, Illinois. Her second book of poetry, *Song*, was the 1994 Lamont Poetry Selection of the Academy of American Poets. Her first collection, *To the Place of Trumpets*, was awarded the 1987 Yale Series of Younger Poets Prize.

THE FALCON TO THE FALCONER

Unleash me from your hand
And I will lance the light for you
I'll cut a swordblade on the wind
And pennant it with flight for you
To signal I am yours
If you will free me to be true to you

Unleash me from your hand
And I will mock the sky for you
I'll pull the anger from the air
And make the breezes sigh for you
To show that I am yours
If you will free me to be true to you

Unleash me from your hand
And I will jewel it bright for you
I'll hunt the treasures of the wind
And pluck them into sight for you
To show that I am yours
If you will free me to be true to you

O, cast me from your hand
That I may show my love for you
And throw me to the wind
That I may know my need for you

The falcon to the falconer

All darkness on your hand
I'm hooded, pinned and held by you
O, give me back my wings
That they may bring me back to you

Jonathan Steffen
(5 October 1958 –)

Jonathan Steffen lives in Heidelberg in Germany. This poem was published in *The Spectator* in September 1992.

CROSSING THE BAR

Sunset and evening star,
  And one clear call for me!
And may there be no moaning of the bar,
  When I put out to sea,

But such a tide as moving seems asleep,
  Too full for sound and foam,
When that which drew from out the boundless deep
  Turns again home.

Twilight and evening bell,
  And after that the dark!
And may there be no sadness of farewell,
  When I embark;

For tho' from out our bourne of Time and Place
  The flood may bear me far,
I hope to see my Pilot face to face
  When I have crost the bar.

Alfred, Lord Tennyson
(6 August 1809 - 6 October 1892)

Tennyson's son Hallam wrote that this poem was "made in my father's eighty-first year, after his serious illness in 1888-9, on a day in October 1889, while crossing the Solent, as we came from Aldworth to Farringford. When he repeated it to me in the evening, I said, 'That is the crown of your life's work.' He answered, 'It came in a moment.'" It is claimed that the idea for this poem was "planted by his nurse, who told him to stop grumbling; she said he might better offer a hymn of praise to his God."

7 OCTOBER

JEWELS IN MY HAND

I hold dead friends like jewels in my hand
Watching their brilliance gleam against my palm
Turquoise and emerald, jade, a golden band

All ravages of time they can withstand
Like talismans their grace keeps me from harm
I hold dead friends like jewels in my hand

I see them standing in some borderland
Their heads half-turned, waiting for my arm
Turquoise and emerald, jade, a golden band

I'm not afraid they will misunderstand
My turning to them like a magic charm
I hold dead friends like jewels in my hand
Turquoise and emerald, jade, a golden band.

Sasha Moorsom
(25 January 1931 - 22 June 1993)

Sophie Young, Sasha's daughter, writes: "This poem was written in hospital when Sasha was first being treated for cancer, expressing the hope and comfort that is much needed at such times. She faced her illness as she had lived her life: so graceful, so dignified and so unself-concerned that it was a real honour to be in her presence. Not long before she died, she said how important it was to accept whatever happens with equanimity. And this is what she did."

Heaven-haven

A NUN TAKES THE VEIL

I have desired to go
  Where springs not fail,
To fields where flies no sharp and sided hail
  And a few lilies blow.

And I have asked to be
  Where no storms come,
Where the green swell is in the havens dumb,
  And out of the swing of the sea.

Gerard Manley Hopkins
(28 July 1844 - 8 June 1889)

On this day in 1865, Hopkins recorded in his journal speculations about converting to Catholicism and added that he talked "about Dr. Newman at dinner etc. in a foolish way likely to produce unhappiness and pain." This poem was probably drafted in 1864 at a time when Hopkins, an undergraduate at Balliol College, Oxford, was first attracted to Catholicism and the priesthood.

KIND OF AN ODE TO DUTY

O Duty,
Why hast thou not the visage of a sweetie or a cutie?
Why glitter thy spectacles so ominously?
Why art thou clad so abominously?
Why art thou so different from Venus
And why do thou and I have so few interests mutually in common
    between us?
Why art thou fifty per cent martyr
And fifty-one per cent Tartar?

Why is it thy unfortunate wont
To try to attract people by calling on them either to leave undone
    the deeds they like, or to do the deeds they don't?
Why art thou so like an April post-mortem
Or something that died in the ortumn?
Above all, why dost thou continue to hound me?
Why art thou always albatrossly hanging around me?

Thou so ubiquitous,
And I so iniquitous.
I seem to be the one person in the world thou art perpetually
    preaching at who or to who;
Whatever looks like fun, there art thou standing between me and it,
    calling you-hoo.
O Duty, Duty!
How noble a man should I be hadst thou the visage of a sweetie or
    a cutie!

Kind of an Ode to Duty

But as it is thou art so much forbiddinger than a Wodehouse hero's
   forbiddingest aunt
That in the words of the poet, When Duty whispers low, Thou must,
   this erstwhile youth replies, I just can't.

Ogden Nash
(19 August 1902 - 19 May 1971)

Ogden Nash, America's most popular comic poet, described himself as a "wersifier." In the 1930s, he gave up trying to write serious verse and settled for his own brew, where, as Archibald MacLeish remarked, "Nothing . . . suggests the structure of verse but the rhymes." Nash retired from his job at the *New Yorker* to give himself more time to write and concluded that "When I consider how my life is spent, / I hardly ever repent."

SOLAR CREATION

The sun, of whose terrain we creatures are,
Is the director of all human love,
Unit of time, and circle round the earth,

And we are the commotion born of love
And slanted rays of that illustrious star,
Peregrine of the crowded fields of birth,

The crowded lane, the market and the tower.
Like sight in pictures, real at remove,
Such is our motion on dimensional earth.

Down by the river, where the ragged are,
Continuous the cries and noise of birth,
While to the muddy edge dark fishes move,

And over all, like death, or sloping hill,
Is nature, which is larger and more still.

Charles Madge
(*10 October 1912 -)

Charles Madge was born in Johannesburg and educated at Winchester and Magdalene College, Cambridge. His first wife was Kathleen Raine and his first poetry collection, in which "Solar Creation" appeared, was *The Disappearing Castle* (1937). The 52-year gap between his second volume, *Father Found* (1941), and the third, *Of Love, Time and Places* (1993), is explained in part by his work as a sociologist, founding Mass Observation in 1937 and publishing works with titles such as *Survey Before Development in Thai Villages* and *Art Students Observed*.

They flee from me

They flee from me that sometime did me seek
With naked foot stalking in my chamber.
I have seen them gentle, tame, and meek
That now are wild and do not remember
That sometime they put themselves in danger
To take bread at my hand; and now they range
Busily seeking with a continual change.

Thankèd be Fortune, it hath been otherwise
Twenty times better; but once in special,
In thin array after a pleasant guise,
When her loose gown from her shoulders did fall,
And she me caught in her arms long and small;
Therewith all sweetly did me kiss,
And softly said, 'Dear heart, how like you this?'

It was no dream: I lay broad waking.
But all is turnèd, thorough my gentleness,
Into a strange fashion of forsaking;
And I have leave to go of her goodness,
And she also to use newfangleness.
But since that I so kindly am servèd,
I would fain know what she hath deservèd.

Sir Thomas Wyatt (1503 - 11 October 1542)

Wyatt was twice imprisoned during his career: in 1536, when Henry VIII executed Anne
Boleyn's other lovers and merely put Wyatt in the Tower; and in 1541, for alleged treason.
Nevertheless, he was despatched by the king to Falmouth on 3 October 1542 to welcome
and escort a Spanish envoy to London. He died in Sherborne in Dorset and was buried in
the great church there.

SON AND HEIR

He's up. And off, a tipsy
  tightrope turn
juggling with gravity.
  The ascent of man
starts here. Like one spotlit

  he makes his stand
on the brink of a big-top
  drop. The ground
sways. One false step
  and . . .

Will he take it stonily
  like Sitting Bull?
Like holy Job? Or melancholy
  Charlie, fall-
guy to the old joke? Will he

  heck! He's baby-bald
Khrushchev, blamming a shoe
  on the diplomatic table –
'WE WILL BURY YOU . . .'

No joke. He will.

Philip Gross
(27 February 1952 -)

On this day in 1960, Khrushchev slammed his shoe down on the desk at the United Nations. Philip Gross comments: "When I wrote this in the mid 1980's, part of the irony was that Khrushchev was already part of history, succeeded as Soviet leader several times over."

ROMANCE

When I was but thirteen or so
  I went into a golden land;
Chimborazo, Cotopaxi
  Took me by the hand.

My father died, my brother too,
  They passed like fleeting dreams,
I stood where Popocatapetl
  In the sunlight gleams.

I dimly heard the master's voice
  And boys far-off at play;
Chimborazo, Cotopaxi
  Had stolen me away.

I walked in a great golden dream
  To and fro from school –
Shining Popocatapetl
  The dusty streets did rule.

I walked home with a gold dark boy
  And never a word I'd say;
Chimborazo, Cotopaxi
  Had taken my speech away:

I gazed entranced upon his face
  Fairer than any flower –
O shining Popocatapetl,
  It was thy magic hour:

ROMANCE

The houses, people, traffic seemed
  Thin fading dreams by day;
Chimborazo, Cotopaxi,
  They had stolen my soul away!

W. J. Turner
(13 October 1889 - 18 November 1946)

Turner was born in Melbourne, Australia, and was educated there and in Munich and Vienna. His creative output included: a novel *The Duchess of Popocatapetl*, a play *The Man Who Ate the Popomack*, and three books of poetry. He was also a drama critic, music critic, and literary editor.

i thank You God for most this amazing

i thank You God for most this amazing
day:for the leaping greenly spirits of trees
and a blue true dream of sky;and for everything
which is natural which is infinite which is yes

(i who have died am alive again today,
and this is the sun's birthday;this is the birth
day of life and of love and wings:and of the gay
great happening illimitably earth)

how should tasting touching hearing seeing
breathing any – lifted from the no
of all nothing – human merely being
doubt unimaginable You?

(now the ears of my ears awake and
now the eyes of my eyes are opened)

e. e. cummings
(14 October 1894 – 3 September 1962)

e. e. cummings wrote to his sister Elizabeth in 1954: "if you take Someone Worth Worshipping (alias 'God') away from human beings, they'll (without realizing what they're doing) worship someone-unworthy-of-worship); e.g.; a Roosevelt or Stalin or Hitler – alias themselves."

In the Introduction to his *Collected Poems* e. e. cummings wrote (and the punctuation is his): "Life,for mostpeople,simply isn't . . . What do mostpeople mean by 'living'? They don't mean living. They mean the latest and closest plural approximation to singular pre-natal passivity which science,in its finite but unbounded wisdom,has succeeded in selling their wives . . . With you I leave a remembrance of miracles:they are by somebody who can love and who shall be continually reborn,a human being. . . ."

DELIGHT IN DISORDER

A sweet disorder in the dress
Kindles in clothes a wantonness:
A lawn[1] about the shoulders thrown
Into a fine distraction:
An erring lace, which here and there
Enthrals the crimson stomacher:
A cuff neglectful, and thereby
Ribbons to flow confusedly:
A winning wave, deserving note,
In the tempestuous petticoat:
A careless shoe-string, in whose tie
I see a wild civility:
Do more bewitch me than when art
Is too precise in every part.

Robert Herrick
(24 August 1591 - 15 October 1674)

"Herrick's verse," Louis Untermeyer wrote, is "never rowdy, often lascivious, but seldom rudely lecherous." His life was of a piece with his verse, for as Herrick himself reassured the reader:

Wantons we are; and though our words be such,
Our lives do differ from our lines by much.

1. A light scarf.

THE BITE

I didn't start taking myself seriously as a poet
until the white began to appear in my cheek.
All before was amusement and affection –
now, like a hare, like a hare, like a hare,
I watch the turtle lift one horrible leg
over the last remaining stile and head
for home, practically roaring with virtue.
   Everything, suddenly everything is up there in the mind,
   all the beauty of the race gone
   and my life merely an allegory.

Gerald Stern
(22 February 1925 –)

Gerald Stern notes: "I wrote this poem at a time in my life when I was experiencing the famous "crisis of forty." I think I was forty-one at the time. My endless youth, represented by the lazy hare, was suddenly surprisingly ended, and the tortoise was taking over. My beard was white and my time was limited."

17 OCTOBER

from THE COUNTESS OF PEMBROKE'S ARCADIA

My true love hath my heart, and I have his,
By just exchange one for the other given.
I hold his dear, and mine he cannot miss:
There never was a better bargain driven.
His heart in me keeps me and him in one;
My heart in him his thoughts and senses guides;
He loves my heart, for once it was his own;
I cherish his, because in me it bides.
His heart his wound receivèd from my sight;
My heart was wounded with his wounded heart;
For as from me on him his hurt did light,
So still, methought, in me his hurt did smart;
  Both equal hurt, in this change sought our bliss:
  My true love hath my heart, and I have his.

Sir Philip Sidney
(30 November 1554 - 17 October 1586)

Immoderately favored with high birth, influence, charm, and success, Sidney is remembered as a paragon of nobility – an extreme example of his behavior came during an attack on Spanish forces at Zutphen. He is reported to have left his thigh armour off so as not to be better protected than his subordinates. The musket ball wound that ensued quickly became infected, and he died within three weeks. As he was being carried from the battlefield, he refused a cup of water, preferring to give it to a dying soldier with the words: "Thy necessity is yet greater than mine."

ETERNITY

He who binds to himself a joy
Does the wingèd life destroy;
But he who kisses the joy as it flies
Lives in eternity's sun rise.

William Blake
(28 November 1757 – 12 August 1827)

Blake believed that a bigger force than himself worked through him. He held the pen, the graver, or the brush. He was its agent, never its master, the possessed rather than the possessor.

On 18 October 1831, four years after her husband's death, Catherine Blake died at 17 Upper Charlotte Street, Fitzroy Square. In this last home, a contemporary report states, she called "continually to her William, as if he were in the next room, to say she was coming to him and would not be long now."

ABOU BEN ADHEM

Abou Ben Adhem (may his tribe increase!)
Awoke one night from a deep dream of peace,
And saw, within the moonlight in his room,
Making it rich, and like a lily in bloom,
An angel writing in a book of gold: –
Exceeding peace had made Ben Adhem bold,
And to the presence in the room he said,
'What writest thou?' The vision raised its head,
And with a look made of all sweet accord,
Answered, 'The names of those who love the Lord.'
'And is mine one?' said Abou. 'Nay, not so,'
Replied the angel. Abou spoke more low,
But cheerly still; and said, 'I pray thee, then,
Write me as one that loves his fellow men.'
The angel wrote, and vanished. The next night
It came again with a great wakening light,
And showed the names whom love of God had blest,
And lo! Ben Adhem's name led all the rest.

Leigh Hunt
(19 October 1784 – 28 August 1859)

Leigh Hunt was born in Southgate, the son of a poor immigrant American preacher. He became a great editor and encourager of talent – helping Keats, Tennyson, Shelley, Byron, and others. Imprisoned for two years (1813-1815) for libeling the Prince Regent, he was visited in jail by Bentham and Byron. Dickens caricatured his sunny optimism in the early character of Harold Skimpole in *Bleak House*.

"Abou Ben Adhem" appeared in an anthology, the *Book of Gems*, in 1838. Hunt was proud of this poem, admitting that he was "not unwilling to be judged by 'Ben Adhem'... and by one or two others of the smallest pieces."

ULYSSES

It little profits that an idle king,
By this still hearth, among these barren crags,
Match'd with an aged wife, I mete and dole
Unequal laws unto a savage race,
That hoard, and sleep, and feed, and know not me.
I cannot rest from travel; I will drink
Life to the lees. All times I have enjoy'd
Greatly, have suffer'd greatly, both with those
That loved me, and alone; on shore, and when
Thro' scudding drifts the rainy Hyades
Vext the dim sea. I am become a name;
For always roaming with a hungry heart
Much have I seen and known – cities of men
And manners, climates, councils, governments,
Myself not least, but honour'd of them all –
And drunk delight of battle with my peers,
Far on the ringing plains of windy Troy.
I am a part of all that I have met;
Yet all experience is an arch wherethrough
Gleams that untraveled world, whose margin fades
For ever and for ever when I move.
How dull it is to pause, to make an end,
To rust unburnished, not to shine in use!
As tho' to breathe were life! Life piled on life
Were all too little, and of one to me
Little remains: but every hour is saved
From that eternal silence, something more,
A bringer of new things; and vile it were
For some three suns to store and hoard myself,
And this gray spirit yearning in desire

Ulysses

To follow knowledge like a sinking star,
Beyond the utmost bound of human thought.
   This is my son, mine own Telemachus
To whom I leave the sceptre and the isle –
Well-loved of me, discerning to fulfil
This labour, by slow prudence to make mild
A rugged people, and through soft degrees
Subdue them to the useful and the good.
Most blameless is he, centred in the sphere
Of common duties, decent not to fail
In offices of tenderness, and pay
Meet adoration to my household gods,
When I am gone. He works his work, I mine.
   There lies the port; the vessel puffs her sail;
There gloom the dark broad seas. My mariners,
Souls that have toiled, and wrought, and thought with me,
That ever with a frolic welcome took
The thunder and the sunshine, and opposed
Free hearts, free foreheads—you and I are old;
Old age hath yet his honour and his toil.
Death closes all; but something ere the end,
Some work of noble note, may yet be done,
Not unbecoming men that strove with gods.
The lights begin to twinkle from the rocks;
The long day wanes; the slow moon climbs; the deep
Moans round with many voices. Come, my friends,
'Tis not too late to seek a newer world.
Push off, and sitting well in order smite
The sounding furrows; for my purpose holds

Ulysses

To sail beyond the sunset, and the baths
Of all the western stars, until I die.
It may be that the gulfs will wash us down;
It may be we shall touch the Happy Isles,
And see the great Achilles, whom we knew.
Though much is taken, much abides; and though
We are not now that strength which in old days
Moved earth and heaven; that which we are, we are;
One equal temper of heroic hearts,
Made weak by time and fate, but strong in will
To strive, to seek, to find, and not to yield.

Alfred, Lord Tennyson
(6 August 1809 - 6 October 1892)

Written on this day in 1833, less than three weeks after Tennyson received the painful
news of the death of Arthur Hallam, "Ulysses" is, according to the poet, a more immediate outpouring of grief for his friend than *In Memoriam*: "There is more about myself in
'Ulysses'... It was more written with the feeling of his loss upon me than many poems in
In Memoriam ... It gives the feeling about the need of going forward and braving the
struggle of life." Sir Robert Peel, on reading this poem, decided to give Tennyson a pension of £200 a year.

KUBLA KHAN

OR, A VISION IN A DREAM. A FRAGMENT

In Xanadu did Kubla Khan
A stately pleasure-dome decree:
Where Alph, the sacred river, ran
Through caverns measureless to man
   Down to a sunless sea.
So twice five miles of fertile ground
With walls and towers were girdled round:
And here were gardens bright with sinuous rills,
Where blossomed many an incense-bearing tree;
And here were forests ancient as the hills,

Enfolding sunny spots of greenery.
But oh! that deep romantic chasm which slanted
Down the green hill athwart a cedarn cover!
A savage place! as holy and enchanted
As e'er beneath a waning moon was haunted
By woman wailing for her demon-lover!
And from this chasm, with ceaseless turmoil seething
As if this earth in fast thick pants were breathing,
A mighty fountain momently was forced:
Amid whose swift half-intermitted burst
Huge fragments vaulted like rebounding hail
Or chaffy grain beneath the thresher's flail:
And 'mid these dancing rocks at once and ever
It flung up momently the sacred river.
Five miles meandering with a mazy motion
Through wood and dale the sacred river ran,
Then reached the caverns measureless to man,
And sank in tumult to a lifeless ocean:

And 'mid this tumult Kubla heard from far
Ancestral voices prophesying war!

  The shadow of the dome of pleasure
  Floated midway on the waves;
  Where was heard the mingled measure
  From the fountain and the caves.
It was a miracle of rare device,
A sunny pleasure-dome with caves of ice!

  A damsel with a dulcimer
  In a vision once I saw:
  It was an Abyssinian maid,
  And on her dulcimer she played,
  Singing of Mount Abora.
  Could I revive within me
  Her symphony and song,
  To such a deep delight 'twould win me,
That with music loud and long,
I would build that dome in air,
That sunny dome! those caves of ice!
And all who heard should see them there,
And all should cry, Beware! Beware!
His flashing eyes, his floating hair!
Weave a circle round him thrice,
And close your eyes with holy dread,
For he on honey-dew hath fed,
And drunk the milk of Paradise.

Samuel Taylor Coleridge
(21 October 1772 - 25 July 1834)

ALL THINGS PASS

All things pass
A sunrise does not last all morning
All things pass
A cloudburst does not last all day
All things pass
Nor a sunset all night
All things pass
What always changes?

Earth . . . sky . . . thunder . . .
mountain . . . water . . .
wind . . . fire . . . lake . . .

These change
And if these do not last

Do man's visions last?
Do man's illusions?

Take things as they come

All things pass

Lao-Tzu (6th century BC)
from translations adapted by Timothy Leary
(22 October 1920 - 31 May 1996)

This version appears in Leary's *Psychedelic Prayers* (Academy Editions, London, 1972). Leary had half a dozen English translations to work from. In the foreword, he writes that "these translations from English to psychedelese were made while sitting under a bamboo tree on a grassy slope of the Kumaon Hills overlooking the snow peaks of the Himalayas."

The sun rising

Busy old fool, unruly Sun,
Why dost thou thus,
Through windows, and through curtains, call on us?
Must to thy motions lovers' seasons run?
Saucy pedantic wretch, go chide
Late school-boys and sour prentices,°   *apprentices*
Go tell court-huntsmen that the king will ride,
Call country ants to harvest offices;°   *duties*
Love, all alike, no season knows nor clime,
Nor hours, days, months, which are the rags of time.

Thy beams so reverend and strong
Why should'st thou think?
I could eclipse and cloud them with a wink,
But that I would not lose her sight so long.
If her eyes have not blinded thine,
Look, and to-morrow late tell me,
Whether both th' Indias of spice and mine
Be where thou left'st them, or lie here with me.
Ask for those kings whom thou saw'st yesterday
And thou shalt hear, 'All here in one bed lay.'

She's all states, and all princes I:
Nothing else is;
Princes do but play us; compared to this,
All honour's mimic,° all wealth alchemy.°   *fake; a fraud*

THE SUN RISING

Thou, Sun, art half as happy as we,
In that the world's contracted thus;
Thine age asks ease, and since thy duties be
To warm the world, that's done by warming us.
Shine here to us, and thou art everywhere;
This bed thy centre is, these walls thy sphere.

John Donne
(c. June 1572 - 31 March 1631)

On this day in 1584, Donne was admitted to Hart Hall, Oxford University, aged 12,
which was exceptionally young even for the time. In his twenties, Donne enjoyed independence of means, popularity at court, and a degree of sexual promiscuity, reflected in
his early lyrics. Jonson told Drummond that after 1615 Donne "repented highly, and
sought to destroy all his poems."

from MATINS

v

Stir the holy grains, set
the bowls on the table and
call the child to eat.

While we eat we think,
as we think an undercurrent
of dream runs through us
faster than thought
towards recognition.

Call the child to eat,
send him off, his mouth
tasting of toothpaste, to go down
into the ground, into a roaring train
and to school.

His cheeks are pink
his black eyes hold his dreams, he has left
forgetting his glasses.

Follow down the stairs at a clatter
to give them to him and save
his clear sight.

Cold air
comes in at the street door.

Denise Levertov
(24 October 1923 ‑)

TEARS, IDLE TEARS
from THE PRINCESS

Tears, idle tears, I know not what they mean,
Tears from the depth of some divine despair
Rise in the heart, and gather to the eyes,
In looking on the happy autumn-fields,
And thinking of the days that are no more.

Fresh as the first beam glittering on a sail,
That brings our friends up from the underworld,
Sad as the last which reddens over one
That sinks with all we love below the verge;
So sad, so fresh, the days that are no more.

Ah, sad and strange as in dark summer dawns
The earliest pipe of half-awakened birds
To dying ears, when unto dying eyes
The casement slowly grows a glimmering square;
So sad, so strange, the days that are no more.

Dear as remembered kisses after death,
And sweet as those by hopeless fancy feigned
On lips that are for others; deep as love,
Deep as first love, and wild with all regret;
O Death in Life, the days that are no more!

Alfred, Lord Tennyson
(6 August 1809 - 6 October 1892)

Tennyson wrote: "This song came to me on the yellowing autumn-tide [of October 1834, in the Wye Valley] at Tintern Abbey, full for me of its bygone memories. It is the sense of the abiding in the transient ... It is what as a boy I called the 'passion of the past.'"

O WESTERN WIND

O western wind, when wilt thou blow
  That the small rain down can rain?
Christ, that my love were in my arms,
  And I in my bed again.

Anonymous
(early 16th century)

On this day in 1529, Henry VIII appointed Sir Thomas More, the poet and author of *Utopia*, as his Lord Chancellor, against More's strongest wish. Henry VIII had him beheaded six years later.

THE FORCE THAT THROUGH THE GREEN
FUSE DRIVES THE FLOWER

The force that through the green fuse drives the flower
Drives my green age; that blasts the roots of trees
Is my destroyer.
And I am dumb to tell the crooked rose
My youth is bent by the same wintry fever.

The force that drives the water through the rocks
Drives my red blood; that dries the mouthing streams
Turns mine to wax.
And I am dumb to mouth unto my veins
How at the mountain spring the same mouth sucks.

The hand that whirls the water in the pool
Stirs the quicksand; that ropes the blowing wind
Hauls my shroud sail.
And I am dumb to tell the hanging man
How of my clay is made the hangman's lime.

The lips of time leech to the fountain head;
Love drips and gathers, but the fallen blood
Shall calm her sores.
And I am dumb to tell a weather's wind
How time has ticked a heaven round the stars.

And I am dumb to tell my lover's tomb
How at my sheet goes the same crooked worm.

Dylan Thomas
(27 October 1914 – 9 November 1953)

WHEN YOU ARE OLD

When you are old and gray and full of sleep
　　And nodding by the fire, take down this book,
　　And slowly read, and dream of the soft look
Your eyes had once, and of their shadows deep;

How many loved your moments of glad grace,
　　And loved your beauty with love false or true;
　　But one man loved the pilgrim soul in you,
And loved the sorrows of your changing face.

And bending down beside the glowing bars,
　　Murmur, a little sadly, how love fled
　　And paced upon the mountains overhead,
And hid his face amid a crowd of stars.

William Butler Yeats
(13 June 1865 – 28 January 1939)
based on a French sonnet by Pierre De Ronsard
(11 September 1524 – 27 December 1585)

This poem was written for the beautiful Irish revolutionary Maud Gonne in October 1891. Both Maud Gonne and later her daughter Iseult turned down offers of marriage from Yeats. The poem is based on Ronsard's sonnet "Quand vous serez bien vielle" in which an old woman by the graveside regrets her proud refusal of the poet's love.

SONNET 73

That time of year thou mayst in me behold,
When yellow leaves, or none, or few do hang
Upon those boughs which shake against the cold,
Bare ruin'd choirs, where late the sweet birds sang.
In me thou see'st the twilight of such day,
As after sunset fadeth in the west,
Which by and by black night doth take away,
Death's second self that seals up all in rest.
In me thou see'st the glowing of such fire,
That on the ashes of his youth doth lie,
As the death bed, whereon it must expire,
Consum'd with that which it was nourish'd by.
   This thou perceiv'st, which makes thy love more strong,
   To love that well, which thou must leave ere long.

William Shakespeare
(23 April 1564 - 23 April 1616)

One of Shakespeare's editors has suggested that "to love that well" in the last line of this sonnet refers to loving not only the poet but the beholder's own youth.

from the Introduction to
SONGS OF EXPERIENCE

Hear the voice of the Bard!
Who Present, Past, & Future sees,
Whose ears have heard
The Holy Word
That walk'd among the ancient trees;

Calling the lapsèd Soul
And weeping in the evening dew;
That might controll
The starry pole,
And fallen fallen light renew!

"O Earth O Earth return!
Arise from out the dewy grass;
Night is worn,
And the morn
Rises from the slumberous mass.

Turn away no more:
Why wilt thou turn away
The starry floor
The watry shore
Is giv'n thee till the break of day."

William Blake
(28 November 1757 - 12 August 1827)

Notice the imperative first line, that marks the poet as prophet. The Bard is Blake himself. Bards were Celtic poet-prophets, their craft destroyed in Wales by Edward III and in Ireland by the Plantation of the seventeenth century.

On first looking into Chapman's Homer[1]

Much have I travelled in the realms of gold,
  And many goodly states and kingdoms seen;
  Round many western islands have I been
Which bards in fealty° to Apollo hold.   *allegiance*
Oft of one wide expanse had I been told
  That deep-browed Homer ruled as his demesne;° *domain*
  Yet did I never breathe its pure serene°   *atmosphere*
Till I heard Chapman speak out loud and bold:
Then felt I like some watcher of the skies
  When a new planet swims into his ken;
Or like stout Cortez when with eagle eyes
  He stared at the Pacific – and all his men
Looked at each other with a wild surmise –
  Silent, upon a peak in Darien.

John Keats
(*31 October 1795 – 23 February 1821*)

Keats was the oldest son of a livery stables manager. His father died in a fall from a horse when Keats was eight, and his mother of tuberculosis when he was 14. Apprenticed to an Edmonton surgeon, Keats canceled his apprenticeship at 19 and moved to London.

This sonnet was written in October 1816, after a night spent reading aloud translations from Homer with his old school friend Cowden-Clarke. At daybreak, Keats parted from Clarke and walked over London Bridge back to Dean Street, and at once wrote this sonnet. They parted, said Clarke, "at day-spring, yet he contrived that I should receive the poem from a distance of, may be, two miles by ten o'clock." In 1816 Leigh Hunt included this sonnet in a survey of young poets in *The Examiner*, and Hunt introduced Keats to Shelley, Coleridge, and Wordsworth.

1. Translations from Homer by George Chapman (1559-1634) completed in 1616.

from THE TEMPEST

ACT IV SCENE I

Prospero. Be cheerful, sir:
Our revels now are ended. These our actors,
As I foretold you, were all spirits and
Are melted into air, into thin air:
And, like the baseless fabric of this vision,
The cloud-capp'd towers, the gorgeous palaces,
The solemn temples, the great globe itself,
Yea, all which it inherit,[1] shall dissolve
And, like this insubstantial pageant faded,
Leave not a rack[2] behind. We are such stuff
As dreams are made on, and our little life
Is rounded with a sleep.

William Shakespeare
(23 April 1564 – 23 April 1616)

The first mention of *The Tempest* is in the royal Account Books of the Revels Office: On Hallowmass night, November 1st 1611, "a play called the Tempest" was performed before that most cultured of kings, James I.

W. Raleigh commented in his book *Shakespeare* (1907) that "*The Tempest* was probably his last play – in the sense, at least, that he designed it for his farewell to the stage. The thought that occurs at once to almost every reader of the play, that Prospero resembles Shakespeare himself, can hardly have been absent from the mind of the author . . . In all the work of Shakespeare there is nothing more like himself than those quiet words of parting – 'Be cheerful, sir: our revels now are ended.'"

1. i.e., occupy it.
2. cloud.

from A SHROPSHIRE LAD

XXXI

On Wenlock Edge the wood's in trouble;
  His forest fleece the Wrekin heaves;
The gale, it plies the saplings double,
  And thick on Severn snow the leaves.

'Twould blow like this through holt and hanger
  When Uricon the city stood:
'Tis the old wind in the old anger,
  But then it threshed another wood.

Then, 'twas before my time, the Roman
  At yonder heaving hill would stare:
The blood that warms an English yeoman,
  The thoughts that hurt him, they were there.

There, like the wind through woods in riot,
  Through him the gale of life blew high;
The tree of man was never quiet:
  Then 'twas the Roman, now 'tis I.

The gale, it plies the saplings double,
  It blows so hard, 'twill soon be gone:
To-day the Roman and his trouble
  Are ashes under Uricon.

A. E. Housman
(26 March 1859 – 30 April 1936)

SONG

Life is ours in vain
Lacking love, which never
Counts the loss or gain.
But remember, ever
Love is linked with pain.

Light and sister shade
Shape each mortal morrow
Seek not to evade
Love's companion, Sorrow,
and be not dismayed.

Grief is not in vain,
It's for our completeness.
If the fates ordain
Love to bring life's sweetness
Welcome too its pain.

Oodgeroo of the Noonuccal
(3 November 1920 - 16 September 1993)

Oodgeroo of the Noonuccal was born on North Stradbroke Island, Queensland, Australia, and described her Aboriginal Noonuccal tribe heritage in the autobiographical *Stradbroke Dreaming* (1970). Her first poetry collection, *We Are Going* (1964), has been a best-seller in Australia. Her other publications include *The Dawn is at Hand* (1966), *My People* (1970), and *Quandamooka: The Art of Kath Walker* (1985). She changed her name from Kath Walker in 1988 in protest at the bicentennial year of the European invasion. As Kath Walker, she had been awarded the MBE in 1971 for services to her people.

GREATER LOVE

Red lips are not so red
  As the stained stones kissed by the English dead.
Kindness of wooed and wooer
Seems shame to their love pure.
O Love, your eyes lose lure
  When I behold eyes blinded in my stead!

Your slender attitude
  Trembles not exquisite like limbs knife-skewed,
Rolling and rolling there
Where God seems not to care;
Till the fierce Love they bear
  Cramps them in death's extreme decrepitude.

Your voice sings not so soft, –
  Though even as wind murmuring through raftered loft, –
Your dear voice is not dear,
Gentle, and evening clear,
As theirs whom none now hear,
  Now earth has stopped their piteous mouths that coughed.

Heart, you were never hot,
  Nor large, nor full like hearts made great with shot;
And though your hand be pale,
Paler are all which trail
Your cross through flame and hail:
  Weep, you may weep, for you may touch them not.

Wilfred Owen
(18 March 1893 – 4 November 1918)

from THE PRINCESS

The splendour falls on castle walls
   And snowy summits old in story:
The long light shakes across the lakes,
   And the wild cataract leaps in glory.
Blow, bugle, blow, set the wild echoes flying,
Blow, bugle; answer, echoes, dying, dying, dying.

O hark, O hear! how thin and clear,
   And thinner, clearer, farther going!
O sweet and far from cliff and scar
   The horns of Elfland faintly blowing!
Blow, let us hear the purple glens replying:
Blow, bugle; answer, echoes, dying, dying, dying.

O love, they die in yon rich sky,
   They faint on hill or field or river:
Our echoes roll from soul to soul,
   And grow for ever and for ever.
Blow, bugle, blow, set the wild echoes flying,
And answer, echoes, answer, dying, dying, dying.

Alfred, Lord Tennyson
(6 August 1809 – 6 October 1892)

On this day in 1850, Tennyson was offered the honor of becoming Poet Laureate (after it had been declined by Samuel Rogers). Tennyson accepted, as long as he was not required to write birthday odes.

   Of this song Tennyson noted that it was "written after hearing the echoes at Killarney in 1848. When I was there I heard a bugle blown beneath the 'Eagle's Nest,' and eight distinct echoes."

6 NOVEMBER

EGYPTIAN POEM

Death is before me to-day,
Like the recovery of a sick man,
Like going forth into a garden after sickness;
Death is before me to-day,
Like the odour of myrrh,
Like sitting under the sail on a windy day;

Death is before me to-day,
Like the odour of lotus flowers,
Like sitting on the shore of drunkenness;
Death is before me to-day,
Like the course of the freshet,
Like the return of a man from the war-galley to his house,
When he has spent years in captivity.

Anonymous

On this day in 1956, the United States backed the United Nations in its condemnation of the British bombing of Egyptian airfields and bases and its airborne assault on Port Said. Aldous Huxley selected this "Egyptian Poem" as one of his favorite poems on death and dying for his anthology *Texts and Pretexts* (1932).

THE GREAT DAY

Hurrah for revolution and more cannon-shot!
A beggar upon horseback lashes a beggar on foot.
Hurrah for revolution and cannon come again!
The beggars have changed places, but the lash goes on.

William Butler Yeats
(13 June 1865 - 28 January 1939)

On this day in 1793, at the height of the period of Terror in Paris, with Christianity under attack and Notre Dame turned into a Temple of Reason, the Bishop of Paris was forced to resign and to announce that in the future "there should be no other public cult than liberty and equality." Twenty-five thousand people were guillotined in France during these years, in the name of liberty and equality.

On this day in 1917 (October 25th Old Style), the Bolshevik Red Guards staged a coup, storming the Winter palace and ousting Kerensky's cabinet.

Yeats himself was vigilant in defense of human rights and liberties under the new Irish Free State. In a speech to the Senate in 1925 he said: "I think it tragic that within three years of this country gaining its independence, we should be discussing a measure [on divorce] which the [Protestant] minority considers grossly oppressive."

Sonnet XIX

ON HIS BLINDNESS

When I consider how my light is spent
Ere half my days in this dark world and wide,
And that one talent which is death to hide
Lodged with me useless, though my soul more bent
To serve therewith my Maker, and present
My true account, lest He returning chide;
'Doth God exact day-labour, light denied?'
I fondly ask. But Patience, to prevent
That murmur, soon replies, 'God doth not need
Either man's work or his own gifts. Who best
Bear his mild yoke, they serve him best. His state
Is kingly: thousands at his bidding speed,
And post o'er land and ocean without rest;
They also serve who only stand and wait.'

John Milton
(9 December 1608 – c. 8 November 1674)

By 1651 Milton was totally blind. He believed that his blindness had been brought on by his labors in writing treatises such as *Aereopagitica*, his defense of freedom of the press and his *Defence of the English People*. As he put it in Sonnet XXII "To Cyrick Skinner," he lost his eyes "overplied / In liberty's defence, my noble task, / Of which all Europe talks from side to side." This Sonnet XIX was only given the title "On His Blindness" in 1752. It is probably as much concerned with Milton's feeling that his prose works had caused him to neglect his true talent for poetry.

Louis Untermeyer recounts how Milton's older daughters, Anne and Mary, rebelled against the drudgery of reading aloud to their blind father, cheated him, and disposed of many of his books: "When Milton, at fifty-four, married his third wife, Elizabeth Minshull, twenty-four, Mary remarked that a wedding was no news, but 'if she could hear of his death that would be something' . . . In his old age, the disappointed poet, 'on evil days fallen and evil tongues,' made a kind of peace with the world and himself. He refused to argue; he declined to attend church and permitted no religious observances in his home.

AND DEATH SHALL HAVE NO DOMINION

And death shall have no dominion.
Dead men naked they shall be one
With the man in the wind and the west moon;
When their bones are picked clean and the clean bones gone,
They shall have stars at elbow and foot;
Though they go mad they shall be sane,
Though they sink through the sea they shall rise again;
Though lovers be lost love shall not;
And death shall have no dominion.

And death shall have no dominion.
Under the windings of the sea
They lying long shall not die windily;
Twisting on racks when sinews give way,
Strapped to a wheel, yet they shall not break;

Faith in their hands shall snap in two,
And the unicorn evils run them through;
Split all ends up they shan't crack:
And death shall have no dominion.

And death shall have no dominion.
No more may gulls cry at their ears
Or waves break loud on the seashores;
Where blew a flower may a flower no more
Lift its head to the blows of the rain;
Though they be mad and dead as nails

AND DEATH SHALL HAVE NO DOMINION

Heads of the characters hammer through daisies;
Break in the sun till the sun breaks down,
And death shall have no dominion.

Dylan Thomas
(27 October 1914 - 9 November 1953)

This pantheistic early poem first appeared in his 1933 notebook and was finally revised for *Twenty-Five Poems,* published in 1936, the year of his marriage to Caitlin Macnamara. Dylan, an alcoholic, described himself at the age of 35 as "old, small, dark, intelligent, and daring-doting-dotting eyed . . . balding and toothlessing." In 1953, during his fourth lecture tour in America, he was living in New York on a diet of raw eggs and booze; in the early hours of November 4th he checked out of the Chelsea Hotel and into a bar, went into a coma and died on November 9th, a few days after his 39th birthday. He was buried in Laugharne Churchyard in Wales.

THE LEADEN-EYED

Let not young souls be smothered out before
They do quaint deeds and fully flaunt their pride.
It is the world's one crime its babes grow dull,
Its poor are ox-like, limp and leaden-eyed.

Not that they starve, but starve so dreamlessly,
Not that they sow, but that they seldom reap,
Not that they serve, but have no gods to serve,
Not that they die but that they die like sheep.

Vachel Lindsay
(10 November 1879 – 5 December 1931)

As a young man Lindsay tramped throughout the Midwest and southern states of the United States on a mission to spread poetry. An extraordinary figure with a strong puritan streak, part minstrel, part missionary, and wholly in love with the figure of the pioneer, he carried a pamphlet called *Rhymes to be Traded for Bread*, which he took to the door of every farmhouse. There he would relate stories, recite poetry, and entertain children in return for a night's bed and food.

Lindsay became a national figure famous for his inspired poetry performances, but gradually he began to despise his audiences believing they were responsible for turning him from a visionary into an entertainer. As he grew older in extreme poverty, self-doubt developed into a mental turmoil of hallucination, hearing voices, and imagining persecution from every quarter. On 5 December 1931, aged 52, he committed suicide by drinking lysol.

GETHSEMANE
1914-18

The Garden called Gethsemane
In Picardy it was,
And there the people came to see
The English soldiers pass.
We used to pass – we used to pass
Or halt, as it might be,
And ship our masks in case of gas
Beyond Gethsemane.

The Garden called Gethsemane,
It held a pretty lass,
But all the time she talked to me
I prayed my cup might pass.
The officer sat on the chair,
The men lay on the grass,
And all the time we halted there
I prayed my cup might pass.

It didn't pass – it didn't pass –
It didn't pass from me.
I drank it when we met the gas
Beyond Gethsemane.

Rudyard Kipling
(30 December 1865 – 18 January 1936)

The armistice ending the First World War was signed on 11 November 1918. Kipling's son John was killed in the Battle of Loos on 27 September 1915.

from THE CIRCUS ANIMALS' DESERTION

Those masterful images because complete
Grew in pure mind, but out of what began?
A mound of refuse or the sweepings of a street,
Old kettles, old bottles, and a broken can,
Old iron, old bones, old rags, that raving slut
Who keeps the till. Now that my ladder's gone,
I must lie down where all the ladders start,
In the foul rag-and-bone shop of the heart.

William Butler Yeats
(13 June 1865 - 28 January 1939)

"The Circus Animals' Desertion" was composed in the last year or so of Yeats' life. For Yeats, the "circus animals" were his own early works.

13 NOVEMBER

REQUIEM

Under the wide and starry sky
Dig the grave and let me lie:
Glad did I live and gladly die,
   And I laid me down with a will.

This be the verse you grave for me:
Here he lies where he long'd to be;
Home is the sailor, home from sea,
   And the hunter home from the hill.

Robert Louis Stevenson
(13 November 1850 – 3 December 1894)

Stevenson's grandfather invented the"'intermittent" lights for lighthouses, and planned or constructed 23 lighthouses. Robert Louis Stevenson was prevented by ill health from becoming a lighthouse engineer in his turn. He suffered all his life from hemorrhages and a bronchial condition and traveled in an attempt to find a healthy climate. He met a divorcée, Fanny Osbourne, in France, and pursued her by emigrant ship and train to California. With her and his stepson Lloyd, he settled for the last five years of his life in Western Samoa where he was known as "Tusitala" (The Story Teller). According to various accounts, he was either making mayonnaise or fetching wine from the cellar, when he collapsed from a brain hemorrhage. Sixty natives carried him to a peak overlooking the Pacific and carved this requiem on a tablet as his epitaph.

THE TYGER

Tyger, tyger, burning bright
In the forests of the night,
What immortal hand or eye
Could frame thy fearful symmetry?

In what distant deeps or skies
Burnt the fire of thine eyes?
On what wings dare he aspire?
What the hand dare seize the fire?

And what shoulder and what art
Could twist the sinews of thy heart?
And, when thy heart began to beat,
What dread hand and what dread feet?

What the hammer? What the chain?
In what furnace was thy brain?
What the anvil? What dread grasp
Dare its deadly terrors clasp?

When the stars threw down their spears,
And water'd heaven with their tears,
Did He smile His work to see?
Did He who made the lamb make thee?

THE TYGER

Tyger, tyger, burning bright
In the forests of the night,
What immortal hand or eye
Dare frame thy fearful symmetry?

William Blake
(28 November 1757 - 12 August 1827)

Blake was "in a way to do well" as an engraver, wrote his artist friend Flaxman on this day in 1805, "if he will only condescend to give that attention to his worldly concerns which everyone does that prefers living to starving." In the event, Blake remained poor all his life. Of Blake and his poem Charles Lamb wrote: "There is one [poem] to a tiger . . . which is glorious . . . I must look on him as one of the most extraordinary persons of the age."

"The Tyger" was written in 1793 when the French Revolution was consuming "the forests of the night" i.e., the French Church and State. It has a Gnostic background, viz., that there are two Gods. The first, Jehovah, the inadequate author of an imperfect creation and, beyond him, the ultimate divinity. To explain himself Blake invented his own mythology but wrote no key to it. It was not until our own time that his code was broken – see S. Foster Damon's *A Blake Dictionary*. The tyger, symbol of wrath, is the product of *Urizen*, the spirit of calculating rationality and materialism. *Urizen* is a fallen titan engaged in a historic struggle with *Los*, who is the spirit of imagination and the arts. Their ultimate reconciliation is the climactic moment that makes *Jerusalem* possible. Blake equates the Lamb (Jesus) with spirituality i.e., the arts.

THE CALL

From our low seat beside the fire
  Where we have dozed and dreamed and watched the glow
Or raked the ashes, stopping so
We scarcely saw the sun or rain
  Above, or looked much higher
Than this same quiet red or burned-out fire.
      To-night we heard a call,
      A rattle on the window-pane,
      A voice on the sharp air,
And felt a breath stirring our hair,
  A flame within us: Something swift and tall
Swept in and out and that was all.
Was it a bright or a dark angel? Who can know?
  It left no mark upon the snow,
    But suddenly it snapped the chain
    Unbarred, flung wide the door
    Which will not shut again;
And so we cannot sit here any more.
     We must arise and go:
     The world is cold without
     And dark and hedged about
     With mystery and enmity and doubt,
      But we must go
     Though yet we do not know
Who called, or what marks we shall leave upon the snow.

Charlotte Mew (15 November 1869 – 24 March 1928)

Hardy said of Charlotte Mew that she was "the least pretentious but undoubtedly the best woman poet of our day." Nevertheless, increasing financial problems combined with protracted family difficulty made life unbearable, and at 58 she committed suicide.

EVOLUTION

Out of the dusk a shadow,
  Then, a spark;
Out of the cloud a silence,
  Then, a lark;
Out of the heart a rapture,
  Then, a pain;
Out of the dead, cold ashes,
  Life again.

John Banister Tabb
(22 March 1845 - 19 November 1909)

Tabb was a convert to Roman Catholicism, and ordained in 1884 two years after his first book of poetry was brought out through private publication. Born in Virginia and a blockade runner for the Confederacy, Tabb called himself an "unreconstructed Rebel," though he taught English at St. Charles' College in Maryland until he was made to retire in 1907 probably due to the loss of his eyesight.

EGOTIST

Megaceph, chosen to serve the State
In the halls of legislative debate,
One day with all his credentials came
To the capitol's door and announced his name.
The doorkeeper looked, with a comical twist
Of the face, at the eminent egotist,
And said: "Go away, for we settle here
All manner of questions, knotty and queer,
And we cannot have, when the speaker demands
To be told how every member stands,
A man who to all things under the sky
Assents by eternally voting 'I'."

Ambrose Bierce
(24 June 1842 – 11 January 1914?)

Known best for writing about the worst in human nature, Bierce was a master of the mordant and wryly caustic definition; a collection of which appeared under the title, *The Devil's Dictionary*. He was a successful San Franciscan journalist and used his experience as a Union soldier to draw together in a number of short stories a vivid account of his war years. In October 1913, Bierce headed for Mexico and was never heard from again.

INVICTUS[1]

Out of the night that covers me,
  Black as the Pit from pole to pole,
I thank whatever gods may be
  For my unconquerable soul.

In the fell clutch of circumstance
  I have not winced nor cried aloud.
Under the bludgeonings of chance
  My head is bloody, but unbowed.

Beyond this place of wrath and tears
  Looms but the horror of the shade,
And yet the menace of the years
  Finds, and shall find me, unafraid.

It matters not how strait the gate,
  How charged with punishments the scroll,
I am the master of my fate:
  I am the captain of my soul.

W. E. Henley
(23 August 1849 - 11 June 1903)

On this day in 1898, W. E. Henley wrote to Charles Whibley, after yet another operation: "They say I'm bettering and perhaps I am ... the pain is considerable, the inconvenience almost beyond bearing ... also often a passion of itching ... a mass of blisters."

Of this poem, which dates from 1875, at the end of a two-year stay in hospital, Stan Smith writes that "Henley often expresses a desperate carefree nihilism ... yet even when attitudinizing about 'the fell clutch of circumstance' or 'the bludgeonings of chance,' he preserves a sententious, overwrought dignity that aches with the pain of real feeling."

1. Latin for "Unconquered"

THE CONNOISSEUSE OF SLUGS

When I was a connoisseuse of slugs
I would part the ivy leaves, and look for the
naked jelly of those gold bodies,
translucent strangers glistening along the
stones, slowly, their gelatinous bodies
at my mercy. Made mostly of water, they would shrivel
to nothing if they were sprinkled with salt,
but I was not interested in that. What I liked
was to draw aside the ivy, breathe the
odor of the wall, and stand there in silence
until the slug forgot I was there
and sent its antennae up out of its
head, the glimmering umber horns
rising like telescopes, until finally the
sensitive knobs would pop out the ends,
delicate and intimate. Years later,
when I first saw a naked man,
I gasped with pleasure to see that quiet
mystery reenacted, the slow
elegant being coming out of hiding and
gleaming in the dark air, eager and so
trusting you could weep.

Sharon Olds
(19 November 1942 -)

Sharon Olds was brought up in California but has since lived in New York. She has written of paying attention to the small beauties of the physical world "as if it were our duty to / find things to love, to bind ourselves to this world."

ON THE VANITY OF EARTHLY GREATNESS

The tusks that clashed in mighty brawls
Of mastodons, are billiard balls.

The sword of Charlemagne the Just
Is ferric oxide, known as rust.

The grizzly bear whose potent hug
Was feared by all, is now a rug.

Great Caesar's bust is on the shelf,
And I don't feel so well myself.

Arthur Guiterman
(20 November 1871 - 11 January 1943)

Arthur Guiterman was born in Vienna of American parents. *The Laughing Muse* is his collection of mock-heroic ballads, parodying the ballads of chivalry. He also initiated the concept of reviews in rhyme, for *Life* magazine; wrote *Ballads of New York* about the quaint, historical side of New York; translated *L'Ecole des Maris*, a play by Molière into rhymed verse for the American stage; and wrote the lyrics and libretto for the opera *The Man Without a Country*.

TO A MOUSE
(ON TURNING HER UP IN HER NEST WITH THE PLOUGH, NOVEMBER, 1785)

Wee, sleekit,° cow'rin', tim'rous beastie,   *sleek*
O what a panic's in thy breastie!
Thou need na start awa sae hasty,
         Wi' bickering brattle!°   *hurrying scamper*
I wad be laith° to rin an' chase thee,   *loath*
         Wi' murd'ring pattle!°   *ploughstaff*

I'm truly sorry man's dominion
Has broken Nature's social union,
An' justifies that ill opinion
         Which makes thee startle
At me, thy poor earth-born companion,
         An' fellow-mortal!

I doubt na, whiles,° but thou may thieve;   *sometimes*
What then? poor beastie, thou maun° live!   *must*
     A daimen-icker in a thrave°   *the odd corn-ear from a bundle*
         'S a sma' request:
I'll get a blessin' wi' the lave,°   *rest*
         And never miss 't!

Thy wee bit housie, too, in ruin!
Its silly° wa's the win's are strewin'!   *frail*
An' naething, now, to big° a new ane,   *build*
         O' foggage° green!   *moss*
An' bleak December's winds ensuin',
         Baith snell° an keen!   *bitter*

To a mouse

Thou saw the fields laid bare and waste,
An' weary winter comin' fast,
An' cozie here, beneath the blast,
       Thou thought to dwell,
Till crash! the cruel coulter° past   *ploughshare*
       Out-thro' thy cell.

That wee bit heap o' leaves an' stibble°   *stubble*
Hast cost thee mony a weary nibble!
Now thou's turned out, for a' thy trouble,
       But house or hald,°   *Without house or holding*
To thole° the winter's sleety dribble,   *endure*
       An' cranreuch° cauld!   *hoar-frost*

But, Mousie, thou art no thy lane,°   *alone*
In proving foresight may be vain:
The best laid schemes o' mice an' men
       Gang aft a-gley,°   *Go often astray*
An' lea'e us nought but grief an' pain
       For promised joy.

Still thou art blest, compared wi' me!
The present only toucheth thee:
But oh! I backward cast my e'e
       On prospects drear!
An' forward tho' I canna see,
       I guess an' fear!

Robert Burns
(25 January 1759 - 21 July 1796)

THE PASSING OF ARTHUR
from Idylls of the King

Then murmured Arthur, 'Place me in the barge.'
So to the barge they came. There those three Queens
Put forth their hands, and took the King, and wept.
But she, that rose the tallest of them all
And fairest, laid his head upon her lap,
And loosed the shattered casque, and chafed his hands,
And called him by his name, complaining loud,
And dropping bitter tears against a brow
Striped with dark blood: for all his face was white
And colourless, and like the withered moon
Smote by the fresh beam of the springing east;
And all his greaves and cuisses dashed with drops
Of onset; and the light and lustrous curls –
That made his forehead like a rising sun
High from the daïs-throne – were parched with dust;
Or, clotted into points and hanging loose,
Mixed with the knightly growth that fringed his lips.
So like a shattered column lay the King;
Not like that Arthur who, with lance in rest,
From spur to plume a star of tournament,
Shot through the lists at Camelot, and charged
Before the eyes of ladies and of kings.

Then loudly cried the bold Sir Bedivere:
'Ah! my Lord Arthur, whither shall I go?
Where shall I hide my forehead and my eyes?
For now I see the true old times are dead,
When every morning brought a noble chance,
And every chance brought out a noble knight.

THE PASSING OF ARTHUR

Such times have been not since the light that led
The holy Elders with the gift of myrrh.
But now the whole Round Table is dissolved
Which was an image of the mighty world,
And I, the last, go forth companionless,
And the days darken round me, and the years,
Among new men, strange faces, other minds.'

And slowly answered Authur from the barge:
'The old order changeth, yielding place to new,
And God fulfills himself in many ways,
Lest one good custom should corrupt the world.
Comfort thyself: what comfort is in me?
I have lived my life, and that which I have done
May He within himself make pure! but thou,
If thou shouldst never see my face again,
Pray for my soul. More things are wrought by prayer
Than this world dreams of. Wherefore, let thy voice
Rise like a fountain for me night and day.

Alfred, Lord Tennyson
(6 August 1809–6 October 1892)

The Camelot of Arthurian legend became associated with the years of John F. Kennedy's presidency because of his fondness for the musical of the same name. This fabled kingdom stood in utopian contrast to the political realities of Vietnam, the civil rights movement, and the War Against Poverty. On this day in 1963 Kennedy was assassinated and Camelot undone.

BIBLE DEFENCE OF SLAVERY

Take sackcloth of the darkest dye,
  And shroud the pulpits round!
Servants of Him that cannot lie,
  Sit mourning on the ground.

Let holy horror blanch each cheek,
  Pale every brow with fears;
And rocks and stones, if ye could speak,
  Ye well might melt to tears!

Let sorrow breathe in every tone,
  In every strain ye raise;
Insult not God's majestic throne
  With th' mockery of praise.

A "reverend" man, whose light should be
  The guide of age and youth,
Brings to the shrine of Slavery
  The sacrifice of truth!

For the direst wrong by man imposed,
  Since Sodom's fearful cry,
The word of life has been unclos'd,
  To give your God the lie.

BIBLE DEFENCE OF SLAVERY

Oh! when ye pray for heathen lands,
And plead for their dark shores,
Remember Slavery's cruel hands
Make heathens at your doors!

Frances Ellen Watkins Harper
(24 September 1824 - 22 February 1911)

Born in Baltimore, Harper became galvanized by the anti-slavery movement. After meeting William Grant Still, a black abolitionist, she moved to Philadelphia, joining efforts with him on the Underground Railway and lecturing from the western states to Maine. After the death of her husband to whom she had been married a brief four years, she carried her message to the South. She was an indefatigable organizer who aided in establishing the National Association of Colored Women in 1896.

LOUISA

AFTER ACCOMPANYING HER ON A MOUNTAIN EXCURSION

I met Louisa in the shade,
And, having seen that lovely Maid,
Why should I fear to say
That, nymph-like, she is fleet and strong;
And down the rocks can leap along
Like rivulets in May?

And she hath smiles to earth unknown;
Smiles, that with motion of their own
Do spread, and sink, and rise;
That come and go with endless play,
And ever, as they pass away,
Are hidden in her eyes.

She loves her fire, her cottage-home;
Yet o'er the moorland will she roam
In weather rough and bleak;
And, when against the wind she strains,
Oh! might I kiss the mountain rains
That sparkle on her cheek.

Take all that's mine 'beneath the moon,'
If I with her but half a noon
May sit beneath the walls

LOUISA

Of some old cave, or mossy nook,
When up she winds along the brook
To hunt the waterfalls.

William Wordsworth
(7 April 1770 - 23 April 1850)

On this day in 1815, Sara Hutchinson (the sister of Wordsworth's wife, Mary) wrote that
Thomas De Quincey had been up all night with William at Elleray, dosing himself with
opium and drinking like a fish.

The poem "Louisa" was composed in 1802. The last line is echoed in Dorothy
Wordsworth's journal for 11 October 1802: "A beautiful day. We walked to the Easedale
hills to hunt waterfalls. William and Mary left me sitting on a stone on the solitary
mountains."

To hell with commonsense

More kicks than pence
We get from commonsense
Above its door is writ
All hope abandon. It
Is a bank will refuse a post
Dated cheque of the Holy Ghost.
Therefore I say to hell
With all reasonable
Poems in particular
We want no secular
Wisdom plodded together
By concerned fools. Gather
No moss you rolling stones
Nothing thought out atones
For no flight
In the light.
Let them wear out nerve and bone
Those who would have it that way
But in the end nothing that they
Have achieved will be in the shake up
In the final Wake Up
And I have a feeling
That through the hole in reason's ceiling
We can fly to knowledge
Without ever going to college.

Patrick Kavanagh
(21 October 1905 – 30 November 1967)

from KING LEAR
ACT III SCENE II

Lear. Blow, winds, and crack your cheeks! rage! blow!
You cataracts and hurricanoes, spout
Till you have drench'd our steeples, drown'd the cocks!
You sulphurous and thought-executing fires,
Vaunt-couriers to oak-cleaving thunderbolts,
Singe my white head! And thou, all-shaking thunder,
Strike flat the thick rotundity o' the world!
Crack nature's moulds, all germens° spill at once   *germs or forms*
That make ingrateful man!

   Rumble thy bellyful! Spit, fire! spout, rain!
Nor rain, wind, thunder, fire, are my daughters:
I tax not you, you elements, with unkindness;
I never gave you kingdom, call'd you children,
You owe me no subscription: then, let fall
Your horrible pleasure; here I stand, your slave,
A poor, infirm, weak, and despis'd old man.
But yet I call you servile ministers,
That have with two pernicious daughters join'd
Your high-engender'd battles 'gainst a head
So old and white as this. O! O! 'tis foul.

William Shakespeare
(23 April 1564 – 23 April 1616)

King Lear was entered on the Stationer's Register on this day in 1607.
  "... to see Lear acted –" wrote Lamb in his *On the Tragedies of Shakespeare*, "to see an old man tottering about the stage with a walking stick, turned out of doors by his daughters on a rainy night, has nothing in it but what is painful and disgusting. We want to take him in to shelter and relieve him. That is all the feeling which the acting of Lear ever produced in me. But the Lear of Shakespeare cannot be acted."

SONNET 29

When, in disgrace with fortune and men's eyes,
  I all alone beweep my outcast state,
And trouble deaf heaven with my bootless cries,
  And look upon myself, and curse my fate,
Wishing me like to one more rich in hope,
  Featured like him, like him with friends possessed,
Desiring this man's art and that man's scope,
  With what I most enjoy contented least;
Yet in these thoughts myself almost despising,
  Haply I think on thee, and then my state,
Like to the lark at break of day arising
  From sullen earth, sings hymns at heaven's gate;
    For thy sweet love remembered such wealth brings
    That then I scorn to change my state with kings.

William Shakespeare
(23 April 1564 – 23 April 1616)

On this day in 1582, a marriage licence was issued to Shakespeare and Anne Hathaway.
He married at the age of 18; she was eight years his senior.

INFANT SORROW

My mother groan'd! my father wept.
Into the dangerous world I leapt:
Helpless, naked, piping loud:
Like a fiend hid in a cloud.

Struggling in my father's hands,
Striving against my swadling bands,
Bound and weary I thought best
To sulk upon my mother's breast.

William Blake
(28 November 1757 – 12 August 1827)

Many of Blake's *Songs of Innocence* pair with those of *Experience*. This one pairs with "Infant Joy" (qv). But now the child is self-aware, with a will of its own, capable of defying both parents. He, or she, has entered "experience," potential alienation.

Blake was born at 28 Broad Street in London, the third son of a hosier and haberdasher. From the start he disliked discipline and his father decided not to send him to school, "thinking it most prudent to withhold from him the liability of receiving punishment." Before the age of ten, Blake saw a vision of angels in a tree, "bright angelic wings bespangling every bough like stars."

FULL MOON THAT STRIKES THE EARTH COLD

PLAINS CREE

Winter came early this year,
that's why, under my duvet,
I'm wondering about feathers,
the way some things so insubstantial,
so hardly there, can make all the difference.

I'm wondering too about geese.
Where do the souls of naked geese
go? Do they rise red like fire
from the coals, or gather
on some lonely neck of beach,

or do they, like idle pensioners,
throw dominoes on small blue tables
in the hills of Tenerife? Perhaps
they are speaking in ancient tongues
of honk or quack, about how one can adjust

to anything, make do without the fluff,
appreciate the lack of upper air disturbance
that so often fouled their course.
I wonder if they ever
want their feathers back,

Full moon that strikes
the earth cold

or to be young geese again
on the night of their first
migration: two angled lines
joined only at the vertex.
A week ago the full moon

that strikes the earth cold
began as thin blue air
in the distance that parted
for the V of your leaving.

Karen McCosker
(10 January 1948 -)

Karen McCosker notes: "Living in a severe climate clarifies how subject to nature we humans are and how dependent the two existences on each other. It seems no matter how simply we keep our lives, so much more is received than we can ever give back."

from THE BALLAD OF READING GAOL

6

In Reading gaol by Reading town
　There is a pit of shame,
And in it lies a wretched man
　Eaten by teeth of flame,
In a burning winding-sheet he lies,
　And his grave has got no name.

And there, till Christ call forth the dead,
　In silence let him lie:
No need to waste the foolish tear,
　Or heave the windy sigh:
The man had killed the thing he loved,
　And so he had to die.

And all men kill the thing they love,
　By all let this be heard,
Some do it with a bitter look,
　Some with a flattering word,
The coward does it with a kiss,
　The brave man with a sword!

Oscar Wilde
(16 October 1854 - 30 November 1900)

The Marquis of Queensbury, father of Wilde's companion Lord Alfred Douglas, left a card at Wilde's club "To Oscar Wilde posing as a Somdomite (sic)." Wilde took him to court for libel, lost the action, and was tried and sentenced to two years in jail for homosexual offenses. He was released in 1897, went into exile in France, and published *The Ballad of Reading Gaol* in 1898 under the pseudonym Sebastian Melmoth, a martyr character in a novel by his great-uncle.

A BALLAD OF TREES AND THE MASTER

Into the woods my Master went,
  Clean forspent, forspent.
Into the woods my Master came,
  Forspent with love and shame.
But the olives they were not blind to Him,
The little gray leaves were kind to Him:
The thorn-tree had a mind to Him
  When into the woods He came.

Out of the woods my Master went,
  And He was well content.
Out of the woods my Master came,
  Content with death and shame.
When Death and Shame would woo Him last,
From under the trees they drew Him last:
'Twas on a tree they slew Him – last
  When out of the woods He came.

Sidney Lanier
(3 February 1842 – 7 September 1881)

Lanier's two aesthetic loves were music and poetry, neither of which provided him a decent income until late in his brief life. Lanier's poetry was often denounced by critics because of his unconventional use of meter and the extended, rhythmic line. This poem, however, gives no evidence of Lanier the rebel poet, rather Lanier the musician. It is a ballad and the lines read like lyrics. Born in Macon, Georgia, Lanier died in North Carolina of tuberculosis contracted during his four-month captivity as a signal officer on a seized Confederate blockade runner.

THE CHARGE OF THE LIGHT BRIGADE

Half a league, half a league,
  Half a league onward,
All in the valley of Death
  Rode the six hundred.
'Forward, the Light Brigade!
Charge for the guns!' he said;
Into the valley of Death
  Rode the six hundred.

'Forward, the Light Brigade!'
Was there a man dismayed?
Not tho' the soldier knew
  Some one had blundered:
Their's not to make reply,
Their's not to reason why,
Their's but to do and die:
Into the valley of Death
  Rode the six hundred.

Cannon to right of them,
Cannon to left of them,
Cannon in front of them
  Volleyed and thundered;
Stormed at with shot and shell,
Boldly they rode and well,
Into the jaws of Death,
Into the mouth of Hell
  Rode the six hundred.

Flashed all their sabres bare,
Flashed as they turned in air,
Sabring the gunners there,
Charging an army, while
    All the world wondered:
Plunged in the battery-smoke
Right thro' the line they broke;
Cossack and Russian
Reeled from the sabre-stroke
    Shattered and sundered.
Then they rode back, but not,
    Not the six hundred.

Cannon to right of them,
Cannon to left of them,
Cannon behind them
    Volleyed and thundered;
Stormed at with shot and shell,
While horse and hero fell,
They that had fought so well
Came thro' the jaws of Death
Back from the mouth of Hell,
All that was left of them,
    Left of six hundred.

When can their glory fade?
O the wild charge they made!
    All the world wondered.
Honour the charge they made!
Honour the Light Brigade,
    Noble six hundred!

Alfred, Lord Tennyson
(6 August 1809 – 6 October 1892)

ALONE

From childhood's hour I have not been
As others were – I have not seen
As others saw – I could not bring
My passions from a common spring –
From the same source I have not taken
My sorrow – I could not awaken
My heart to joy at the same tone –
And all I lov'd – I lov'd alone –
Then – in my childhood – in the dawn
Of a most stormy life – was drawn
From ev'ry depth of good and ill
The mystery which binds me still –
From the torrent, or the fountain –
From the red cliff of the mountain –
From the sun that 'round me roll'd
In its autumn tint of gold –
From the lightning in the sky
As it pass'd me flying by –
From the thunder, and the storm –
And the cloud that took the form
(When the rest of Heaven was blue)
Of a demon in my view –

Edgar Allan Poe
(19 January 1809 – 7 October 1849)

Poe was raised by a foster family, the Allans, in Richmond, Virginia after the death of his mother. Having left the University of Virginia because of an unmet gambling debt, Poe received an appointment to West Point from which he was (not to his displeasure) dismissed for gross neglect of duty. He married Virginia Clemm when she was thirteen. She would die of tuberculosis twelve years later.

SONNETS TO ORPHEUS

IV

O you lovers that are so gentle, step occasionally
into the breath of the sufferers not meant for you,
let it be parted by your cheeks,
it will tremble, joined again, behind you.

You have been chosen, you are sound and whole,
you are like the very first beat of the heart,
you are the bow that shoots the arrows, and also their target,
in tears your smile would glow forever.

Do not be afraid to suffer, give
the heaviness back to the weight of the earth;
mountains are heavy, seas are heavy.

Even those trees you planted as children
became too heavy long ago – you couldn't carry them now.
But you can carry the winds . . . and the open spaces . . .

Rainer Maria Rilke
(4 December 1875 – 29 December 1926)
translated by Robert Bly
(23 December 1926 –)

Rainer Maria Rilke, an Austrian, was born in Prague and deserted the military academy there to study art history. He was influenced by Tolstoy, whom he met in Russia, and by Rodin, whose pupil, Klara Westhoff, he married in 1901. Rilke became Rodin's secretary in Paris, publishing *Das Rodin-Buch* in 1907. *Die Sonnette an Orpheus*, published in 1923, is seen as some of Rilke's finest work.

AGAINST

Against the bolts and welder's bloom of rhetoric
chamfer the waggon, scoop and shave the grain
to serviceable lightness, take the rein.

Against the packs of fighters shocking screes to fall
gaze on the heron, watch the wings yield their long
elegance over the water, echo the call.

Against the precipitate action of the angry father
loosen the mother, wait for the snow, hold
in a gloved finger his gloved hand, walk the lane.

Adam Thorpe
(5 December 1956 -)

Novelist and poet Adam Thorpe, author of *Ulverton*, was born in Paris. He Founded
the Equinox Travelling Theatre. Adam Thorpe comments:"I wrote this in our first year
in France, during the Gulf War. It's about all kinds of aggression, though, including
one's own."

HE WISHES FOR THE CLOTHS OF HEAVEN

Had I the heavens' embroidered cloths,
Enwrought with golden and silver light,
The blue and the dim and the dark cloths
Of night and light and the half-light,
I would spread the cloths under your feet:
But I, being poor, have only my dreams;
I have spread my dreams under your feet;
Tread softly because you tread on my dreams.

W. B. Yeats
(13 June 1865 – 28 January 1939)

On this day in 1921, the Anglo-Irish treaty was signed creating an Irish Free State with dominion status within the British Empire. Yeats wrote about the treaty to Mrs. Shakespeare: "I am in deep gloom about Ireland . . . I see no hope of escape from bitterness, and the extreme party may carry the country. When men are very bitter, death and ruin draw them on as a rabbit is supposed to be drawn on by the dancing of the fox." He was wondering whether Dublin would be a safe place to bring up his children, but he soon returned and was full of plans for a State Theatre, an Irish Academy of Letters and the creation of a Ministry of Fine Arts.

THE DARK HILLS

Dark hills at evening in the west,
Where sunset hovers like a sound
Of golden horns that sang to rest
Old bones of warriors under ground,
Far now from all the bannered ways
Where flash the legions of the sun,
You fade – as if the last of days
Were fading and all wars were done.

Edwin Arlington Robinson
(22 December 1869 – 6 April 1935)

Robinson, a descendant of Anne Bradstreet, acknowledged Theodore Roosevelt's attention to his poetry and his offer of a position in the New York City custom house by
dedicating his book *The Town Down the River* (1910) to him. Robinson went on to receive
three Pulitzer Prizes for works he may not have written had he not been freed by
Roosevelt from his job as inspector of subway construction. However, it was his early
poems that prompted one reviewer to comment, "The world is not beautiful to him, but
a prison house." Robinson replied, "The world is not a prison house, but a kind of spiritual kindergarten where bewildered infants are trying to spell God with the wrong
blocks."

AN APPEAL TO CATS IN THE
BUSINESS OF LOVE

Ye cats that at midnight spit love at each other,
Who best feel the pangs of a passionate lover,
I appeal to your scratches and your tattered fur,
If the business of love be no more than to purr.
Old Lady Grimalkin with her gooseberry eyes
Knew some thing when a kitten, for why she was wise;
You find by experience, the love-fit's soon o'er,
Puss! Puss! lasts not long, but turns to *Cat-whore*!

    Men ride many miles,
    Cats tread many tiles,
Both hazard their necks in the fray;
    Only cats, when they fall
    From a house or a wall,
Keep their feet, mount their tails, and away!

Thomas Flatman
(21 February 1637 - 8 December 1688)

Thomas Flatman was born in London and educated at Winchester and New College, Oxford. He became a barrister in 1626, but also acquired a reputation as a painter of miniatures – a self-portrait done when he was 38 is kept in the Victoria and Albert Museum. His *Poems and Songs* were published when he was 39 and include "The Dying Christian to his Soul," a poem that Alexander Pope later imitated.

SONNET VII
HOW SOON HATH TIME

How soon hath Time, the subtle thief of youth,
  Stolen on his wing my three and twentieth year!
  My hasting days fly on with full career,
  But my late spring no bud or blossom shew'th.°   *showeth*
Perhaps my semblance° might deceive the truth,   *appearance*
  That I to manhood am arrived so near,
  And inward ripeness doth much less appear,
  That some more timely-happy spirits endu'th.°   *endoweth*
Yet be it less or more, or soon or slow,
  It shall be still in strictest measure even°   *corresponding*
  To that same lot, however mean or high,
Toward which Time leads me, and the will of Heaven;
  All is, if I have grace to use it so,
  As ever in my great Taskmaster's eye.

John Milton
(9 December 1608 – 8 November 1674)

This sonnet was probably composed on or about 9 December 1632, Milton's 24th birthday. Milton transcribed it at the bottom of a letter to a former Cambridge tutor, in which he defended his love of learning and his reluctance to get a job or take holy orders.

Milton's father was a usurer, who made his money from loans and property. He supported Milton in years of study at home, after leaving Cambridge. In a Latin poem to his father, Milton wrote: "So I, who already have a place, though a low one, in the ranks of the learned, shall one day sit among those who wear the ivy and laurels of victory. Now I shall no longer mix with the brainless mob: my steps will shun the sight of common eyes." Milton had been unpopular at Cambridge, where the undergraduates nicknamed him "The Lady of Christ's." He thought that he may have alienated them by "a certain niceness of nature, an honest haughtiness."

THIS WORLD IS NOT CONCLUSION

This World is not Conclusion.
A Species stands beyond –
Invisible, as Music –
But positive, as Sound –
It beckons, and it baffles –
Philosophy – don't know –
And through a Riddle, at the last –
Sagacity, must go –
To guess it, puzzles scholars –
To gain it, Men have borne
Contempt of Generations
And Crucifixion, shown –
Faith slips – and laughs, and rallies –
Blushes, if any see –
Plucks at a twig of Evidence –
And asks a Vane, the way –
Much Gesture, from the Pulpit –
Strong Hallelujahs roll –
Narcotics cannot still the Tooth
That nibbles at the soul –

Emily Dickinson
(10 December 1830 – 15 May 1886)

Dickinson described her art with typical, striking economy: "If I read a book and it makes my whole body so cold I know no fire can ever warm me, I know that is poetry. If I feel physically as if the top of my head were taken off, I know that is poetry. These are the only ways I know it. Is there any other way?"

from VACILLATION
III

Get all the gold and silver that you can,
Satisfy ambition, animate
The trivial days and ram them with the sun,
And yet upon these maxims meditate:
All women dote upon an idle man
Although their children need a rich estate;
No man has ever lived that had enough
Of children's gratitude or woman's love.

No longer in Lethean foliage caught
Begin the preparation for your death
And from the fortieth winter by that thought
Test every work of intellect or faith,
And everything that your own hands have wrought,
And call those works extravagance of breath
That are not suited for such men as come
Proud, open-eyed and laughing to the tomb.

William Butler Yeats
(13 June 1865 – 28 January 1939)

On this day in 1920, the British Government declared martial law in Ireland, less than a fortnight before ceding Home Rule to Ireland. Yeats was appointed a Senator by the new Free State – but less thanks to his poetry or his work at the Abbey Theatre than to his previous membership in the Irish Republican Brotherhood. Yeats wrote "Vacillation" in his late sixties.

PROSPICE

Fear death? – to feel the fog in my throat,
  The mist in my face,
When the snows begin, and the blasts denote
  I am nearing the place,
The power of the night, the press of the storm,
  The post of the foe;
Where he stands, the Arch Fear in a visible form,
  Yet the strong man must go:
For the journey is done and the summit attained,
  And the barriers fall,
Though a battle's to fight ere the guerdon be gained,
  The reward of it all.
I was ever a fighter, so – one fight more,
  The best and the last!
I would hate that death bandaged my eyes, and forbore,
  And bade me creep past.
No! let me taste the whole of it, fare like my peers
  The heroes of old,
Bear the brunt, in a minute pay glad life's arrears
  Of pain, darkness and cold.
For sudden the worst turns the best to the brave,
  The black minute's at end,
And the elements' rage, the fiend-voices that rave,
  Shall dwindle, shall blend,
Shall change, shall become first a peace out of pain,
  Then a light, then thy breast,
O thou soul of my soul! I shall clasp thee again,
  And with God be the rest!

Robert Browning (7 May 1812 – 12 December 1889)

NICE DAY FOR A LYNCHING

The bloodhounds look like sad old judges
In a strange court. They point their noses
At the Negro jerking in the tight noose;
His feet spread crow-like above these
Honourable men who laugh as he chokes.

I don't know this black man.
I don't know these white men.

But I know that one of my hands
Is black, and one white. I know that
One part of me is being strangled,
While another part horribly laughs.

Until it changes,
I shall be forever killing; and be killed.

Kenneth Patchen
(13 December 1911 – 8 January 1972)

Kenneth Patchen was born and educated in Ohio, and attended, for one year only, the Experimental College at the University of Wisconsin, where he excelled as an athlete. He held a succession of jobs until the success of his first poetry collection *Before the Brave* in 1936 led him to focus on his (thereafter prolific) writing – the flavor of which is indicated by the title of his 1945 collection *An Astonished Eye Looks Out of the Air: Being Some Poems Old and New Against War and in Behalf of Life*. Some of his books were hand-bound and hand-painted and he exhibited "talismanic wall-hangings warning Fear and Stupidity that Love is in town and well-armed." For the last twenty years and more of his life, he had a spinal ailment and was cared for and protected by his wife, Miriam (née Oikemus). Eliot, Auden, and others gave money to help support this widely admired poet.

EVERNESS

One thing does not exist: Oblivion.
God saves the metal and he saves the dross,
And his prophetic memory guards from loss
The moons to come, and those of evenings gone.
Everything *is*: the shadows in the glass
Which, in between the day's two twilights, you
Have scattered by the thousands, or shall strew
Henceforward in the mirrors that you pass.
And everything is part of that diverse
Crystalline memory, the universe;
Whoever through its endless mazes wanders
Hears door on door click shut behind his stride,
And only from the sunset's farther side
Shall view at last the Archetypes and the Splendors.

Jorge Luis Borges
(24 August 1889 - 14 June 1986)
translated by Richard Wilbur
(1 March 1921 -)

Richard Wilbur comments: "This translation was done with the linguistic and other advice of Norman Thomas di Giovanni, who was putting together a bilingual *Selected Poems* (1971) of Jorge Luis Borges. Borges went over all of the translations done, by various hands, for that book, and delighted me by saying that, in one line of another sonnet, I had improved on the original. I am sure that, in so saying, Borges was merely giving further proof of his notorious love of the English language."

EL DORADO

Gaily bedight,
A gallant knight,
In sunshine and in shadow,
Had journeyed long,
Singing a song,
In search of El Dorado.

But he grew old –
This knight so bold –
And o'er his heart a shadow
Fell as he found
No spot of ground
That looked like El Dorado.

And, as his strength
Failed him at length,
He met a pilgrim shadow –
'Shadow,' said he,
'Where it can be –
This land of El Dorado?'

'Over the mountains
Of the moon,
Down the Valley of the Shadow,
Ride, boldly ride,'
The shade replied, –
'If you seek for El Dorado!'

Edgar Allan Poe
(19 January 1809 – 7 October 1849)

THE LAST WORD

Creep into thy narrow bed,
Creep, and let no more be said!
Vain thy onset! all stands fast;
Thou thyself must break at last.

Let the long contention cease!
Geese are swans, and swans are geese.
Let them have it how they will!
Thou art tired; best be still!

They out-talk'd thee, hiss'd thee, tore thee.
Better men fared thus before thee;
Fired their ringing shot and pass'd,
Hotly charged – and broke at last.

Charge once more, then, and be dumb!
Let the victors, when they come,
When the forts of folly fall,
Find thy body by the wall.

Matthew Arnold
(24 December 1822 – 15 April 1888)

Arnold wrote to his mother regarding his prospects as a poet: "I have less poetical senti-
ment than Tennyson and less intellectual vigour and abundance than Browning. Yet
because I have more of a fusion than either of them, and have more regularly applied that
fusion to the main line of modern development, I am likely to have my turn."

On Arnold's death, Browning wrote: "I shall hold in veneration – to my own dying day –
the memory of one of the noblest and best men I ever knew and ever loved."

Upon julia's clothes

Whenas in silks my Julia goes,
Then, then methinks, how sweetly flows
That liquefaction of her clothes!

Next, when I cast mine eyes and see
That brave vibration each way free;
O how that glittering taketh me!

Robert Herrick
(24 August 1591 – 15 October 1674)

Though he flirted wildly with his sweethearts, real and imaginary, the vicar of Dean Prior lived as a bachelor, excepting his brief and uncharacteristically impetuous affair with Tomasin Parsons. He filled his house with pets, including a tame pig that would drink from a tankard to the delight of Herrick's visitors.

from CONTEMPLATION[1]

From stones and poets you may know,
Nothing so active is, as that which least seems so.

For he, that conduit running wine of song,
Then to himself does most belong,
When he his mortal house unbars
To the importunate and thronging feet
That round our corporal walls unheeded beat;
Till, all containing, he exalt
His stature to the stars, or stars
Narrow their heaven to his fleshly vault:
When, like a city under ocean,
To human things he grows a desolation,
And is made a habitation
For the fluctuous universe
To lave° with unimpeded motion.   *bathe*
He scarcely frets the atmosphere
With breathing, and his body shares
The immobility of rocks;
His heart's a drop-well of tranquility;
His mind more still is than the limbs of fear,
And yet its unperturbed velocity
The spirit of the simoon[2] mocks.
He round the solemn centre of his soul
Wheels like a dervish, while his being is
Streamed with the set of the world's harmonies,
In the long draft of whatsoever sphere
He lists the sweet and clear
Clangour of his high orbit on to roll,
So gracious is his heavenly grace;

from CONTEMPLATION

And the bold stars does hear,
Every one in his airy soar,
For evermore
Shout to each other from the peaks of space,
As thwart ravines of azure shouts the mountaineer.

Francis Thompson
(18 December 1859 – 13 November 1907)

Francis Thompson, author of *The Hound of Heaven*, was born in Preston, the son of a Roman Catholic doctor. Failing to become either a priest or a doctor, he drifted as a homeless opium addict until befriended by the Meynells.

1. Lines 46 - 78.
2. An oppressively hot desert wind.

MUSEUM PIECE

The good grey guardians of art
Patrol the halls on spongy shoes,
Impartially protective, though
Perhaps suspicious of Toulouse.

Here dozes one against the wall,
Disposed upon a funeral chair.
A Degas dancer pirouettes
Upon the parting of his hair.

See how she spins! The grace is there,
But strain as well is plain to see.
Degas loved the two together:
Beauty joined to energy.

Edgar Degas purchased once
A fine El Greco, which he kept
Against the wall beside his bed
To hang his pants on while he slept.

Richard Wilbur
(1 March 1921 -)

Richard Wilbur writes: "The concluding anecdote of this 1947 poem is true, and may be found in the art-dealer Vollard's memoir of Degas. What the poem conveys, I hope, is that artists are less gravely reverential about art than its custodians are. The usual shorter form of Toulouse-Lautrec is Lautrec rather than Toulouse, but 'Lautrec' has the defect of not rhyming with 'shoes.'"

THE WORLD IS TOO MUCH WITH US

The world is too much with us; late and soon,
Getting and spending, we lay waste our powers:
Little we see in nature that is ours;
We have given our hearts away, a sordid boon!
This Sea that bares her bosom to the moon;
The Winds that will be howling at all hours,
And are up-gathered now like sleeping flowers;
For this, for everything, we are out of tune;
It moves us not. – Great God! I'd rather be
A Pagan suckled in a creed outworn;
So might I, standing on this pleasant lea,
Have glimpses that would make me less forlorn;
Have sight of Proteus coming from the sea;
Or hear old Triton blow his wreathèd horn.

William Wordsworth
(7 April 1770 – 23 April 1850)

On this day in 1799, William Wordsworth and his sister Dorothy reached their new home, Dove Cottage, after overnight stays at Sedbergh and Kendall. Beset by the wintry weather, they were soon to fall ill with colds. It was left to Dorothy to do her best to make the damp and empty house comfortable.

THE GOOD-MORROW

I wonder by my troth, what thou and I
Did, till we loved? were we not weaned till then?
But sucked on country pleasures, childishly?
Or snorted we in the seven sleepers' den?
'Twas so; but this, all pleasures fancies be.
If ever any beauty I did see,
Which I desired, and got, 'twas but a dream of thee.

And now good-morrow to our waking souls,
Which watch not one another out of fear;
For love all love of other sights controls,
And makes one little room an everywhere.
Let sea-discoverers to new worlds have gone,
Let maps to others, worlds on worlds have shown,
Let us possess one world, each hath one, and is one.

My face in thine eye, thine in mine appears,
And true plain hearts do in the faces rest;
Where can we find two better hemispheres
Without sharp North, without declining West?
What ever dies, was not mixed equally;
If our two loves be one, or thou and I
Love so alike that none do slacken, none can die.

John Donne
(c. June 1572 - 31 March 1631)

On this day in 1614, Donne wrote to his friend Sir Henry Goodere to tell him he would
be printing "forthwith" a collection of his poems "not for much public view, but at mine
own cost, a few copies."

'DONG, SOUNDS THE BRASS IN THE EAST'

Dong, sounds the brass in the east,
As if to a funeral feast,
But I like that sound the best
Out of the fluttering west.

The steeple ringeth a knell,
But the fairies' silvery bell
Is the voice of that gentle folk,
Or else the horizon that spoke.

Its metal is not of brass,
But air, and water, and glass,
And under a cloud it is swung,
And by the wind it is rung.

When the steeple tolleth the noon,
It soundeth not so soon,
Yet it rings a far earlier hour,
And the sun has not reached its tower.

Henry David Thoreau
(12 July 1817 – 6 May 1862)

In 1845, Thoreau constructed a cabin for twenty-eight dollars on a piece of property belonging to his mentor and friend, Ralph Waldo Emerson, on Walden Pond in Massachusetts for what was to be a twenty-six month experiment in simple living. Thoreau's lifestyle, however, did not remove him from society and did not conflict with the writer's robust social life in Concord.

Almost unknown as a writer during his lifetime, Thoreau's books, expanded from notes in his journals, reveal a man of tenacious individualism who believed in the power of one person's actions, an anarchist who would rather immerse himself in nature or be locked in a prison cell than dissipate his energy and time in fruitless debate.

23

from IDEA

61

Since there's no help, come let us kiss and part:
Nay, I have done; you get no more of me,
And I am glad, yea, glad with all my heart,
That thus so cleanly I myself can free;
Shake hands for ever, cancel all our vows,
And when we meet at any time again,
Be it not seen in either of our brows
That we one jot of former love retain.
Now at the last gasp of love's latest breath,
When, his pulse failing, passion speechless lies,
When faith is kneeling by his bed of death,
And innocence is closing up his eyes,
Now, if thou wouldst, when all have given him over,
From death to life thou mightst him yet recover.

Michael Drayton
(1563 – 23 December 1631)

Michael Drayton was born in Hartshill, Warwickshire. It is conjectured that he became a page in the household of Sir Henry Goodere and that his *Idea* sonnet sequence is addressed to Ann, Sir Henry's younger daughter. The sonnets were first published in 1594, but this particular sonnet was not added until the publication of *Ideas Mirrour* in 1619.

The authorities took offense at Drayton's first published work, metrical paraphrases from the Bible, entitled *The Harmony of the Church* (1592), and gave orders for it to be destroyed. Drayton went on to write odes, dramas, mythological poems, historical tales, and patriotic poems such as "The Battle of Agincourt." His *Poems, Lyric and Pastoral* (c. 1606) contained the poem "Fair Stood the Wind for France." His mammoth multi-volume poem, *Poly-olbion*, aimed to provide "a chronological description of all the tracts, rivers, mountains, forests, and other parts of Great Britain."

He died in relative poverty, and it was left to Lady Anne Clifford, countess of Dorset, to sponsor the construction and installation of his monument in Westminster Abbey.

THE BALLAD OF BOUILLABAISSE

A street there is in Paris famous,
  For which no rhyme our language yields,
Rue Neuve des Petits Champs its name is –
  The New Street of the Little Fields;
And here's an inn, not rich and splendid,
  But still in comfortable case;
The which in youth I oft attended,
  To eat a bowl of Bouillabaisse.

This Bouillabaisse a noble dish is –
  A sort of soup or broth, or brew,
Or hotchpotch of all sorts of fishes,
  That Greenwich never could outdo;
Green herbs, red peppers, mussels, saffern,
  Soles, onions, garlic, roach, and dace;
All these you eat at Terré's tavern,
  In that one dish of Bouillabaisse.

Indeed, a rich and savoury stew 'tis;
  And true philosophers, methinks,
Who love all sorts of natural beauties,
  Should love good victuals and good drinks.
And Cordelier or Benedictine
  Might gladly, sure, his lot embrace,
Nor find a fast-day too afflicting
  Which served him up a Bouillabaisse.

I wonder if the house still there is?
  Yes, here the lamp is, as before;
The smiling red-cheeked écaillère is

Still opening oysters at the door.
Is Terré still alive and able?
  I recollect his droll grimace;
He'd come and smile before your table,
  And hope you liked your Bouillabaisse.

We enter – nothing's changed or older.
  'How's Monsieur Terré, waiter, pray?'
The waiter stares and shrugs his shoulder –
  'Monsieur is dead this many a day.'
'It is the lot of saint and sinner,
  So honest Terré's run his race.'
'What will Monsieur require for dinner?'
  'Say, do you still cook Bouillabaisse?'

'Oh oui, Monsieur,' 's the waiter's answer;
  'Quel vin Monsieur désire-t-il?'
'Tell me a good one.' – 'That I can, Sir:
  The Chambertin with yellow seal.'
'So Terré's gone,' I say, and sink in
  My old accustomed corner-place;
'He's done with feasting and with drinking,
  With Burgundy and Bouillabaisse.'

My old accustomed corner here is,
  The table still is in the nook;
Ah! vanished many a busy year is,
  This well-known chair since last I took.
When first I saw ye, *cari luoghi*,°   *dear places*
  I'd scarce a beard upon my face,
And now a grizzled, grim old fogy,
  I sit and wait for Bouillabaisse.

Where are you, old companions trusty,
  Of early days, here met to dine?
Come, waiter! quick, a flagon crusty –

I'll pledge them in the good old wine.
The kind old voices and old faces.
My memory can quick retrace;
Around the board they take their places,
And share the wine and Bouillabaisse.

There's Jack has made a wondrous marriage;
There's laughing Tom is laughing yet;
There's brave Augustus drives his carriage;
There's poor old Fred in the Gazette;
On James's head the grass is growing:
Good Lord! the world has wagged apace
Since here we set the Claret flowing,
And drank, and ate the Bouillabaisse.

Ah me! how quick the days are flitting?
I mind me of a time that's gone,
When here I'd sit, as now I'm sitting,
In this same place – but not alone.
A fair young form was nestled near me,
A dear, dear face looked fondly up,
And sweetly spoke and smiled to cheer me.
– There's no one now to share my cup.

I drink it, as the Fates ordain it.
Come, fill it, and have done with rhymes:
Fill up the lonely glass, and drain it
In memory of dear old times.
Welcome the wine, whate'er the seal is;
And sit you down and say your grace
With thankful heart, whate'er the meal is.
– Here comes the smoking Bouillabaisse!

William Makepeace Thackeray
(18 July 1811 – 24 December 1863)

THE SECOND COMING

Turning and turning in the widening gyre
The falcon cannot hear the falconer;
Things fall apart; the centre cannot hold;
Mere anarchy is loosed upon the world,
The blood-dimmed tide is loosed, and everywhere
The ceremony of innocence is drowned;
The best lack all conviction, while the worst
Are full of passionate intensity.

Surely some revelation is at hand;
Surely the Second Coming is at hand.
The Second Coming! Hardly are those words out
When a vast image out of *Spiritus Mundi*
Troubles my sight: somewhere in sands of the desert
A shape with lion body and the head of a man,
A gaze blank and pitiless as the sun,
Is moving its slow thighs, while all about it
Reel shadows of the indignant desert birds.
The darkness drops again; but now I know
That twenty centuries of stony sleep
Were vexed to nightmare by a rocking cradle,
And what rough beast, its hour come round at last,
Slouches towards Bethlehem to be born?

William Butler Yeats (13 June 1865 - 28 January 1939)

The poem was written in January 1919, no doubt with the Russian revolution and the troubles in Ireland in mind. Yeats, in annotating this poem, wrote: "All our scientific, democratic, fact-accumulating, heterogeneous civilisation belongs to the outward gyre [spiral revolution] and prepares not the continuance of itself but the revelation as in a lightning flash, though in a flash that will not strike only in one place, and will for a time be constantly repeated, of the civilisation that must slowly take its place."

SIMPLE GIFTS

'Tis the gift to be simple, 'tis the gift to be free,
'Tis the gift to come down where we ought to be,
And when we find ourselves in the place just right,
'Twill be in the valley of love and delight.
When true simplicity is gain'd,
To bow and to bend we shan't be asham'd,
To turn, turn will be our delight
'Till by turning, turning we come round right.

Anonymous

Composed around the late 1840s, "Simple Gifts" is a Shaker hymn. The sect originated in England in 1747, and emigrated to America in 1772. The Shakers practiced celibacy and an ascetic communal life.

27 DECEMBER

from VARIATIONS DONE FOR GERALD VAN DE WIELE[1]

what soul
isn't in default?

can you afford not to make
the magical study

which happiness is? do you hear
the cock when he crows? do you know the charge,

that you shall have no envy, that your life
has its orders, that the seasons

seize you too, that no body and soul are one
if they are not wrought

in this retort? that otherwise efforts
are efforts? And that the hour of your flight

will be the hour of your death?

Charles Olson (27 December 1910 - 10 January 1970)
based around "Le Bonheur" by Arthur Rimbaud (20 October 1854 - 10 November 1891)

Charles Olson was born in Chicago, the son of a postman, and educated at the university there. He married twice and had four children. Toward the end of his life he concentrated on his long poem *Maximus*. He died of cancer at the age of 60. He is identified as a Black Mountain poet, having been rector at this experimental Black Mountain College in North Carolina, influencing the poets Robert Creeley and Denise Levertov among others.

1. From Section II, *The Charge*, lines 55 to 67.

SONNET 129

The expense of spirit in a waste of shame
Is lust in action; and till action, lust
Is perjur'd, murderous, bloody, full of blame,
Savage, extreme, rude, cruel, not to trust;
Enjoy'd no sooner but despisèd straight;
Past reason hunted; and no sooner had,
Past reason hated, as a swallow'd bait,
On purpose laid to make the taker mad:
Mad in pursuit, and in possession so;
Had, having, and in quest to have, extreme;
A bliss in proof, – and prov'd, a very woe;
Before, a joy propos'd; behind, a dream.
  All this the world well knows; yet none knows well
  To shun the heaven that leads men to this hell.

William Shakespeare
(23 April 1564 – 23 April 1616)

On this day in 1594, Queen Elizabeth I watched Shakespeare, William Kemp, and Richard Burbage act in an unidentified comedy. The three actors received £20 by "waye of her Majesties rewarde."

SONG

When I am dead, my dearest,
  Sing no sad songs for me;
Plant thou no roses at my head,
  Nor shady cypress tree:
Be the green grass above me
  With showers and dewdrops wet;
And if thou wilt, remember,
  And if thou wilt, forget.

I shall not see the shadows,
  I shall not feel the rain;
I shall not hear the nightingale
  Sing on, as if in pain:
And dreaming through the twilight
  That doth not rise nor set,
Haply I may remember,
  And haply may forget.

Christina Rossetti
(5 December 1830 – 29 December 1894)

This poem was written on 12 December 1848, just after Christina Rossetti's 18th birthday, as an engagement present to the painter James Collinson. She broke off the engagement when he returned to the Catholic faith – and never married. "Grown old before my time," as she put it, she suffered from ill health most of her life and was operated on for cancer. She died later, according to one report, while "in the act of prayer."

If –

If you can keep your head when all about you
   Are losing theirs and blaming it on you,
If you can trust yourself when all men doubt you,
   But make allowance for their doubting too;
If you can wait and not be tired of waiting,
   Or being lied about, don't deal in lies,
Or being hated, don't give way to hating,
   And yet don't look too good, nor talk too wise:

If you can dream – and not make dreams your master;
   If you can think – and not make thoughts your aim;
If you can meet with Triumph and Disaster
   And treat those two impostors just the same;
If you can bear to hear the truth you've spoken
   Twisted by knaves to make a trap for fools,
Or watch the things you gave your life to, broken,
   And stoop and build 'em up with worn-out tools:

If you can make one heap of all your winnings
   And risk it on one turn of pitch-and-toss,
And lose, and start again at your beginnings
   And never breathe a word about your loss;
If you can force your heart and nerve and sinew
   To serve your turn long after they are gone,
And so hold on when there is nothing in you
   Except the Will which says to them: 'Hold on!'

I F –

If you can talk with crowds and keep your virtue,
     Or walk with Kings – nor lose the common touch,
If neither foes nor loving friends can hurt you,
     If all men count with you, but none too much;
If you can fill the unforgiving minute
     With sixty seconds' worth of distance run,
Yours is the Earth and everything that's in it,
     And – which is more – you'll be a Man, my son!

Rudyard Kipling
(30 December 1865 – 18 January 1936)

Kipling based this masculine ideal on Dr. Jameson, leader of the fiasco that came to be
known as the Jameson raid (29 December 1895 to 2 January 1896). The raid was intended
to surprise the Transvaal Boers but ended ignominiously with Jameson being led off to a
Pretoria jail in tears.

Auld lang syne

Should auld acquaintance be forgot,
  And never brought to min'?
Should auld acquaintance be forgot,
  And auld lang syne?

  For auld lang syne, my dear.
    For auld lang syne,
  We'll tak a cup o' kindness yet,
    For auld lang syne.

We twa hae run about the braes,
  And pu'd the gowans° fine;   daisies
But we've wandered mony a weary foot
  Sin' auld lang syne.

We twa hae paidled° i' the burn,   paddled
  From morning sun till dine;
But seas between us braid hae roared
  Sin' auld lang syne.

And there's a hand, my trusty fiere,°   comrade
  And gie's a hand o' thine;
And we'll tak a right guid-willie waught,° hearty draught
  For auld lang syne.

And surely ye'll be your pint-stowp,
And surely I'll be mine;
And we'll tak a cup o' kindness yet
For auld lang syne.

Robert Burns
(25 January 1759 - 21 July 1796)

On this day in 1792, Burns told Mrs. Dunlop that hard drinking was "the devil to him." Burns contributed this song to James Thomson's Scots Musical Museum, writing to Thomson in September 1793 that it was "the old song of olden times, and which has never been in print, nor even in manuscript, until I took it down from an old man's singing." This reference to the old man singing may have been made "merely in a playful humor," says one editor, for "the song offers evidence of our Bard himself being the author." In which case, Burns had again been playful when he sent this song to Mrs. Dunlop on 17 December 1788, with a letter to say: "Light be the turf on the breast of the Heaven-inspired poet who composed this glorious fragment. There is more fire of native genius in it than in half a dozen Modern English Bacchanalians."

Acknowledgments

If this acknowledgments section appears curiously redundant, there is a reason. This book was originally published in Britain as *Poem for the Day*. Proceeds from sale of the books were given over to The Natural Death Centre, a London-based "educational charity which assists families who are looking after a dying person at home or who are trying to arrange a funeral, with or without using undertakers." My task as U.S. editor was to remove a portion of the poems, replacing them with works mainly by American poets.

—*Karen McCosker*

From Nicholas Albery and The Natural Death Centre:

The Natural Death Centre is grateful to Wendy Cope, Peter Ratcliffe, Matthew Mezey, Christine Mills, Emma Whiting, Peter Cadogan, Gillian Rathbone, John-David Papworth, Merlyn Albery, Josefine Speyer and Yvonne Ackroyd for their work on this book, and to the many people and organizations that contributed poems, suggestions or research, including Heather Albery, Anne Ashworth, Tim Beaumont, Judith Becque-Rowley, Rosemary Bett, Dr Irene Campbell, Betsy Cook, Theo Dorgan, Marie Louise Grennert, Karen McCosker, Yvonne Malik, Marianne Nault, Marcelle Papworth, John Rowan, Pattie Powell, Diana Senior, Guida Swan, Janet Whitaker, Heathcote Williams and Valerie Yule.

Much of the source material for the biographical information on the poets was compiled from the following reference works, to which the reader is directed for further information: *The Oxford Companion to English Literature* (Drabble, OUP), *The Oxford Companion to Twentieth Century Poetry in English* (Hamilton, OUP), *Contemporary Poets* (Vinson, St James Press), *Chamber's Biographical Dictionary* (Magnusson, Chambers) and *The Dictionary of National Biography* (OUP). The Natural Death Centre is also grateful for help from librarians at the British Museum, the London Library, the Poetry Library, the Bodleian Library, and the Kensington and Chelsea Library.

The Natural Death Centre gratefully acknowledges the following for their patient help and for their most generous permission to reproduce copyright material (and is apologetic for any errors or omissions – this was our first venture into the minefield of poem permissions):

Virago Press Ltd for a poem by Maya Angelou from *And Still I Rise* ©1978; Faber and Faber Ltd and Simon Armitage for a poem by Simon Armitage; Peters Fraser & Dunlop for a poem by Hilaire Belloc; Duncan Cotterill & Co on behalf of the Estate of Ursula Bethell for a poem by Ursula Bethell; John Murray (Publishers) Ltd for poems by John Betjeman from *Collected Poems*; Earle Birney for a poem from *The Collected Poems of Earle Birney* (McClelland & Stewart Ltd); Farrar, Straus & Giroux, Inc for 'Casabianca' and 'One Art' by Elizabeth Bishop from *The Complete Poems 1927-1979* ©1979, 1983 by Alice Helen Methfessel; Robert Bly for his translations of poems by Antonio Machado, Rainer Maria Rilke, Kabir and Juan Ramón Jiménez; Grove/Atlantic Inc for a poem by Raymond Carver from *A New Path to the Waterfall* published by The Atlantic Monthly Press ©1989; TRO Essex Music Ltd for a song by Leonard Cohen ©1966 Leonard Cohen Stranger Music Inc USA, London for UK and Commonwealth (ex Canada), Republics of Ireland and South Africa. All rights reserved. Used by permission; Faber and Faber Ltd and Wendy Cope for 'Summer Vilanelle' and 'Giving up Smoking' from *Making Cocoa for Kingsley Amis*, and 'Bloody Men' from *Serious Concerns*, both books by Wendy Cope; Random House UK Ltd and the estate of Frances Cornford for a poem from her *Collected Poems* (Cresset Press); Marion Boyars Publishing Ltd for a poem by Robert Creeley; Anvil Press Ltd for '6 A.M. Thoughts' by Dick Davis from *Dick Davis: Devices and Desires* (Anvil Press Poetry 1989); Theo Dorgan for his poem from *The Ordinary House of Love* (Salmon Publishing); Anvil Press Poetry and Carol Ann Duffy for 'Valentine' by Carol Ann Duffy from *Meantime* ©1993; Random House UK Ltd and Gavin Ewart for poems by Gavin Ewart from *The Complete Little Ones* (Hutchinsons); Peters, Fraser & Dunlop for a poem by James Fenton; New Directions Publishing Corp. for a poem by Lawrence Ferlinghetti from *A Coney Island of the Mind* copyright ©1958 by Lawrence Ferlinghetti; Duncan Forbes for ' Recension Day'; Faber and Faber Ltd and Philip Gross for 'Son and Heir' by Philip Gross; Faber and Faber Ltd and Thom Gunn for a poem by Thom Gunn; Liveright Publishing Corporation for 'Those Winter Sundays' by Robert Hayden from *Collected Poems of Robert Hayden* edited by Frederic Glaysher Copyright ©1985 by Erma Hayden; Roger Garfit, executor of the estate of Frances Horovitz for a poem by Frances Horovitz; Faber and Faber Ltd and Ted Hughes for his poem; Bloodaxe Books Ltd for a poem by Kathleen Jamie from *The Way We Live* (Bloodaxe Books 1987); By kind permission of the trustees of the Estate of Patrick Kavanagh, c/o Peter Fallon, Literary Agent, Loughcrew, Oldcastle, Co. Meath, Ireland, for a poem by Patrick Kavanagh; Curtis Brown Ltd for poems by X. J. Kennedy ©1961; Timothy Leary for his poem; Andre Deutsch Ltd and Laurie Lee for his poems from *Selected Poems* (Penguin Books); New Directions Publishing Corp. and Laurence Pollinger Ltd for a poem by Denise Levertov from *Poems 1960-1967* copyright ©1960 by Denise Levertov Goodman; Rogers, Coleridge & White and Edward Lucie-Smith for a poem by Edward Lucie-Smith from *A Tropical Childhood and Other Poems*; John McGrath for his poem; Houghton Mifflin Co (New York) for a poem by Archibald MacLeish; Faber and Faber Ltd and Charles Madge for 'Solar Creation' by Charles Madge; Aidan Carl Mathews for his poem 'Woodniche'; Alfred A. Knopf Inc for a poem by William Meredith from *The Cheer* ©1980; The Regents of the University of California for a poem by Josephine Miles from *Poetry and Change: Donne, Milton, Wordsworth and the Equilibrium of the Present* ©1974; Elizabeth Barnett, literary executor of the estate of Edna St Vincent Millay for a poem by Edna St Vincent Millay; Sophie and Michael Young for poems by Sasha Moorsom, which will be published in November '94 by Carcanet entitled *Your Head in Mine*; Little Brown and Company for 'Kind of an ode to duty' by Ogden Nash; Lothian Books for a poem by Bernard O'Dowd ©Thomas C. Lothian Pty Ltd, Port Melbourne, Australia; Alfred A. Knopf for a poem by Sharon Olds from her *The Dead and the Living* Copyright ©1983; University of California Press for 'Variations Done for Gerald Van De Wiele' by Charles Olson from *Maximus Poems* edited/translated by George Butterick ©1983 The Regents of the University of California; Jacaranda Wiley (Australia) for a Poem by Oodgeroo of the Noonuccal/Kath Walker; Gerald Duckworth & Co Ltd for a poem by Dorothy Parker; New Directions Publishing Corp. for a poem by Kenneth Patchen from *Collected Poems of Kenneth Patchen* copyright ©1939 by New Directions Publishing Corp.; Faber And Faber Ltd on behalf of the estate of Sylvia Plath for 'Words' by Sylvia Plath from *Ariel* © Frieda and Nicholas Hughes; Bloodaxe Books for a poem by Irina Ratushinskaya from her book *No I'm Not Afraid* (Bloodaxe Books,1986); Oxford University Press for 'Naming of Parts' by Henry Reed from *Collected Poems* edited by John Stallworthy (1991); Faber and Faber Ltd and Anne Ridler for her poem, which is also included in her *Collected Poems* published by Carcanet Press, Manchester, in October 1994; Methuen London for a poem by Michèle Roberts from *The Mirror of The Mother*; Curtis Brown Ltd on behalf of the author's estate for a poem by Vita Sackville-West; George T. Sassoon for a poem by Siegfried Sassoon; Sheil Land Associates and Vikram Seth for 'Protocols' and 'All you who sleep tonight' by Vikram Seth; Carcanet Press Ltd for a poem by C.H. Sisson from *Selected Poems*; James MacGibbon, executor of the estate of Stevie Smith, for poems by Stevie Smith; Jonathan Steffen for his poem 'The Falcon to the Falconer'; Hubert Nicholson for a poem by A.S.J. Tessimond; Adam Thorpe for his poem (Secker and Warburg); Oxford University Press and Elaine Feinstein for her translation of a poem by Marina Tsvetayeva; Harcourt Brace & Company for 'Museum piece' by Richard Wilbur from *Ceremony and Other Poems* ©1950 renewed 1978 and 'For K.R.on her Sixtieth Birthday' from *Waking to Sleep: New Poems And Translations* ©1968 and to Richard Wilbur for his permissions; Michael Young for his poem, which appeared in the London Review of Books, January 9th 1992 – Carcanet in November '94 publish his poems jointly with those of his wife, Sasha Moorsom, under the title *Your Head in Mine*.

From Karen McCosker:

I am most grateful to Nicholas Albery for giving me the chance to try and do something I hadn't done before; to Tom Powers, Suzanne Shepherd, and Chip Fleischer at Steerforth Press for their guidance; to Kurt Brown for the numbers; to my colleagues at the University of Maine at Presque Isle, including Kenneth Lee Taylor, Ph.D., Professor of English, and Dr. George Hall for use of their libraries; to James William Brown for his time; and to those who gave to this project in ways they have no way of knowing, especially Cassie Baughman, Gwen Bell, Linda Berube, Dr. Alice Bolstridge, Paul Erb, Dr. Brian Fitzgerald, Janet Foley, Ginger Hall, Marie McCosker, Mary McDonald, Wes McNair, Bob Papworth, Nancy Swanson, Troy Terry, and Mary Todd.

⚮

I wish to acknowledge the poets and publishers and to thank them for their understanding as well as their generous permission to reproduce the following copyright material and as yet unpublished poems (with apologies for any errors or omissions):

"Sonnet 115" from *Berryman's Sonnets* by John Berryman. Copyright ©1967 by John Berryman. Reprinted by permission of Farrar, Straus & Giroux, Inc.; "Hope," copyright ©1992 by Philip Booth, from *Pairs* by Philip Booth. Used by permission of the author and of Penguin, a division of Penguin Books USA Inc.; "Fall" by Laure-Anne Bosselaar. Used by permission of the author; "Yerokastrinos" by Karen Chamberlain. Used by permission of the author; "o sweet spontaneous," copyright 1923, 1951, ©1991 by the Trustees for the E. E. Cummings Trust. Copyright ©1976 by George James Firmage; "i thank You God for most this amazing," copyright 1950, ©1978, 1991 by the Trustees for the E. E. Cummings Trust. Copyright 1979 by George James Firmage, from *Complete Poems: 1904–1962* by E. E. Cummings, Edited by George J. Firmage. Page 147 letter excerpt from "Selected Letters of E. E. Cummings, Edited by F. W. Dupee and George Stade. Copyright ©1969 by the Trustees for the E. E. Cummings Trust. Page 371 excerpt from the Introduction to *New Poems* [from *Collected Poems*], copyright ©1938, 1966, 1991 by the Trustees for the E. E. Cummings Trust. Reprinted by permission of Liveright Publishing Corporation; "Sunlight" and "Mossbawn" from *Selected Poems 1966–1987* by Seamus Heaney. Copyright ©1990 by Seamus Heaney. Reprinted by permission of Farrar, Straus & Giroux, Inc.; "The Leaving," by Brigit Pegeen Kelly, from *To the Place of Trumpets*, copyright 1988. Used by permission of the author and of Yale University Press; "I Remember Clifford," ©Philip Levine, from *One for the Rose*, Atheneum, 1981. Used by permission of the author; "The Voyage" by Charles Baudelaire, translated by Robert Lowell from *Imitations* by Robert Lowell. Copyright ©1961 by Robert Lowell, and copyright renewed ©1989 by Caroline, Harriet, and Sheridan Lowell. Reprinted by permission of Farrar, Straus & Giroux; "People Like Us" by William Matthews. Used by permission of the author; "The Bite," copyright Gerald Stern, from *Rejoicings*, Cummington Press, 1973, reprinted in *Leaving Another Kingdom*, Harper, 1990; "The Power of Maples," copyright Gerald Stern from *Lucky Life*, Houghton-Mifflin, 1977, reprinted in *Leaving Another Kingdom*, Harper, 1990. Used by permission of the author; "And Death Shall Have No Dominion," by Dylan Thomas, from *The Poems of Dylan Thomas*. Copyright ©1943 by New Directions Publishing Corp.; "Do Not Go Gentle into That Good Night," by Dylan Thomas, from *The Poems of Dylan Thomas*. Copyright ©1952 by Dylan Thomas. Reprinted by permission of New Directions Publishing Corp.; "The Force That Through the Green Fuse Drives the Flower," by Dylan Thomas, from *The Poems of Dylan Thomas*. Copyright ©1939 by New Directions Publishing Corp. Reprinted by permission of New Directions Publishing Corp.; "The Waking," copyright 1953 by Theodore Roethke, from *The Collected Poems of Theodore Roethke* by Theodore Roethke. Used by permission of Doubleday, a division of Bantam Doubleday Dell Publishing Group, Inc.; "For K. R. on Her Sixtieth Birthday" from *Walking to Sleep: New Poems and Translations*, copyright ©1968 by Richard Wilbur, reprinted by permission of the author and Harcourt Brace & Company.

Index